Growth Management for a Sustainable Future

Growth Management for a Sustainable Future

Ecological Sustainability as the New Growth Management Focus for the 21st Century

Gabor Zovanyi

Westport, Connecticut
London

Library of Congress Cataloging-in-Publication Data

Zovanyi, Gabor, 1943–
    Growth management for a sustainable future : ecological
sustainability as the new growth management focus for the 21st
century / Gabor Zovanyi.
        p.   cm.
    Includes bibliographical references and index.
    ISBN 0–275–96135–4 (alk. paper)—ISBN 0–275–97349–2 (pbk.: alk. paper)
    1. Sustainable development—United States.   2. Economic
development—Environmental aspects—United States.   3. Land use—
Environmental aspects—United States.   4. Land use—United States—
Planning.   I. Title.
HC110.E5Z68   1998
338.9′0973—dc21   97–35138

British Library Cataloguing in Publication Data is available.

Library of Congress Catalog Card Number: 97–35138
ISBN: 0–275–97349–2 (pbk.)

First published in 1998

Praeger Publishers, 88 Post Road West, Westport, CT 06881
An imprint of Greenwood Publishing Group, Inc.
www.praeger.com

Printed in the United States of America

The paper used in this book complies with the
Permanent Paper Standard issued by the National
Information Standards Organization (Z39.48–1984).

P

In order to keep this title in print and available to the academic community, this edition
was produced using digital reprint technology in a relatively short print run. This would
not have been attainable using traditional methods. Although the cover has been changed
from its original appearance, the text remains the same and all materials and methods
used still conform to the highest book-making standards.

COPYRIGHT NOTICES

To Carrie
friend, partner, confidant, editor,
and quite simply the brightest star in my galaxy.

Contents

Tables

Preface

The arrival of a new century and millennium represents a watershed in human history. More than two centuries of exponential demographic, economic, and urban growth are now altering our relationship to the natural world in an unprecedented manner. As the scale of the human enterprise has grown exponentially, ecosystems and their species have been subjected to an assault that represents the antithesis of sustainable behavior. Our current impact on the earth's nonhuman community of life has come to be characterized as biological meltdown. Some estimates suggest the loss of fully half of the world's species by the year 2050. There also is mounting evidence that the present scale of the human enterprise can no longer be supported by the planet's income, and that our species is already living off its capital. Consumption of that capital resource base is causing serious environmental deterioration. These and other ecological realities increasingly reveal the currency of limits to any further physical expansion of the human enterprise on our planet. The opening chapter of this book documents the case for existing global limits to growth and advances the premise that we have no alternative but to relinquish the growth imperative driving the human enterprise and to undertake a transition to sustainable behavior. Given that premise, this work takes the position that growth management programs must now be directed at efforts to stop growth.

The second chapter portrays the evolution of the growth management movement in the United States. In its characterization of growth management efforts undertaken by local governments, the chapter shows how local programs directed at regulating the amount, location, rate, or quality of growth have with few exceptions been implemented within the context of ongoing growth accommodation. A portrayal of statewide growth management laws passed to date illustrates the growth accommodation bias of these enactments and reveals that the majority of these laws actually mandate ongoing growth accommodation by local governments. In short, documentation is provided to illustrate that the overwhelming majority of growth management programs in the United States have allowed, facilitated, or actually mandated ongoing growth accommodation. As a result, the growth management movement in this country represents an institutionalized form of ongoing growth accommodation that is incongruous with sustainable behavior. Existing books on growth management in the United States advance the concept of "balanced growth," which suggests that growth and environmental protection represent equally legitimate objectives, and that a balance can be achieved between these ends without compromising either. This book takes issue with that position, argues that further growth is unsustainable, and maintains that the focus of growth management must change from accommodating ongoing growth to ensuring sustainable behavior. The second chapter concludes by arguing that the growth management movement continues to support allegiance to the growth imperative, and that this wholehearted endorsement of ongoing growth accommodation increasingly will be seen as irresponsible support for an obsolete ideology as further growth induces increasing environmental havoc.

Chapter three reveals the historical pro-growth bias of the planning profession in the United States. As key players in the growth management movement, planners are able to influence the development process that brings ongoing growth to communities. Their positions allow them to take part in structuring the policy agenda that addresses growth in America's communities, and they also are able to influence development policy as they help create comprehensive plans and associated development regulations that spell out prospects for future growth. Unfortunately, the profession's historical pro-growth bias has tended to limit the planning profession's role in growth management to activity directed toward a "managing to grow" option, rather than management efforts to limit or stop future growth. Even during the growth management era, the profession has continued to align itself with the forces of development and growth. The profession's unwillingness to concede that growth is relentlessly eliminating nonhuman species and ecosystems on a global basis makes it possible for most of its members to ignore the possibility of an alternative to the development facilitation activity that has characterized the profession since its inception. As each year of exponential growth presents further evidence of our unsustainable assault on the natural world, the profession increasingly will be pressured to reassess its legacy of pro-growth ideas and behavior. Continuing to base professional theory and practice on the oxymoronic idea of sustainable growth will invariably become less tenable with time. If the planning profession is to play a meaningful role in helping society transition to a sustainable future, it will have to begin by letting go of the growth imperative. The third chapter closes with speculation on changes the profession must undergo if it is to successfully participate in the essential societal transformation to a sustainable future.

Chapter four of this work addresses the role of the courts in shaping growth management efforts in the United States. The essence of the growth management movement in this country has been its regulatory nature. As the movement implemented an expanded array of land-use regulations to achieve its ends, the increase in regulatory interference with the use of private property produced litigation. Proponents of private property rights have sought to curb new restrictions on the use of private land associated with growth management programs by challenging the legality of many growth management efforts in the courts. The chapter opens with a treatment of the nature of property rights in the United States, and then presents standards used by courts in deciding the legality of growth management regulations that limit the use of private property. A subsequent survey of the legality of growth management techniques implemented to date concludes that the courts have upheld the majority of challenged management efforts in spite of the pro-growth orientation of the judiciary illustrated in the chapter. This willingness of courts to sanction most growth management programs may, however, be attributed to the fact that the overwhelming majority of these programs have continued to provide for ongoing growth. The fourth chapter concludes with consideration of whether courts might be expected to sanction growth management programs designed to stop growth with land-use regulations. A case is made for the claim that land-use law presents very real obstacles to shutting down further growth with land-use controls, but that these obstacles do not represent an insurmountable barrier to growth controls directed at stopping growth.

Chapter five advances the view that ecological sustainability must become the primary focus of future growth management activity. The chapter begins with a review of environmental planning considerations that have been subsumed under the rubric of growth management. A review of the three major environmental planning responses under growth management—planning based on impact assessments, planning based on land-suitability analyses, and planning based on the carrying capacities of natural systems—reveals that none of these approaches has effectively advanced the idea of ecological sustainability within the growth management movement. A subsequent survey of the idea of sustainable development and its impact on the growth management movement illustrates the extent to which the notion of sustainable development is linked to the oxymoronic idea of sustainable growth and the minimal impact it has had on the growth management movement in spite of its general endorsement of prospects for ongoing growth. Consideration of operational measures of sustainability is then used to illustrate the primacy of ecological concerns in any assessment of sustainability. The human economy and civilization itself are utterly dependent on the life-support services provided by sound ecosystems. Ultimately, human well-being is incapable of being realized at the expense of ecological integrity. In acknowledgment of this self-evident reality, the fifth chapter closes with the identification of operational measures of ecological sustainability and argues that these measures must become the primary focus of both the growth management movement and society at large. Final observations on future prospects for the growth management movement conclude that the movement must shift from its current irresponsible growth accommodation focus to overseeing the required downsizing and redesigning of the human enterprise to an ecologically sustainable level and form. To make that shift, the central challenge facing the growth management movement is portrayed as one of having to replace the growth imperative currently driving the movement with the imperative of ecological sustainability.

1

The Growth
Management
Context

> Perpetual growth in the scale of the human enterprise is an impossibility; *its growth will cease.*
>
> Paul and Anne Ehrlich[1]

The growth imperative driving the culture of the global civilization complex has increasingly come to be associated with the demise of the natural world.[2] To associate growth in general, and population, economic, and urban growth in particular, with such a dire consequence as the destruction of the natural world represents a stunning reversal in what has been an historical perception of growth as a social good. It has been common under the traditional viewpoint to equate growth with progress.[3] When viewing it in this light, one might expect growth to be pursued indefinitely, and that expectation has in fact become the social orientation of an emerging global culture. In just a few recent decades, "the evolving industrial culture has implanted within the human mind the expectation of ever-continuing growth."[4] During the same period, such growth has increasingly come to be linked with dire environmental consequences.

While growth of human populations and their associated socioeconomic activities has a history tracing back to the origins of our species, growth on a scale capable of affecting our planetary ecosystem is a relatively recent phenomenon. Exponential growth as a fundamental feature of modern society only dates back to the time of the Industrial Revolution. However, that growth and the quantities it has generated has now had more than two centuries to leave its mark on the natural world. As has been recently observed, "Growth has been the dominant behavior of the [global] socioeconomic system for more than two hundred years."[5] In terms of the most significant effects of this growth on the natural world, it has only been during the 20th century that "humanity has become a truly planetary ecological force."[6] Moving beyond the transformation of regional landscapes, our species is now altering the global atmosphere, modifying the global climate, and effecting the extermination of other species on a global scale. Growth on a scale capable of producing these effects has been referred to as "terminal growthism,"[7] and in the minds of some portends such malevolent prospective consequences as "biosuicide"[8] and "ecocide."[9]

Within a mere two decades our perceived relationship to the natural world has shifted from what was labeled as the environmental crisis of the 1970s to what is now seen as the global ecological crisis of the 1990s. The focus of the 1970s on local matters like air and water pollution harmful to humans quickly expanded to encompass regional concerns like acid rain and desertification, and increasingly considered the effects of these regional alterations on other species. By the 1990s the focus was increasingly becoming one of a concern with global ecosystem alterations and their consequences for all life on the planet. The role of population, economic, and urban growth, and their related consequences, in bringing about a breakdown in the world's ecology has brought us to the point of a forced reassessment of the societal value of the growth imperative. At the very least it has produced a willingness to accept the need for a control of growth, in the form of growth management, if we are to maintain the habitability of the planet. For many, however, existing growth-induced effects call for an outright rejection of the growth imperative and the acceptance of sustainable development as the central guiding principal for our global community. In order to understand how this shift in public perceptions toward the desirability of further growth has come about, it is necessary to examine how exponential growth has brought us to the point of questioning unending growth as one of the basic tenets of the world's dominant social paradigm.

A PRO-GROWTH LEGACY

The world's dominant social paradigm—the collection of beliefs, values, norms, and ideals that form the world view representative of an emerging world culture—has been directly implicated in the ongoing destruction of the natural world.[10] Such a paradigm influences thinking and behavior, and many components of the dominant social paradigm have been faulted for the role they play in undermining the ability of the global ecosystem to support life. Components that have been called into question because of their antienvironmental attributes include: an unwavering faith in science and technology; a belief in the industrialism development model; a conviction in the merit of consumerism and materialism; a view of nature limited by utilitarian and property-rights perspectives; certitude regarding the propriety of anthropocentrism; optimism concerning unending social progress; and allegiance to the growth imperative. While all these components and others associated with the dominant social paradigm have been criticized on environmental grounds, the principal focus here will be on the growth imperative and the role that a pro-growth legacy has played in dismantling the natural world. In order to understand the current controversy surrounding the merit of ongoing growth, one needs to consider the historical reasoning that has been employed to support ongoing population, economic, and urban growth.

Traditional Views Toward Population Growth

While the origins of favorable views toward population growth may be obscure and elusive, it may be surmised that some of the earliest explanations for popular attitudes toward population growth derive from familial or small-group settings and, more specifically, from the concern of people in such contexts with survival. "When famine and pestilence frequently decimated the population, it was important that [people] should breed at every opportunity."[11] In the familial context, "large numbers of children were necessary to insure survival of the species, given the high infant and child death rates."[12] The meaning attributed to survival came to encompass both biological and economic survival in traditional societies, because offspring in those settings were felt to "contribute to the family economy from an early age and represent old-age insurance to boot."[13]

The fact that biological and economic survival came to be associated early on with high levels of reproductivity found expression in, and formal support from, the dictates of numerous religions. It has been noted that "the laws of the Hindus, the Jews, the Zoroastrians, and many other ancient religious groups revere fertility and regard procreation as both a blessing and a duty."[14] Religious writings reveal such a posture toward fertility as evidenced by the directive from the Bible endorsing procreation: "Be fruitful, and multiply." These pronatalist pronouncements in the sacred writings of religions, coupled with individual perceptions concerning ties between childbearing and biological and economic survival, have produced positive attitudes toward fertility that are revealed in the daily language of some cultures. In India, for example, a standard greeting to a woman—"May you have many sons"—conveys the extent to which popular verbal communications may incorporate and then reflect such positive attitudes toward fertility.[15]

Previously noted associations between childbearing and the concern with economic survival illustrate the difficulty of disassociating supportive rationales for population growth from economic considerations. Population growth has, for example, not only been credited with promoting economic growth,[16] it has also been linked to the pace of potential economic growth.[17] Economically, population growth is viewed positively mainly because of its association with the production and consumption potential of additional people.[18] There have, however, been a host of other economic-based reasons for supporting population growth. Mention has, for example, been made of the specific prospects of realizing "economies of scale" or "increased returns to scale" with the large-scale production processes that large numbers of people make possible.[19] Population increases, it is believed, contribute positively to the formation of such "economies of mass production," because they are credited with making specialization of function and the division of labor possible.[20] Another economic-based rationale behind favorable attitudes toward population increases is based on the logic of reduced per capita burdens in the cost of social overhead like transportation and communication under a larger population.[21] A similar argument identifies population growth with an increased capacity for sharing in the provision of such public goods as scientific and medical research.[22] Yet another economic-based rationale in support of population growth derives from the favorable impact that such growth is felt to exert on the promotion of a "bullish investment psychology."[23] To risk negative investment outcomes via inadequate population increases under this line of reasoning is to risk the specter of large-scale, persistent unemployment.

All of the noted rationales serve to illustrate why population growth has long been considered a social good. The positive perceptions toward population growth have in fact existed for so long that they have been credited with finding their way into the values and norms of present-day societies.[24] Such pronatalist perspectives are reinforced by a range of societal influences such as tax credits that reward the addition of each child. The United States has, for example, been described as a setting where "fertility has always occurred in the context of massive collective intervention of a pronatalist type" that has "encouraged parenthood and discouraged nonparenthood using virtually the entire spectrum of available pressures to induce conformity."[25] When taken together, all of the noted pronatalist rationales have served as powerful genetic and cultural inducements to a continued pro-growth posture regarding population increases.

Traditional Views Toward Economic Growth

In examining the historical reasoning that has been employed to argue the desirability of economic growth, one also finds an extensive set of rationales utilized to support ongoing economic expansion. A global economic culture has come to view "development," "modernization," and "progress" in terms of a single economic index of advancement: the gross national product (GNP).[26] Such "GNP fetishism"[27] is based on the increased levels of individual affluence and consumption that GNP increases are assumed to afford. This affluence and consumption has been equated with increased economic welfare, and because it has been assumed that economic welfare and general welfare are closely correlated,[28] increased affluence and increased consumption have come to represent desirable social goals. Increased affluence is valued under this line of reasoning because it is believed to increase the range of individual and collective choice.[29] The increased choices and expanded capabilities for doing more of whatever people want to do, in turn, come to be expressed principally in terms of increased prospects for consumption. Such a consumption focus has been described in the American context as the full-grown ideology of "consumerism."[30] Economists have contributed to the development of such an ideology with their endorsement of the postulate of non-satiety, which generally assumes that consumers' material wants are unlimited.[31] While economists recognize that increased affluence permits increased consumption of services, the main emphasis of "consumerism" has been on the increased consumption of material goods. As has been observed: "All modern societies conduct their economies on the basis of rising material standards for their citizens."[32] In the United States and elsewhere, there has quite simply been a tendency to define prosperity in a materialistic way,[33] to associate materialism with happiness,[34] and even to identify material well-being with spiritual well-being.[35] The value placed on increased material consumption at least partially explains the widespread endorsement of technology in an increasingly industrial world. Technology assumes a pivotal role in increasing material output for consumption,[36] and is embraced because of its accepted contribution to what has been called an "industrial society geared to achieving a materialist paradise."[37]

Under this reasoning, increased consumption of material goods is assumed to represent a societal good because it is believed to reflect the exercise of choice and the attainment of happiness. Increased consumer choices are made dependent on the prior state of affluence, as evidenced by high per capita incomes, which in turn require economic growth in the form of an increasing GNP. This, however, provides only a partial explanation of the reasoning that has been employed to support ongoing economic growth. As was the case with population growth, a rather extensive set of rationales have evolved to justify the merit of continued economic expansion. Ongoing economic growth has been linked to such disparate factors as peace,[38] security,[39] control over negative environmental forces such as famine, plague, or pestilence,[40] increased likelihood of greater exercise of compassion,[41] forestallment of otherwise unbearable social tension,[42] and resolution of a host of societal problems.[43]

With respect to the relationship between continued economic growth and reduced prospects for a host of social ills, such growth has been seen as a prerequisite to reduced prospects for unemployment problems and avoidance of the related ills of recession and depression.[44] It is also common to associate economic growth with prospects for the reduction, or even the elimination, of poverty,[45] as well as the reduction of disparities between nations.[46] Arguments have been advanced linking the availability of natural resources, or the derivation of suitable substitutes, to higher prices capable of being absorbed under further growth.[47] The future outlook for social expenditures, ranging from social programs to defense spending, has been directly tied to economic growth.[48] Perhaps the most curious argument advanced in support of further economic growth is the one that suggests growth is needed to pay for pollution abatement while ignoring the role growth itself plays in generating additional pollution.[49] These and other rationales have been employed to support the economic growth element of the growth imperative and to instill the belief that a viable future without such growth is simply unattainable. The dominant social paradigm representative of an emerging world culture therefore has most of the world's people deifying economic growth in the same fashion that they have traditionally deified population growth.

Traditional Views Toward Urban Growth

To the extent that population growth and economic growth have been viewed as desirable phenomena and identified with societal progress,[50] a similar positive attitude has accompanied the observed growth of urban places. Under a traditional perspective, population growth, economic growth, and the growth of urban places have been portrayed as mutually supportive phenomena. For some, the connection between population and urban growth was so direct that population increases were seen as inevitably involving increases in the size of cities.[51] For others, the assumed interconnection between economic and urban growth was viewed in terms of a basic, long-term, multifold trend toward inexorable increases in industrialization and urbanization.[52] In Lewis Mumford's terms: "An expanding economy demanded an expanding population; and an expanding population demanded an expanding city."[53]

Reasons for the positive view that has traditionally accompanied urban growth appear in the literature of development economics. While the global quest for increases in GNP and per capita incomes may be pursued through such avenues as expanded agricultural production and the expansion and diversification of exports, top priority has traditionally been given to increased industrial output through deliberate policies of industrialization.[54] In much the same way that development has come to be associated with industrialization, similar associations have evolved with regard to industrialization and urbanization. Even when those associations have been qualified, both industrialization and urbanization have been expressed as preconditions for, and results of, each other,[55] as well as in terms of "mutually reinforcing links"[56] that appear to preclude the consideration of one without at the same time considering the other. To the extent that development has been equated with industrialization, and industrialization with urbanization, the circle has been closed with the equation of urbanization with development.[57] The degree to which they have been equated has ranged from discussion of the "effects of urbanization favorable to economic progress,"[58] to urbanization being viewed "as both a prerequisite for and a result of economic development,"[59] to a position where urbanization is treated as "an inevitable concomitant of economic development."[60]

Urban places formed by the urbanization process have tended to be viewed positively for a number of reasons. The scarcity of investment capital needed for industrial development serves as an effective barrier to simultaneous development throughout the countryside, and therefore has development planners evidencing a natural bias toward a more limited number of urban centers.[61] Urban places are also credited with making possible a more rational deployment of certain vital but scarce facilities and personnel than would be possible under a population scattered about in villages and small towns.[62] The favorable attitude also derives from the belief that urban centers are initiators of the development process. This latter view is expressed in widespread acceptance of the concept of "urban growth poles" as communicators of growth,[63] which is to say that they are alleged to possess the ability of spreading economic development to areas beyond their borders.[64] Urban places have additionally been credited with inducing new ways of thinking and acting that are seen as conducive to economic development[65] and have even been viewed "as the essential environment in which economic capacities are created."[66]

The reasoning illustrated previously has produced a positive view of an increase in both the number of urban places and the growth of specific urban centers. Within the body of development literature support for urbanization in general at one time progressed to the point of proposals directed at actually accelerating the rate of urbanization in developing countries.[67] Under this traditional pro-growth orientation, large urban centers have been credited with being better suited to the accomplishment of economic development objectives than small or intermediate centers.[68] Large centers are favored on several grounds under such reasoning, including the advantages of a large and concentrated labor and consumer market, their economics of scale and their juxtaposition of industries and specialists, their function as centers from which innovations are most likely to diffuse, and their alleged advantages in instilling the skills and values of an industrial system. Such views lead to the conclusion that "location in the largest cities provides the best physical setting for effective industrialization and economic growth"[69] and that large metropolitan centers are necessary conditions for advanced industrialization.[70] When the noted reasoning is viewed collectively, one has an elaborate set of rationales to support urban growth that are a natural consequence of the rationales that have evolved to support population and economic growth.

Supportive rationales for population growth and economic growth lead to a natural endorsement of both urbanization in general and the growth of specific urban places in particular under the line of reasoning described here. With the dominant social paradigm's growth imperative reinforcing population increases on a massive scale during the current century, it was inevitable that urban places should be assigned a positive role in accepting that growth. A social paradigm that equates development and progress with economic growth, credits industrialization with providing the greatest impetus to furthering such growth,[71] and argues that industrialization presupposes conditions that tend to produce agglomeration of population[72] would also inevitably produce a positive view of urban growth. When taken together, the rationales that have evolved to support population, economic, and urban growth comprise a pro-growth legacy that has played a key role in generating the growth called for by the dominant social paradigm's growth imperative. The imperative's success in generating growth has in fact brought us to the point of questioning this central tenet of the world's dominant social paradigm. A review of the extent of the growth that has been generated to date and of some of its critical consequences will serve to illustrate why the growth imperative has come under fire.

THE GROWTH DEBATE OF THE 1970s

By the 1970s the growth imperative was being assailed on a number of different fronts. The very rationales traditionally used to defend the desirability of ongoing growth were increasingly coming under attack.[73] For example, even the United States, with its phenomenal economic growth prior to the 1970s, had not been able to eliminate poverty or alter a distribution of income that the Census Bureau had been tracking for a quarter of a century.[74] On a global scale, the number of people living in poverty was increasing rather than decreasing, and the gap between the rich and the poor on a worldwide basis was revealed to be increasing.[75] There was, in short, what came to be described as a "stunning discovery": "that growth does not bring about certain desired ends or arrest certain undesired trends."[76] In striking contrast to the conventional wisdom of the day, growth was actually being implicated as the cause of problems rather than an avenue for their prospective solutions. With the rising interest in the environment during the early 1970s, such environmental problems as air and water pollution were increasingly being attributed to growth.[77] For an expanding number of observers the pollution effects of growth translated directly into "an ultimate certitude about the problem of environmental deterioration."[78] So while some were questioning a broad range of rationales underlying the merit of continued growth, many were basing their increasing skepticism of the growth imperative on a single consideration, their observation of worsening environmental conditions.

Acknowledged Limits to Growth

Another attack on the growth imperative during the 1970s was epitomized by the central argument put forth by a book published in 1972, *The Limits to Growth*.[79] That argument advanced the incontrovertible axiom that infinite growth is impossible in a finite system. The authors examined growth trends in world population, industrialization, resource depletion, pollution, and food production by using a computer model and concluded that under existing trends the limits to growth on this planet would be reached within 100 years. Under the standard run of the model it collapsed because of nonrenewable resource depletion. When that constraint was assumed away the model collapsed due to the level of pollution generated by growth. In a subsequent run the resource and pollution constraints were both relaxed and the collapse occurred because of food shortages. Even with the most optimistic assumptions introduced into the model regarding impending constraints, the basic behavioral mode of the modeled world system under ongoing exponential growth of population and capital was consistently one of sudden and uncontrollable decline in both population and industrial capacity. Defenders of the growth imperative tended to reject such findings, based largely on a faith in human ingenuity and a belief that the automatic adjustment mechanisms of the market-price system and technology would continue to make ongoing growth possible.[80] The argument of impending limits to growth was rejected by these optimists, who discounted the idea of limits as too distant of a concern to warrant serious short-term consideration.[81] There were others, however, for whom consideration of limits represented a matter of current concern.[82]

Limits to Population Growth

By the 1970s the concept of limits had evoked what would be described as "the debate of the century, anti-growth versus pro-growth."[83] While much of the debate was being waged on a theoretical level, some preferred to focus attention on the magnitudes being generated by population, economic, and urban growth. For these observers, the quantities associated with growth by the 1970s provided additional grounds for assailing the growth imperative. With respect to population growth, it became fashionable by the early 1970s to illustrate the changing nature of population increases in terms of "doubling time"—the time required for population to double in size.[84] These sources noted that until about 10,000 years ago it took some 35,000 years for the population to double.[85] With the introduction of agriculture around 8,000 B.C. that changed dramatically, instituting a progressive reduction in doubling times that is illustrated in Table 1.1. The 100-fold population increase between 8000 B.C. and 1650 A.D. required between six and seven doublings in just under 10,000 years, representing an average doubling time of around 1,500 years for each of the doublings during that era. As the table indicates, subsequent doublings occurred in dramatically shorter time frames.

Another approach for illustrating the extraordinary nature of population increases by the 1970s consisted of reference to changes in the number of people being added to the world's population each year.[86] In the year 1650, when the human population numbered around 500 million, and was growing at about 0.3% per year, the number of people on the planet was only increasing by 1.5 million people a year. The escalating character of those annual additions under exponential growth during the current century is illustrated in Table 1.2. For some observers, the annual increases in excess of 70 million people a year by

Table 1.1
Doubling Times for World Population

Date	Estimated world population	Time for population to double
8000 B.C.	5 million	
		1,500 years
1650 A.D.	500 million	
		200 years
1850 A.D.	1,000 million (1 billion)	
		80 years
1930 A.D.	2,000 million (2 billion)	
		45 years
1975 A.D.	4,000 million (4 billion)	
		41 years
2016 A.D.	8,000 million (8 billion)	

Source: Adapted from a table in Paul R. Ehrlich and Anne H. Ehrlich, 1970, *Population, Resources, and Environment: Issues in Human Ecology*, San Francisco, California: WH Freeman, 6; with the current estimated time for the next doubling taken from Oliver S. Owen and Daniel D. Chiras, 1995, *Natural Resource Conservation: Management for a Sustainable Future*, Englewood Cliffs, New Jersey: Prentice Hall, 68.

the 1970s, and the associated implication in the form of a current doubling time of some 40 years for the world's population, represented sufficient grounds for abandoning the population-growth element of the growth imperative during this period.[87]

The growth of population in the United States by the 1970s similarly led some to reject the merit of ongoing population increases in the American context.[88] Centuries of growth had only succeeded in generating an American population of some 76 million people by the year 1900. In the next 50 years that population nearly doubled, putting the 1950 population figure at approximately

Table 1.2
Annual Additions to World Population 1900-1970

Year	Population (millions)	x	Growth rate (per year)	=	People added (millions)
1900	1500	x	0.5%	=	7.5
1950	2500	x	1.7%	=	42.5
1970	3600	x	2.1%	=	75.6

Sources: Such figures on annual additions to the global population appear in The Report of the Commission on Population Growth and the American Future, 1972, *Population and the American Future*, New York: Signet, 9; and in Edward Goldsmith, Robert Allen, Michael Allaby, John Davoll, Sam Lawrence, editors, 1974, *Blueprint for Survival*, NY: Signet, 3.

150 million. By 1970, that figure had increased to 205 million, and was growing at about 2.25 million a year, of which some 400,000 were legal immigrants.[89] The Commission on Population Growth and the American Future projected population growth from the 1970 figure of 205 million to the year
2000.[90] Under an assumption of two-child families on the average and immigration continuing at the then existing rate, the population was projected to reach
271 million by the end of the century. Under an assumption of three-child families on the average and a continued annual immigration of 400,000, the population was projected to reach 322 million by the year 2000. The fact that a difference of only one child per family would translate into a difference of an additional 51 million Americans in only three decades clearly revealed the significance of different growth rates even in this country. This awareness produced
skepticism regarding the value of further population growth even in a country as
large and as wealthy as the United States.

Limits to Economic Growth

That skepticism had surfaced by the 1970s regarding the desirability of ongoing economic growth is illustrated by treatment of global economic growth in
The Limits to Growth book.[91] Using world-wide industrial production as an indicator of global economic growth, the authors questioned the ability to maintain
future increases in industrial output when it was growing significantly faster
than the notable growth evidenced by the human population. The historically
high population growth rate of just over 2% a year in the early 1970s represented
a doubling time of just under 35 years for the world's population, whereas the
7% per year average growth rate in the world's industrial output during a five-
year period in the 1960s represented a doubling time of only 10 years for global
industrial production.[92] The resource consumption and pollution generation consequences of maintaining such a phenomenal growth rate led the authors of the
book to question the ongoing viability of the economic element of the growth
imperative. They simply doubted the feasibility of doubling industrial output
every 10 years, when 10 doublings over the course of a century would create an
output 1000 times larger than the starting level, with related implications for resource needs and pollution generation.[93]

The magnitudes generated by economic growth in the form of industrial output by the 1970s may be illustrated by reference to global increases being
recorded in the manufacture of motor vehicles. In 1950 total annual production
of motor vehicles globally amounted to 10.5 million units. By 1970 that figure
had increased to 29.3 million. Such production levels increased the total number
of registered motor vehicles from approximately 70 million in 1950 to about
246 million in 1970. The number of passenger cars registered during the same
interval increased from about 54 million to over 193 million, altering the ratio
of one car for every 46 people worldwide in 1950 to one car for every 18 people
by 1970.[94] In a time interval when population increased from 2.5 billion to 3.6
billion (44% increase) the number of registered motor vehicles increased from 70
million to 246 million (251% increase). With the growth rate for vehicles exceeding even the phenomenal growth rate of the human population, economic
growth began to come under fire by the 1970s. A great deal of the criticism was
environmentally based. The environmental implications of the growth in the

number of passenger cars from 54 million in 1950 to 193 million in 1970 (257% increase) may in part be illustrated by the corresponding increase in global gasoline consumption by passenger cars, from 45 billion gallons in 1950 to about 145 billion gallons in 1970 (222% increase).[95]

The phenomenal numbers associated with economic growth by the 1970s challenged continuing allegiance to this element of the growth imperative in the same fashion that numbers associated with population growth had contributed to an altered view of population increases. However, a questioning of the merit of continued economic growth during this period was much more limited than the attacks being directed at further population growth. The Commission on Population Growth and the American Future, for example, made it clear in its 1972 report that its rejection of the merit of further population growth did not imply a similar abandonment of ongoing economic growth.[96] While the assault on economic growth was limited in scope during this period, a small group of economists led the way in arguing for a renunciation of economic growth as a social goal.[97] These economists pointed out the flaws in a global economic system that had "become detached from its own biophysical foundations."[98] For these economists, the pursuit of economic growth had already created a disequilibrium between the human economy and the natural ecosystem on which it was based. As a consequence, by the early 1970s they were already inclined to identify the ongoing pursuit of such growth as "growthmania."[99]

Limits to Urban Growth

In much the same fashion that population and economic growth were being repudiated on at least limited fronts by the 1970s, a similar reversal was beginning with respect to the traditional viewpoint regarding the merit of ongoing urban growth. Again, at least part of the altered view toward what had long been considered a social good was attributable to the numbers being generated by growth. Global urbanization was already a very real phenomenon by the 1970s, having altered a worldwide population that was merely 13% urban in the year 1900, to one that was about 29% urban by 1950, and nearly 40% urban by 1970.[100] Statistics of the day revealed that urban populations were growing much more rapidly than overall population increases.[101] Particularly striking was the growth being evidenced by larger urban centers, as is illustrated by the urban population in all cities of 100,000 or more having increased from approximately 392 million in 1950 to over 900 million by the early 1970s.[102] The nature of quantitative changes in some of the largest of the world's urban agglomerations during this century is illustrated in Table 1.3.[103] The unprecedented increases across a range of urban centers and the particularly large increases being recorded by those centers in less developed countries already produced a questioning of urban growth trends by the 1970s.[104] Under the belief that "[t]o a large extent our environmental ills are caused by the demands, functions, and expansion of cities,"[105] it was quite natural that some would come to question the urban growth that was generating urban centers on the scale illustrated here.

Environmental Limits to Growth

The numbers associated with population, economic, and urban growth by the

Table 1.3
Growth of the World's Great Urban Agglomerations

Urban Agglomeration/ Country		Population (millions)		
		1900	1950	1970
London, Britain		6.48	10.40	10.6
New York/NE N.J., USA		4.42	12.40	16.3
Paris, France		3.33	5.50	8.3
Tokyo/Yokohama, Japan		1.50	6.70	14.9
Moscow, Russia		1.12	4.80	7.1
Calcutta, India		1.09	4.40	7.1
Shanghai, China		0.84	10.30	11.4
Buenos Aires, Argentina		0.81	5.30	8.5
Bombay, India		0.78	2.90	5.9
Beijing, China	under	0.50	6.70	8.3
Los Angeles, USA	under	0.50	4.10	8.4
Rio de Janeiro, Brazil	under	0.50	3.50	7.2
Mexico City, Mexico	under	0.50	3.10	9.2
Sao Paulo, Brazil	under	0.50	2.80	8.2
Seoul, Korea	under	0.50	under 2.50	5.4
Cairo/Giza, Egypt	under	0.50	under 2.50	5.4
Jakarta, Indonesia	under	0.50	under 2.50	4.5

Source: The figures are taken from tables appearing in Barclay Jones and William Shepherd,
    1987, Cities of the Future: Implications for the Rise and Relative Decline of the Cities of the
    West, *Journal of Planning Education and Research* 6,3: 162-6.

1970s played a part in producing challenges to the growth imperative during that
period. Rather than viewing each addition to the population base as a blessing,
there were those who were already willing to consider each additional person as
an environmental liability because they were seen to represent a draft on all
aspects of a limited environment.[106] Economic growth, in turn, with its evident
environmental consequences by the 1970s, had at least some willing to suggest
that the ongoing pursuit of such growth represented "a senile ideology that
should be unceremoniously retired."[107] Urbanization and the growth of urban
centers was also drawing criticism in the development literature, again in part
because of the environmental impact associated with such growth, with reference

being made to "overurbanization" and "hyperurbanization" and the parasitic role of large primary cities.

The concern with environmental impact stemming from population, economic, and urban growth was, therefore, a reality by the 1970s. A way of thinking about such impact had been provided by an equation: $I = P \times A \times T$.[108] The total environmental impact (I) is represented as the product of population size (P), times its affluence (A) as measured by consumption, times the damage done by the technologies (T) employed in supplying that consumption. When thought of in these terms population increases are seen as representing an increase in a multiplier that serves to intensify environmental deterioration. The per capita impact represented by $A \times T$ in the equation may, in turn, be viewed as a surrogate for the impact associated with economic growth. Increases in such growth, as reflected by increases in consumption and production ($A \times T$), therefore also comes to be considered in terms of increases to multipliers that act to intensify environmental damage. The placement of most of that population and economic growth in expanding urban centers that serve to concentrate and intensify environmental impacts produces, in turn, a negative view of urban growth. Despite this reasoning the dominant social paradigm was unwilling to give up on the growth imperative by the 1970s. In spite of a litany of environmental ills associated with growth, the era evidenced a general inability to acknowledge limits to growth. When limits where claimed, as in the book *Limits to Growth*, they were portrayed as a future concern of coming generations, specifically as far removed as 100 years in that publication. Such a position on limits would dramatically change by the 1990s, due in large part to the numbers generated by exponential growth over the course of two intervening decades.

THE HYPERACTIVE GROWTH BETWEEN 1970 AND 1990

Population, economic, and urban growth continued their exponential behavior during the course of the two decades between 1970 and 1990. The global population increased from 3.6 billion in 1970 to 5.3 billion in 1990, representing a whopping 47% increase in only 20 years. While the rate of increase declined from an annual rate of 2.1% to a rate of 1.7% over the course of the two decades, Table 1.4 reveals that the lower rate applied to a much larger base still produced a significant increase in the number of people being added to the world's population each year by the 1990s. Whereas the world had to contend with an additional 70 million plus individuals each year during the early 1970s, each year was adding in excess of 90 million persons by the early 1990s.

Another way of illustrating the escalating nature of population change by the 1990s was by reference to the declining number of years required to add each additional billion to the global population base.[109] Table 1.5 reveals the reduced time frames associated with adding each additional billion to the world's population. As the table indicates, the world had the better part of a century to prepare for the addition of the second billion to the standing stock of human beings. The time to make preparations for the arrival of the sixth billion had been reduced to little more than a single decade. There are other ways of illustrating the dramatic nature of population growth during recent decades. It has, for example, been noted that the total world population has increased by more in the past 40

Table 1.4
Annual Additions to World Population 1900-1990

Year	Population (millions)	x	Growth rate (per year)	=	People added (millions)
1900	1500	x	0.5%	=	7.5
1950	2500	x	1.7%	=	42.5
1970	3600	x	2.1%	=	75.6
1990	5300	x	1.7%	=	90.1

Source: The 1990 growth rate and its consequence in terms of the number of people added to the world's population each year appear in Garrett Hardin, 1990, Sheer Numbers: Can Environmentalists Grasp the Nettle of Population? *The Environmental Magazine* 1,6: 41.

years (from 2.5 billion in 1950 to 5.3 billion in 1990) than it did in the previous 3 million years.[110] It has also been noted that we have people living today who represent the first generation to have witnessed a doubling of the world's population during their lifetimes.[111]

Current Views Regarding Population Growth

Unprecedented population growth had finally begun to alter popular perceptions regarding the merit of further additions to the human population by the

Table 1.5
Reduced Time Frames for Adding Each Additional One Billion People to the World's Population Base

One Billion Increments in Population Growth	Year Each Additional Billion Attained	Time Required to Add Each Billion
1st billion	1850	millions of years
2nd billion	1930	80 years
3rd billion	1960	30 years
4th billion	1975	15 years
5th billion	1987	12 years
6th billion	1998	11 years
7th billion	(Projected) 2008	10 years

Source: Figures appearing in World Resources Institute, 1994, *World Resources: 1994-95*, New York: Oxford University Press, 29

mid-1980s. In 1985, more than 40 world leaders, representing more than half of the world's people, signed a "Statement on Population Stabilization" stating that "early population stabilization" was in the interest of all nations.[112] Although the statement offered a number of rationales for such a position, it specifically acknowledged the role overpopulation played in degrading the world's environment. As 1990 approached, another statement of the need for population control surfaced in the form of the 1987 report of the World Commission on Environment and Development. Published under the heading of *Our Common Future*, the Brundtland Report (named after the chair of the commission) simply stated that "Present rates of population growth cannot continue."[113] By 1990 merely altering present rates of growth and moving toward early population stabilization were seen as insufficient responses by some. Paul and Anne Ehrlichs' *The Population Explosion*, for example, published in 1990, advances the case for a needed population *decline*.[114] The environmental consequences of maintaining even the current population had become quite simply untenable for the Ehrlichs and a growing number of other observers by the 1990s.

The implications of ongoing population growth in the United States was also being viewed in an entirely different light by the 1990s. Whereas the conventional wisdom had long advanced the view that America had both the space and the wealth to accommodate population growth into the foreseeable future, the 1990s were providing an alternative perspective. As Table 1.6 shows, while the country did not grow by as much between 1970 and 1990 (45 million) as it had between 1950 and 1970 (55 million), the addition of 100 million people between 1950 and 1990 still ranked the United States as the third most populous country in the world in 1990. Its 250 million put it only behind the 1,134 million of China and the 853 million of India.[115] When the 1990 figure of 250 million people in the United States is considered in terms of its impact on the global environment, it is possible to conclude that its combination of population, affluence, and technology deployment makes it the most overpopulated country in the world. Attempts to calculate the deleterious impact on the environment by way of the environmental impact equation ($I = P \times A \times T$) has produced the claim that

Table 1.6
Population Growth in the United States 1900-1990

Year	Population (millions)	Population Increases (millions)	Population Increases (millions)
1900	76		
1950	150		1900-1950: 74
1970	205	1950-1970: 55	
1990	250	1970-1990: 45	1950-1990: 100

Source: Rounded off figures are from the Bureau of the Census, 1996, *65+ in the United States*, Current Population Reports, Washington, D.C.: U.S. Government Printing Office, Chapter 2, page 3.

the average citizen of the United States has an impact at least 50 times greater than that of an average citizen in some of the desperately poor nations.[116] As the Ehrlichs have put it: "With its huge population (now over a quarter billion), unprecedented affluence, and profligate use of environmentally-damaging technologies, the United States is the world's most overpopulated nation in terms of its impact on Earth's fragile environment."[117] Such information certainly provides grounds for opposing further population growth in the United States, particularly when Census Bureau projections predict the addition of another 100 million Americans in the 40-year period between 1990 and 2030.[118] The population numbers associated with the growth of recent decades had therefore seriously undermined the previously assumed merit of population growth by the 1990s.

Current Views Regarding Economic Growth

Numbers associated with ongoing economic growth between 1970 and 1990 would also serve to further challenge the virtue of growth in the second key element of the growth imperative. Over the 20 years from 1970 to 1990, global industrial output grew by nearly 100%.[119] Although the phenomenal growth rate for output around 1970 of about 7% a year had not been maintained, the 1970-1990 growth rate in total production did average 3.3% per year.[120] Being almost twice the growth rate of about 1.7% a year for population over the course of the two decades, the 3.3% annual rate represents a doubling time for industrial output of about 21 years, while the 1.7% annual rate for population represents a doubling time of about 41 years. So while global population grew by approximately 47% over the course of the two decades, global industrial output recorded an increase of close to 100% during the same period. The doubling of what had already been a large volume of global industrial output in 1970 within a mere two decades contributed to growing skepticism that such a growth-oriented production system could be maintained. The 1992 sequel to the *The Limits to Growth*, titled *Beyond the Limits*, concluded that many of the rates of resource extraction and pollution emission had already grown to an unsupportable level by the 1990s.[121] As a result, the authors again stressed the need to give up on economic growth as a central social goal. The willingness to repudiate this element of the growth imperative was, however, proving to be more difficult than the rejection of population growth as a social good. The previously noted Brundtland Report, for example, while moving toward an acceptance of the need to stabilize the world's population, advocated a 5- to 10-fold increase in global economic activity in the next several decades in an effort to address poverty around the world. Despite the obvious global environmental consequences incurred by the level of economic activity attained by 1990, support for ongoing economic growth clearly seemed to evidence a greater holding power than support for population growth.

It is again possible to illustrate the magnitudes being generated by economic growth in the form of industrial output by illustrating the global increases being recorded in the production of motor vehicles and in the number of registered vehicles worldwide by 1990. As Table 1.7 shows, the two decades between 1970 and 1990 saw significant increases in both the annual number of motor vehicles being produced globally and in the total number of registered passenger cars and

Table 1.7
Motor Vehicle Production and Registration Worldwide 1950-1990

Year	Total Motor Vehicle Production (millions)	Total Registered Passenger Cars (millions)	Total Registered Motor Vehicles (millions)	Population Per Car — Number (millions)	Population Per Car	Per Vehicle
1950	10.5	54.2	70.0	2500	46	36
1970	29.3	193.5	246.4	3600	18	14
1990	48.3	444.9	582.9	5300	12	9

Sources: The figures are from Motor Vehicle Manufacturers Association of the United States, Incorporated, *Facts and Figures*, Detroit, Michigan; with most of the data coming from 1982 and 1992 editions containing comparative figures.

motor vehicles worldwide.[122] The increase in the total annual production of motor vehicles from close to 29 million units in 1970 to over 48 million units in 1990 pushed the totals for worldwide motor vehicle registrations from about 246 million to almost 583 million (137% increase) during the two decades, a period when global population increased from 3.6 billion to 5.3 billion (47%). With the number of registered passenger cars increasing from about 193 million in 1970 to about 445 million in 1990, the ratio of one car for every 18 people in 1970 declined further to a level of one car for every 12 people by 1990. The environmental implications of such an increase in the number of cars may again be illustrated by reference to the increase in global gasoline consumption on the part of passenger cars, which in spite of moves toward more fuel-efficient cars increased from 145 billion gallons annually in 1970 to over 220 billion gallons by 1990.[123]

As the noted figures indicate, the global growth rate for motor vehicles continued to exceed the growth rate of the human population over the 1970 to 1990 time period. An extreme example of the relationship between the growth of industrial output and population may be illustrated by the numbers associated with motor vehicle production and population increases in the United States from 1970 to 1990. Over the course of those two decades, the United States grew by an average of some 2.25 million people per year. During the same two decades motor vehicle production in the country averaged around 10 million units per year. Even this annual production level of four times the rate of the annual population increase was consistently decried as being economically insufficient, with the national goal identified as one of matching or exceeding the highest production year levels of over 12.5 million units a year. To identify success for a national industry in terms of production levels set at five times the annual increase of the country's population amounted to a clear example of "growthmania" for those who had come to question the wisdom or possibility of further economic growth. As noted previously, however, willingness to abandon this element of the growth imperative by the 1990s had not progressed as far as the evolving stance toward population growth.

Current Views Regarding Urban Growth

In much the same way that numbers generated by population and economic growth were altering perceptions regarding the merit of those two forms of growth by the 1990s, the view of urban growth was also being adjusted in response to numbers associated with this third form of growth over the course of the period from 1970 to 1990. By the 1990s the world's population was still urbanizing much faster than it was growing.[124] The location of most of that urbanization was within developing countries over the course of these two decades, and it was occurring at an average annual rate of about 4% between 1970 and 1990 versus a growth rate that averaged less than 2% for population growth during the same period.[125] A 4% growth rate produces a doubling in less than 18 years, and such growth between 1970 and 1990 was producing a very real change in the world's urban landscape. Trends were moving the world from around 40% urban in 1970 toward 50% urban around the year 2005, and more than 60% urban by 2025.[126] Many other trends being reported prior to 1990 revealed the momentous nature of the change occurring with respect to urban growth globally. The approximately 900 million people living in cities of 100,000 or more around 1970 were projected to increase to over 2 billion in such centers by the year 2000.[127] While only one city in the developing world had a population greater than 5 million in 1950, trends predicted the existence of 46 such cities by the year 2000.[128] Trends also indicated that 24 cities were expected to exceed 10 million inhabitants by the year 2000, with 18 of them being in developing countries.[129] Such trends were producing phenomenal results by the year 1990.

The nature of some of the more spectacular increases in urban growth between 1970 and 1990 may be illustrated by again referring to changes that occurred in the size of some of the largest of the world's urban agglomerations. Table 1.8 updates the figures provided in Table 1.3, and shows the nature of ongoing increases in megacities from 1970 to 1990, projected on to the year 2000.[130] The numbers reflecting the growth of some of the megacities shown in Table 1.8 indicate urban growth of unprecedented proportions between 1970 and 1990: Mexico City, 9.2 million to 21.3 million; Sao Paulo, 8.2 million to 18.8 million; Bombay, 5.9 million to 11.9 million; Seoul, 5.4 million to 11.5 million; Cairo/Giza, 5.4 million to 10.0 million. To have urban agglomerations start from population sizes that were already impressive by 1970, and to double those sizes in a mere two decades, contributed to changing views toward urban growth. The growth experienced by the largest centers, as well as that being experienced across a range of lesser-sized cities, caused some to advance the argument that urban areas were outgrowing the capacity of natural and social systems to support them.[131] By the 1990s some observers were willing to label both the growth of human populations and their urban settlements as a malignant, ecopathological process.[132] The numbers generated by urban growth in the few decades prior to 1990 therefore played a part in producing a negative view of urban growth, in much the same fashion that numbers associated with population and economic growth had begun to alter the view of those two forms of growth during the same period.

Growth over the course of the current century had recorded unprecedented increases by the 1990s. Population had almost quadrupled and total environmental impact, as measured by energy use, had increased some 13-fold.[133] It was, however, the growth of the last few decades that was principally responsible for a new view of the implications of ongoing growth. Population increasing by more than 90 million a year, motor vehicle production approaching 50 million units a year, and some of the world's largest cities doubling size in only two decades contributed to an increasing acceptance of the immediacy of limits to growth. Limits to growth, if they had been conceded at all in the previous decades, tended to be viewed as something that would be confronted in the future, perhaps a century away or in the lifetime of today's children.[134] By the 1990s the limits to growth were being treated as an existing reality of the day by a growing list of observers.

ACKNOWLEDGMENT OF EXISTING LIMITS TO GROWTH BY THE 1990s

There were already a limited number of individuals that were claiming the existence of current limits to growth before the 1990s. Lester Brown, for example argued a case for such limits in a 1981 book titled *Building a Sustainable*

Table 1.8
Growth of the World's Great Urban Agglomerations

Urban Agglomeration/ Country	1900		1950	Population (millions) 1970	1990	2000
London, Britain	6.48		10.40	10.6	9.5	9.1
New York/NE N.J., USA	4.42		12.40	16.3	15.3	15.5
Paris, France	3.33		5.50	8.3	9.0	9.2
Tokyo/Yokohama, Japan	1.50		6.70	14.9	17.2	17.1
Moscow, Russia	1.12		4.80	7.1	9.2	10.1
Calcutta, India	1.09		4.40	7.1	12.6	16.6
Shanghai, China	0.84		10.30	11.4	12.0	13.5
Buenos Aires, Argentina	0.81		5.30	8.5	11.7	13.2
Bombay, India	0.78		2.90	5.9	11.9	16.0
Beijing, China	under 0.50		6.70	8.3	9.5	10.8
Los Angeles, USA	under 0.50		4.10	8.4	10.5	11.2
Rio de Janeiro, Brazil	under 0.50		3.50	7.2	11.4	13.3
Mexico City, Mexico	under 0.50		3.10	9.2	21.3	26.3
Sao Paulo, Brazil	under 0.50		2.80	8.2	18.8	24.0
Seoul, Korea	under 0.50	under	2.50	5.4	11.5	13.5
Cairo/Giza, Egypt	under 0.50	under	2.50	5.4	10.0	13.2
Jakarta, Indonesia	under 0.50	under	2.50	4.5	9.3	12.8

Source: The figures are taken from tables appearing in Barclay Jones and William Shepherd, 1987, Cities of the Future: Implications for the Rise and Relative Decline of the Cities of the West, *Journal of Planning Education and Research* 6,3: 162-6.

Society on the basis of a claim that the carrying capacity of biological systems had already been exceeded in many parts of the world.[135] According to that work carrying capacities for many of the planet's fisheries, rangelands, and forests had already been surpassed. In exceeding the sustainable yield of these biological systems, the demands placed on them were already claimed to be consuming the productive resource bases represented by the systems. Expressions of such limits therefore existed prior to the 1990s, but they did not tend to make a case for the existence of current *global* limits to growth. The phenomenal growth in the decades immediately preceding the 1990s served to change that, however, with an increasing number of claims that planetary limits had already shown themselves.

Degradation of the Planet's Carrying Capacity

In their 1990 book, *The Population Explosion*, Paul and Anne Ehrlich argue that the entire planet is already vastly overpopulated on the basis of a single standard: its long-term carrying capacity is being degraded by its current population.[136] For them, carrying capacity consists of a restatement of the biologist's concept of the largest number of any given species that a habitat can support indefinitely, in this case the number of humans capable of being supported indefinitely by an area's resource base and the capacity of the environment to sustain their activities without being degraded. In their opinion the present population can not be maintained without rapidly depleting nonrenewable resources (or converting renewable resources into nonrenewable ones) and without degrading the capacity of the environment to support the population. They offer examples to illustrate the claim that the current population is only being supported by depleting resources that were created over millions of years—fertile topsoils, ice-age groundwater deposits, and other organisms that represent working parts of nature's life-support systems. They also offer several examples to support their claim that the habitability of Earth is rapidly decaying—desertification, the loss of stratospheric ozone, increased acidity of rain, the extermination of other species, etc. For the Ehrlichs the limits to growth were clearly evident by the 1990s, because in their opinion such limits had already been exceeded.

In 1991 the Ehrlichs' next contribution to the debate appeared in the form of their book *Healing the Planet*, in which they again made a case for the currency of limits to growth. In this work they once more assert that the entire globe is overpopulated by a simple standard: the human population can no longer be supported by the planet's income and is instead living largely on its capital (its inheritance of fertile topsoils, ancient groundwater deposits, and the wealth of biodiversity), and by living on that capital it is causing serious environmental deterioration.[137] With respect to losses in the resource of biodiversity, they argue that "[t]he ravaging of biodiversity . . . is the most serious single environmental peril facing civilization."[138] The Ehrlichs use the loss of biodiversity, as one of several indicators treated in the book, to support their contention that the global limits to growth have already been surpassed. For the Ehrlichs, the necessary social response by the 1990s was already one of the earlier noted call for a population decline[139] accompanied by a shrinkage in the current level of economic activity.[140]

Unsustainable Rates of Resource Extraction and Pollution Emission

Twenty years after publication of *The Limits to Growth* in 1972, the authors of that work released the sequel to their first book, this time choosing the title *Beyond the Limits* for the 1992 publication. As the title indicates, Donella Meadows and two coauthors involved in writing the first book had arrived at the conclusion that the world had already overshot some of its limits by the early 1990s. In *The Limits to Growth* it had been argued that if growth trends continued unchanged, the limits to physical growth on the planet would be reached within 100 years. Two decades later the authors were prepared to claim that some of the limits had already arrived. The authors argue that current limits, identified as limits to *throughput*, consist of existing limits to the ability of planetary *sources* to provide sustainable streams of materials and energy, and present limits to the ability of planetary *sinks* to absorb pollution and waste.[141] In the authors' words: "The human world is beyond its limits. The present way of doing things is unsustainable."[142] Because they consider present rates of resource extraction and pollution emission to be environmentally unsustainable, they believe a collapse is imminent, quite possibly within the lifetime of many who are alive today, unless needed changes are implemented.

In spite of such radical conclusions, the authors believe that the "transition to a sustainable society is probably possible without reductions in either population or industrial output."[143] For them, sustainability does not, at least in the short term, mean no growth.[144] Identifying themselves as "technological enthusiasts" the authors argue that given reasonable assumptions about future market efficiency and advances in technology the current throughput limits can temporarily be overcome. Overcoming them would, they believe, make it possible to provide a level of material welfare roughly equivalent to that of present-day Europe for a population of some 8 billion people during the course of slowing and eventually stopping the exponential growth of population and physical capital.[145] So while the work provides a statement of current limits to growth and acknowledges the need to give up on the growth imperative, it also illustrates the difficulty many may have in immediately rejecting both future growth and a classic faith in the market system and technology to make more growth possible.

Pervasive Environmental Constraints

In 1994 Earthwatch Institute released its annual *State of the World* report, and with its publication joined the increasing number of sources claiming that global limits to growth represented a current reality rather than a future prospect. The Institute had been releasing annual reports for a decade, documenting global issues confronting the world, but it had not previously asserted that the scale of the human enterprise had exceeded the planet's carrying capacity. In the 1994 report this claim was made in the following terms: "As a result of our population size, consumption patterns, and technology choices, we have surpassed the planet's carrying capacity."[146] The collection of articles that comprise the report chronicle, among other things, the extent to which current levels of population and economic activity are damaging and depleting the planet's natural capital. Arguing that the earth's ability to sustain life is being severely strained, the report details the nature of pervasive environmental constraints indicating the current existence of limits to further growth: diminished fertility on existing agricultural lands, overgrazed grasslands, overharvested fisheries, depleted and polluted water sources, truncated natural forests, and reduced biodiversity. Taking a look at projected relationships between population size and the availability of renewable resources on a global basis between 1990 and 2010, the report identified the following prospective per capita declines over the course of the two decades: 10% in fish catch, 12% in irrigated land, 21% in cropland, 22% in rangeland and pasture, and 30% in forests.[147] These figures imply that current limits to growth would make themselves much more visible in the next few decades.

Lost Ground in Feeding an Expanding Global Population

Yet another source of claimed limits to further growth by the 1990s appeared with the 1994 release of *Full House: Reassessing the Earth's Population Carrying Capacity*, coauthored by Lester Brown and Hal Kane. The authors of that work argue that "[t]he food sector is the first where our demands are colliding with some of the earth's limits."[148] With respect to oceanic food supplies, the authors cite a report by marine biologists at the U.N. Food and Agricultural Organization claiming that all 17 major oceanic fisheries are now being fished at or beyond capacity, and that 9 are in a state of decline. As a consequence, the record catch of about 100 million tons in 1989 has not been matched, and with population increasing they show the per person share of that catch to have declined by 9% between 1988 and 1993, in contrast to having grown by 126% between 1950 and 1988.[149] They cite other studies indicating that the world's rangelands, a major source of animal protein, are being grazed at or beyond capacity on every continent. With meat production per capita from that source declining, total meat production from rangelands and feedlots is shown to have grown only as fast as the population since 1987, and the authors question the ability to maintain that growth as competing demands for grain to raise that meat become more intense with each passing year.[150] With respect to per person figures for global grain production, they show that after expanding at 3% a year from 1950 to 1984, the growth in grain production slowed to scarcely 1% annually from 1984 to 1993. As a result, grain production per person fell by 12% during this latter period, compared to having increased 40% per person during the 1950 to 1984 period.[151] Brown and Kane provide numerous reasons why future grain production is unlikely to match the production levels that until recently had it increasing more rapidly than population: abandonment of eroded cropland, unsustainable irrigation practices, declining responses to increased fertilizer use, the absence of new advanced yield-raising technologies, and physiological yield limits for many existing cereals. In the end, Brown and Kane describe the limits to growth in the following stark terms: "Even now, the food needs of the 90 million added each year can be satisfied only by reducing consumption among those already here."[152]

As the noted examples illustrate, a number of recurring themes are being used to make a case for the presence of current limits to further physical growth. Some stress that we are living on nature's capital rather than its income. In the process, we are said to be depleting such onetime resource inheritances as deep fertile topsoils and ice-age groundwater deposits and exceeding the sustainable yield of fisheries, rangelands, and forests. Others point to the fact that planetary sources of nonrenewable materials and energy are presently being used on a non-sustainable basis, indicating that limits to growth have been reached. Yet others focus on the reality of serious environmental deterioration, claiming that even the current scale of the human enterprise is progressively degrading the global environment and revealing that we have run into limits to the planet's ability to absorb pollutants. Then there are those who emphasize the reality of declining biodiversity, arguing that growth that drives other species into extinction on a massive scale clearly indicates that limits have been surpassed. There has also been a revival of the Malthusian argument as a basis for making a claim of current limits, pointing out that the food demands of an additional 90 million people each year for grain and seafood are being currently satisfied only by reducing consumption among those already here. Underlying virtually all of these arguments in support of the claim of current limits to growth is recognition of the fact that the present scale of the human enterprise is threatening the planet's life-support systems. The dismantling of these life-support systems is arguably the greatest threat to the future of our species and to the rest of life on this planet.[153]

Assault on Our Life-Support Systems

The planet's ecosystems constitute humanity's life-support apparatus.[154] All life is utterly dependent on these ecosystems to support it, and the continued existence of our species and civilization is not exempt from such dependency. For ecologists the entire biosphere constitutes an ecosystem, as do the innumerable local biotic communities and the physical environments with which the organisms in these communities interact. Such natural ecosystems provide a wide array of essential services that are delivered free. No authors have done more to popularize the idea and further the public understanding of these services than Paul and Anne Ehrlich, whose writings describe some of the critical services provided by our life-support systems.[155] They point out that the global ecosystem maintains a benign mix of gases in the atmosphere essential to life as we know it. Climate control in the form of moderation of the weather constitutes another essential ecosystem service. Regulation of the hydrologic cycle provides fresh water in such a way as to minimize floods and droughts. Ecosystems also serve to purify air and water. Local ecosystems generate and maintain the fertile soils essential for agriculture and forestry. Such ecosystems also dispose of wastes and recycle essential nutrients. They further provide pest control and pollination services for many crops. They directly provide forest products and food from the world's oceans. And they create and maintain the biodiversity that represents the "genetic library" from which our species was able to fashion civilization.

Life-support services provided by the planet's ecosystems are obviously of critical importance. Even the incomplete list of services noted above reveals how completely dependent our species is on the life-support functions of ecosystems. As our species destroys or impairs ecosystems we threaten the very life-support functions on which we depend. The unrelenting expansion of the human enterprise has taken over more and more of the natural landscapes of which ecosystems are comprised, and as a consequence the life-support services performed by these ecosystems have been impaired or lost.[156] As the Ehrlichs put it: "Civilization can't persist without ecosystem services, and these are threatened in innumerable ways by the expanding scale of human activities."[157] Evidence of the extent to which our species is taking over the world's ecosystems and thereby reducing their vital services is revealed by the increasing resources we are being required to commit to such things as sewage treatment, air purification, flood control, pest control, restoration of soil nutrients, and the preservation of species.

Another indicator of the extent to which humans are converting natural ecosystems to human-dominated ones, and thereby diminishing their vital services, comes from research into how much of the biological activity of the planet has been appropriated for the use of human beings. Research has investigated the extent of this appropriation by assessing human impact on the planet's total supply of energy produced in photosynthesis, that is global net primary production.[158] Such net primary production (NPP) is the total amount of solar energy converted into biochemical energy through plant photosynthesis minus the energy used by plants for their own life processes. It represents the basic food source for all life, and the noted research looked into how much of that NPP had already been appropriated by our species. The research concluded that almost 40% of all potential NPP generated on land is now commandeered by people. Although only some 3% is directly consumed, indirectly another 36% of terrestrial NPP goes to crop wastes, forest burning and clearing, desert creation, and conversion of natural areas to settlements.

The 40% appropriation of NPP directly correlates with the global level of land use by humans.[159] Excluding the polar regions, humanity grows crops on about 11% of the planet's land surface and uses another 25% as permanent pasture. Some 2% is occupied by urban settlements. Another 30 to 40% of the land is covered by forest and woodland, much of which is exploited by people. So people already use at least 40% of the planet's land surface intensively, and another 25 to 30% less intensively.[160] To have one species—*Homo sapiens*—appropriate 40% of the terrestrial food supply and at least an equal percentage of the planet's land area, leaving only 60% for the millions of other species of land-based plants and animals, offers some insight into the extent to which humans are replacing the natural world with a human-dominated one. The figures for NPP and land-use appropriation therefore stand as indicators of the extent to which our species is taking over the world's ecosystems and thereby reducing their vital services.

As our species takes over more and more of the planet, taking ever higher percentages of NPP and land area for it own use, the consequence for many other species is clear: extinction. As the Ehrlichs have expressed it: "Since the great majority of the world's species (probably over 95 percent) now exist on land, the 40-percent human appropriation or loss of NPP there goes far to explain the extinction crisis."[161] The extinction of other species has direct implications for the ability of ecosystems to provide vital life-support services. Although the relationship between the loss of biodiversity and the provision of life-support systems is not well understood, there is an awareness that other life forms are intimately involved in delivery of these services.[162] To diminish the complexity of ecosystems through extinctions is therefore a dangerous endeavor, because the losses are likely to result in the disruption of the services that these ecosystems provide. In the Ehrlichs' terms: "The decimation of species in natural ecosystems . . . will almost certainly degrade the services they supply."[163] When viewed in these terms the matter of extinctions takes on a different meaning than that associated with compassion for other forms of life, an interest in protecting esthetic values, or the motive of safeguarding economic interests represented by a species.[164] To allow extinctions is to endanger our own future, because living organisms in natural ecosystems play enormous roles in the provision of life-support services critical to our own well-being.

Even though we now know that the most serious impact of extinctions on our species will be felt through the consequences of disrupting the ecological systems that provide us with essential services, our species has been unable to shut down the growth that is behind the current extinction crisis. The exponential growth of the human enterprise is driving a significant portion of the living world to extinction. As long as the growth imperative drives population, economic, and urban growth at exponential rates, that growth will take over natural ecosystems at exponential rates, and that will in turn push the number of extinctions to increase exponentially. Our understanding of the true extent of biological diversity as measured by the number of species worldwide is still rudimentary. Estimates of the number of species range from 2 million to well over 50 million, with only about 1.4 million having been named and classified. Estimates of the rate of extinctions range from 5,000 to 90,000 species annually, which ecologists believe represents an extinction rate from 10,000 to 150,000 times the "background" rate before our species began practicing agriculture.[165] This extent of species loss may be directly linked to habitat loss. It has been estimated that about half the world's wetlands have been lost to dredging, filling, draining, and ditching,[166] and as places of intense biological activity their loss has contributed to an accelerating rate of global extinction. The same habitat destruction has eliminated about half of the original tropical forests, and under the current accelerating rate of deforestation most of the remaining large tracts will be destroyed by the year 2010.[167] This habitat loss and the resultant extinction process has ecologists referring to the present period as an Era of Impoverishment. It has now been estimated that under current and accelerating trends we may well see half of the planet's species disappear by 2050.[168] One observer has aptly referred to this process as *biological meltdown.*[169]

The United States is not exempt from the extinction process and its associated implications for the ability of ecosystems to provide their vital life-support services. During the course of our history we know that we have eliminated the passenger pigeon, which once existed in numbers capable of blotting out the sun for days; cut back the bison from nearly 60 million to a pathetic population numbering in the thousands; and taken an estimated 100,000 grizzlies and reduced them to two precarious populations in Montana and Wyoming.[170] But these examples represent only the tip of the iceberg in the broad reduction of biodiversity that has occurred in this country to date. Something of the extent of ecosystem disruption is revealed by one study stating that of 23 ecosystem types that once covered about half the coterminous United States, those ecosystems now cover only about 7%.[171] This decline in ecosystem diversity has directly contributed to a reduction of biodiversity. When ecosystem loss is compounded by other adverse effects associated with the expansion of the human enterprise in the setting of the United States, the impacts for a host of species has been devastating. The oyster beds of Chesapeake Bay that once yielded 8 million bushels a year are down to about 300,000 bushels.[172] The 16 million adult salmon that once entered the Columbia River each year are down to about 1.1 million fish, and only approximately 500,000 are non-hatchery fish.[173] Moving to inland waters, 27 species of freshwater fishes have become extinct in North America in the last hundred years.[174] Turning to the skies, recent studies have revealed alarming losses in migrant songbird populations across the United States, exceeding 20% for a range of species since 1980, with such losses attributable at least in part to habitat fragmentation associated with expanding human activities.[175] These examples only begin to convey the cost to other species associated with our takeover of the continent. One recent estimate put some 4,000 domestic species at risk of extinction by the turn of the century.[176] We are obviously involved in the same lethal extermination process that is occurring everywhere else on the planet. By engaging in that process we are simplifying ecosystems and thereby compromising the essential life-support systems they provide. If we are unable to end the extermination of other species on ethical grounds, then perhaps we can be intelligent enough to recognize that such killing represents a threat to our own species and cease on self-serving, anthropocentric grounds. To end the extinction crisis we will have to give up on the growth imperative and accept the Ehrlichs' conclusion of the need for us to reduce the scale of the human enterprise.[177] A central rationale for abandoning the growth imperative would be the realization that we could never successfully or cost effectively replace the life-support systems provided by ecosystems across the globe. One need only look at such examples as past attempts to replace natural flood control systems with artificial ones, and the substitution of synthetic pesticides for natural pest control, to realize how inadequate such replacement measures are destined to be. In reality, life-support systems are provided on such a grand scale it would be impossible to create satisfactory substitutes for them.[178] Since we are utterly dependent on such systems for our survival, and since the growth imperative is unraveling these support systems, growth in the scale of the human enterprise must come to an end and be replaced by a deliberate effort to scale back that enterprise to a level that may be sustained indefinitely.

REQUIEM FOR THE GROWTH IMPERATIVE

Our species finds itself at a watershed in human history. Diverse cultures around the world have incorporated the growth imperative into their own dominant social paradigms. As a result we now have what may be described as a worldwide cultural network united in its pursuit of growth. The pursuit of that growth on the part of a global community has had dramatic consequences since it took on exponential characteristics some two centuries ago. Quantities now being generated by such growth are overwhelming the natural world. As a result of such hyperactive growth during the last few decades, we have witnessed the sudden arrival of limits to further growth as this century comes to a close.

The limits to growth have been revealed in a number of different ways. Sheer magnitudes being created by today's population, economic, and urban growth rates in and of themselves clearly reveal that ongoing growth is simply unsustainable. During the 1970s most of the concern with matters of resource depletion focused on such nonrenewable resources as minerals and fossil fuels. By the 1990s much of the focus had shifted to depletion concerns regarding such renewable resources as groundwater supplies and forests. Difficulties in supplying resources to fuel ongoing growth on both the nonrenewable and renewable resource fronts have therefore provided further evidence that ongoing growth is unsustainable. Pollution levels responsible for the die off of forests across broad regional landscapes and significant changes in the planet's atmospheric mix of gases also indicate that even the current scale of the human enterprise is degrading the capacity of the planet to support life and that further growth is therefore unsustainable. The fact that even the present numbers already generated by growth are serving to kill off a sizable portion of the rest of life on the planet, and in the process degrading the life-support systems needed to sustain our own species, provides more proof of the unsustainable nature of growth by the end of the 1990s. All of these obvious indicators point to the need to recognize that the pursuit of physical growth has now become an obsolete and lethal ideology, and that we are at a point of having to abandon the growth imperative if we are to survive.

Conventional wisdom of the day suggests that some future growth is inevitable. With respect to global population growth, reasoning has it that the current skewed population distribution in favor of age groups in their reproductive years instills a certain momentum that ensures future growth. Such thinking assumes further population growth well into the next century and takes for granted a population at least twice as large as the one currently taxing the limits of the planet. Regarding economic growth, it is widely believed that further expansion of the global economy is necessary to address even current levels of poverty, to say nothing about the needs of those assumed to be inevitable additions to the world's population during coming decades. Traditional thinking therefore assumes a many-fold increase in global economic activity to meet the needs of both current and future populations. And with limited rural land resources in many parts of the world, additional urban growth to house the coming numbers and their associated economic activities has also come to be considered an inevitable aspect of the near future. Even though the current scale of the human enterprise has already exceeded the planet's long-term carrying capacity, the growth imperative component of the world's dominant social paradigm struggles to maintain its hold on our collective consciousness.

There is of course an alternative. We could collectively admit that further growth is unacceptable on numerous grounds. Social action could be taken to reduce birth rates to a single child per family, which would immediately move us toward a stable global population in spite of the large numbers currently in their child-bearing years, and after a few decades begin to produce the needed decline in our numbers. With regard to economics, we could finally admit that any attempt to replicate the current consumer model of developed countries throughout the developing world is unthinkable on environmental grounds. That admission would permit us to reject the idea that human fulfillment is attainable through materialistic satiety and allow us to redirect the global economy toward sustainable activity as we scale back the world's economic enterprise. With population and economic growth brought to a halt and then reversed, it would be possible to begin the task of scaling back the many urban centers that have outgrown the capacity of their social and natural systems to support them and to undertake the task of converting them to sustainable entities.

The premise underlying the remainder of this book is that we have arrived at a point where we have no alternative but to reject the growth imperative. The only acceptable physical growth in population, economic, or urban terms would be growth matched by an equal or greater amount of counterbalancing shrinkage in order to permit the overall human enterprise to be reduced to a level capable of being supported indefinitely. Nature would, of course, be exempt from such a prohibition on future physical expansion, because it would be allowed to regain a sufficient foothold on the planet to permit it to once again provide the full array of life-support services needed by us and other life forms. If we are not yet able to abandon the growth imperative with all that we now know about the arrival of limits to further growth, then our species must surely be in collective denial regarding the urgency of letting go of this particular tenet of the world's dominant social paradigm. As psychologists know, denial acts as a defense mechanism against negative information from the outside world, but continued denial about what the growth imperative is doing to the natural world now runs the risk of shutting down the planet's ability to support life as we now know it.

In addressing the subject matter of growth management for a sustainable future in the remainder of this book, the need to abandon the growth imperative will of course be assumed to apply to the United States. As noted previously, in terms of environmental impact the United States represents the most overpopulated country in the world. The significance of its average annual growth from 1970 to 1990 of 2.25 million people per year may be illustrated by indicating the settlement challenges associated with accommodating such a number under a deliberate new towns policy. If the United States had such a policy, and decided to settle the 2.25 million in small, environmentally sensitive new communities of 30,000 each, it would be necessary to plan and build 75 new towns each year. If the decision were made to locate the additional 2.25 million in urban centers of 100,000, it would be necessary to plan and build 22.5 centers each year. The prospect of locating suitable sites on the American landscape with adequate land, water, and air resources to accommodate such a number of new centers each year, year in and year out, to say nothing of the daunting task of actually planning and building them, ought to have everyone question the sanity of an ongoing accommodation of uncontrolled population increases.

Since we do not have a national new towns settlement policy, these additional people are being absorbed by existing urban agglomerations, a process that may be referred to as growth by accretion. Such growth typically stresses centers that are already at their limits in terms of being able to absorb additional numbers without degrading their environments further. If we do not abandon the growth imperative pressures to settle new Americans will continue, if for no other reason than the change represented by the 1990 Immigration Act, which increased annual immigration into the United States by 40% over previous levels. The Act contained "pierceable caps" making it possible for immigration levels to continue to rise annually. From some 400,000 legal immigrants annually during the early 1970s we are now admitting more than twice that number yearly. Combined with natural increases, and not counting illegal immigrants, we are now forced to accommodate over 3 million a year. The environmental consequences for America's landscape and the planet as a whole clearly point to a need to reject such an ongoing process. As the report of The Commission on Population Growth and the American Future from the early 1970s showed,

Americans could have achieved an immediate cessation of population growth at that time by limiting themselves to one child per family until the year 2000, at which time such reproductive behavior would have actually begun to shrink the country's population. Immigration, in turn, would presently have to be limited to some 200,000, the number who voluntarily leave each year, in order to achieve replacement-level immigration. The next task would then be to abandon our ideology of consumerism, turning our backs on an economic system that has already succeeded in producing one motor vehicle for every 1.6 Americans and is pushing us toward a future where each individual will be expected to own more than one. Facing the same challenge as the rest of the world, we would then be free to devise a sustainable economic system for the future. When contending with population and economic growth no longer represented a full-time preoccupation for the nation, we would also be free to devote time to creating sustainable urban centers.

Having made a case for the need to abandon the growth imperative, and a corresponding need to accept and implement a no-growth philosophy, the remainder of this book will address the implications of such a new posture toward growth for what has been called the growth management movement in the United States. There has been no more fashionable term during the 1990s than that of sustainable development, and the term has started to appear in the field of growth management. That has not, however, meant that growth management activity in the United States has been directed at stopping population, economic, or urban growth. There has instead, as will be shown, been an acceptance of a belief in the oxymoronic idea of sustainable growth. An actual acceptance of abandoning the growth imperative might, therefore, be expected to present challenges to growth management as it has been practiced to date in this country, and the next chapter is intended to reveal the nature of those challenges. That chapter will trace the evolution of the growth management movement in the United States and illustrate the nature of changes that would have to occur in that movement if it is to play a meaningful role in assisting the nation in making a transition to a sustainable future.

2

The Evolution of the Growth Management Movement in the United States

The ethic of growth in America is increasingly being challenged; no longer is it being accepted unquestioningly as a premise of progress. Its effects on the quality of life are widely debated, and its management and control are seen by many as essential elements of modern land use policy.

Randall W. Scott[1]

During the 1970s, literature appeared describing an ideological shift in Americans' attitudes toward growth. The traditional association of population, economic, and urban growth with societal progress was giving way to a new view with respect to these forms of growth. One often quoted source from that period claimed that a "new mood" toward growth was challenging our traditional "growth ethic."[2] A memorandum out of the President's Council on Environmental Quality asserted that "assumptions about the inherent value of growth and change are being discarded in even the more conservative regions."[3] By the 1970s, many Americans, it seemed, were increasingly less willing to endorse the idea that "bigger is better" and to support local growth policies based on "chamber of commerce principles."[4]

This ideological shift did not come easily, because conventional thinking in local governmental contexts had historically associated ongoing population, economic, and urban growth with a range of benefits, including stronger local economies, higher personal incomes, lower taxes, greater upward economic mobility for the poor, and a greater range of lifestyle choices for urban consumers. In spite of this array of supposed benefits, increasing numbers of Americans were rejecting the view of growth as something beneficial by the 1970s. Their own experiences with growth led them to associate it with such ills as overcrowded schools, tax increases, rising crime rates, physical blight, traffic congestion, the loss of open space, the destruction of a "way of life," and increasing air and water pollution. By the mid-1970s a national opinion survey revealed a majority of Americans felt that population and industrial growth should be regulated in the areas where they lived because of its association with such a host of prospective ill effects.[5] That feeling increasingly found expression in what would come to be referred to as the growth management movement.[6] Most participants in that movement had come to think of growth as something to be managed, regulated, or controlled, rather than simply promoted as in the past.

If one reads a description of the changing national perspective toward growth by the 1970s, and considers growth management as a response based on an accepted need to regulate or control growth, one might be tempted to conclude that the growth management movement in the United States represents an acceptance of the need to abandon the growth imperative. As this chapter will illustrate, however, that has not been the case. The premise of this book—that we are at a point of having to abandon the growth imperative—has not been accepted by the overwhelming majority of the participants in the growth management movement. Growth management in the United States has instead reflected a concerted effort to allow continued adherence to the growth imperative by controlling the deleterious effects of growth. Rather than accepting the idea of growth as the central problem of this era, the movement has tended to endorse the viewpoint that it is possible to have quantity with quality if future growth is properly planned and regulated.[7]

ORIGINS OF THE GROWTH MANAGEMENT MOVEMENT IN THE UNITED STATES

Although the so-called growth management movement only emerged during the late 1960s and early 1970s,[8] the management of growth in the form of land-use controls dates back to the opening decades of this century.[9] As acknowledged by one observer, "Long before the term 'growth management' became fashionable, localities had decided that land use decisions would not be left entirely to the marketplace, and developed a reasonably elaborate regulatory system: zoning ordinances, subdivision regulations, and building codes."[10] The management of growth through these regulatory mechanisms therefore grounds such management efforts in the exercise of the police power on the part of local communities. As the inherent power of the government to regulate individual behavior, including the use of private property, for furtherance of the health, safety, and welfare of the community, the police power provides the legal justification for the public imposition of land-use regulations upon private property. In the words of one commentator: "The development and use of the police power to manage growth was a magnificent innovation in 1916, made legitimate in the 1926 Supreme Court case, *Euclid v. Ambler*."[11] The year 1916 represented the adoption date of the first comprehensive zoning code in the United States, and the 1926 Supreme Court decision upheld the general constitutionality of comprehensive zoning. These early zoning ordinances afforded communities the power to regulate: 1) the type of land use permitted at different locations, 2) the amount or intensity of development at specific sites by use of density standards, and 3) the character of development by way of bulk regulations addressing building setbacks from lot lines or streets, maximum lot coverages for buildings, and the height of buildings. Zoning, as the principal police-power regulation of land use in this country, therefore provided opportunities for managing growth since the opening decades of this century. During roughly the same time period subdivision regulations were being developed to ensure that land divided for development sites was adequately serviced by such essential public infrastructure elements as streets and sewers.[12] These two major forms of land-use regulation, coupled with other police-power mechanisms, therefore provided American communities with instruments to manage growth for decades prior to the emergence of the growth management movement during the latter 1960s.

Although the ability to manage growth with land-use regulations based on the police power has existed for the better part of a century, there had only been a limited willingness to utilize zoning and subdivision regulations to effectively manage growth prior to the recent emergence of the growth management movement. Historically, attempts to manage growth encountered the difficulty of "trying to develop land use controls in a country built by unbridled individual rights to property and exploitation of land as a commodity."[13] Efforts to regulate land have had to contend with "the general hostility of Americans to government in general and regulation in particular."[14] Land-use regulations that were applied to property tended to be accepted only because of the role they were seen to play in protecting property rights. Zoning, for example, could be reluctantly supported if it protected land from unacceptable adjoining uses, and subdivision regulations could be unwillingly embraced if they ensured property owners that proper public improvements would enhance development options. As the subsequent chapter will reveal, these traditional land-use regulatory techniques were in fact used to facilitate development rather than to manage the growth that that development represented.

Significant attempts to manage growth through land-use regulations in the United States did not in fact occur until the latter 1960s when the beginnings of an ideological shift in American's attitudes toward growth began to affect popular perceptions regarding land development. Uses of land were increasingly being perceived as the source of a host of societal problems during this period. In addition to the previously noted ill effects attributed to growth, it was also being blamed for such diverse problems as the costly and destructive development patterns associated with urban sprawl, the loss of prime agricultural lands, an inefficient provision of public facilities and services, escalating housing prices, and pervasive environmental degradation beyond the initial focus on matters of air and water pollution. As a result, growth was rapidly coming to be seen as something that had to be managed, and the "ethic of growth" was purportedly said to be giving way to an "ethos of managed growth" by the 1970s.[15]

With an acceptance of the need to manage growth, the objectives of growth management efforts directly reflected an interest in addressing the ill effects attributed to growth. The management movement suggested the possibility of avoiding the loss of open space, prime agricultural tracts, and valuable resource lands. It offered strategies for containing what had increasingly come to be perceived as costly and destructive sprawl development. It put forth techniques for the efficient provision of public facilities and services, including measures designed to have the development community share the cost of providing public improvements. The movement proposed approaches for ensuring housing choices that would further the objective of affordability. It also advanced measures for protecting environmentally-sensitive lands, and held out the promise that properly managed growth would make it possible to avoid further environmental deterioration. The movement also held out the hope that, if managed, growth would not have to represent a destruction of community character and the current way of life.[16] With such a wide range of possible benefits associated with the management of growth, both the term and concept of growth management came to be popularized during the 1970s.[17] By the mid-1970s one observer could claim that "we are entering a new phase of urban development in this country—a phase dominated by the concept of growth management."[18]

As the prior description illustrates, it is possible to attribute the origins of the growth management movement in this country to the development and legalization of land-use regulations during the opening decades of this century. The use of police-power regulations to manage growth therefore predates the recent emergence of the so-called growth management movement by half a century. In this respect, one can argue that the management of growth is, in its generic form, nothing new, and that it has in fact been around for the better part of this century.[19] As one observer recently noted:

> In general, growth management plans or systems are made up of elements that have been well known to planners for years. In that sense, there is nothing unique about them . . . [and] it must be admitted that no absolutely hard line separates growth management from more traditional planning.[20]

This line of reasoning would have one believe that growth management of the present era is not a new phenomenon, and instead merely an integration or synthesis of traditional implementation tools or techniques.[21] However, such generalizations mask a very real difference between former efforts to manage growth and most of the more recent efforts of the current growth management movement. The traditional use of police-power regulations to manage growth tended to reflect a positive view of growth, which in turn produced regulations that were inclined to *promote* and *facilitate* growth during the course of managing it. The current growth management movement, on the other hand, reflected the new sentiment toward growth that had emerged during the 1960s and 1970s, and that ideological shift concerning the popular sentiment toward growth tended instead to produce regulations that were deliberately intended to *regulate* and *control* growth during the course of the management process. In this respect, the growth management movement represented a significant and very real change from the past, both in how growth was to be considered and treated in the American context.

THE GROWTH MANAGEMENT MOVEMENT IN THE UNITED STATES

The emergence of the growth management movement in this country during the latter 1960s and early 1970s may be attributed to a perceived need to respond to a broad range of what had come to be viewed as growth-induced problems. Some students of the movement have, however, credited a few principal forces with providing the impetus for a widespread interest in the management of growth.[22] One of those forces was the concern with the environment that emerged during the 1960s.[23] The movement, "arriving on the heals of the explosive rise in environmental activism at the close of the 1960s,"[24] was so closely associated with the corresponding rise of the environmental movement that "there is no doubt that the growing environmental consciousness of the 1960s and 1970s lent much strength to the growth management movement."[25] Another major force credited with bringing about the movement was the large-scale change associated with the post-war suburbanization movement and the subsequent urbanization of the suburbs.[26] Residents of communities experiencing such change were often willing to support the movement as a way of protecting community character and an existing way of life. A survey of communities engaged in growth management by the mid-1970s revealed another principal motivating force behind the development of the movement. The impacts of growth on community facilities and services prompted an interest in management in order to hold down future costs of providing facilities and services, and in reducing facility and service deficiencies resulting from prior growth.[27] These principal forces created enough of an interest in growth management by the 1970s to have management activity referred to as a movement by that period.

Unwarranted Characterizations of Management Programs as No-Growth Initiatives

If involvement with growth management by the 1970s was sufficient to label it a movement, it would be wrong to infer that the movement was unified in its understanding of what constituted appropriate management behavior. As the previous chapter indicated, the 1970s also represented a period of active debate on the matter of anti-growth versus pro-growth sentiments. Some of those who had come to accept the merit of a no-growth position sought an outlet for their viewpoint in the growth management movement. The nature of growth-control measures advocated by these proponents of a new ideological stance toward growth rarely reflected an actual no-growth posture, but the management proposals elicited considerable controversy nonetheless. By suggesting that the regulation and control of growth were now more appropriate than its promotion and facilitation, these advocates of a new growth orientation challenged the traditional societal posture toward growth sufficiently to have their programs pejoratively labeled as no-growth efforts. In the words of one developer during the 1970s: "Although frequently described as optimum growth, controlled growth, planned growth or balanced growth, the 'new mood' encourages policies that can be more accurately described as no growth."[28] Even though very few growth management proposals have actually advocated a no-growth position, and even these have only proposed some *future* limit to growth in a particular local governmental setting, originally "the term *growth management*, . . . tended to be defined as a no growth, or at least slow growth, phenomenon."[29] As noted by one commentator, "The term as originally used was often synonymous with rigid growth control, especially no-growth or slow-growth programs."[30]

The early association of the growth management movement with a no-growth position was undoubtedly influenced by the willingness of some growth management programs to utilize growth-control measures not previously used by local governments. Although local entities had previously used such land-use regulations as zoning and subdivision ordinances to manage growth, these traditional police-power mechanisms were now being revised to permit a level of growth control that had not previously existed. Zoning, for example, had traditionally only been concerned with controlling the type, density, and character of development at different locations on the landscape, and had left the timing of development to individual property owners.[31] From the perspective of growth management, such zoning was seen as being strong on location controls but weak on timing and cost controls.[32] Growth management programs remedied this weakness by instituting zoning regulations governing the rate of growth— that is, the amount permitted in specified time periods. Cost controls were in turn imposed by linking development permission in such specified time periods to the availability of infrastructure improvements, and by asking property owners to share in the cost of providing improvements. Traditional subdivision regulations were similarly expanded beyond a previous concern with on-site facilities to encompass requirements for owners to also participate in the provision of adequate off-site facilities.[33] These new forms of regulation and the associated cost implications for property owners and developers produced a general condemnation of the new regulatory mechanisms. Many viewed the new regulations as disguised efforts to stop growth, and this produced a corresponding characterization of such management programs as no-growth initiatives.

Typical growth management programs also imposed new land-use regulations designed to contain growth within designated growth boundaries.[34] These measures afforded a means for containing sprawl and thereby avoiding costly and inefficient facility and service provisions across the landscape. When linked with associated requirements for adequate public facilities and services in order to obtain development permission, such measures provided communities with means to contain the cost of future facilities and services, and the opportunity to remedy current facility and service deficiencies. Containing growth within designated growth boundaries was also seen as a way of protecting the environment from sprawling development that could potentially destroy such natural features of the landscape as wetlands and wildlife habitats. Controlling the rate of growth, in conjunction with other regulations designed to influence the quality of development, were in turn seen as ways of protecting community character and allowing sufficient time to absorb new growth without destroying a current way of life. When taken together, the new regulatory responses to growth were seen as necessary to address the very forces that had been credited with creating the growth management movement in the first place.

The arguable point is whether the new land-use regulations utilized by typical growth management programs were really designed to stop growth. Regulations controlling the rate of growth have typically placed a ceiling on the amount of growth allowed on an annual basis, such as the number of new dwelling units permitted per year. While these restrictions limit growth to a specified amount during a designated time period, subsequent time periods are permitted additional growth allotments, and this allows growth to continue. By limiting growth to an amount below what an unconstrained market may desire to build in a specified time period, these efforts might more accurately be characterized as slow-growth programs. The only way that they may be labeled as no-growth measures is by limiting the time frame of consideration to the designated time period associated with rate controls, and then to argue that the imposed limit represents a no-growth measure when the limit has been reached. This position ignores the temporary nature of growth limitations associated with rate of growth controls. Similarly, managing growth on the basis of adequate public facility and service standards may limit growth at particular locations for a period of time, but typical growth management programs have included affirmative programs to provide the future public improvements needed to allow growth to continue. As a result, these measures may also be characterized as slow-growth programs, but they have not typically been directed at putting permanent barriers in the way of continued growth. Growth containment within designated boundaries also places potentially significant limits to growth outside a designated growth zone, although the limits have not pertained to all forms of development in outlying areas. While individual sites outside these containment zones may have a limited range of development options in the short term, such restrictions do not tend to be permanent. As has been noted, "Although many communities have short-range boundaries beyond which they are unlikely to encourage or permit expansion, relatively rigid long-term boundaries are not common."[35] A general willingness to extend such containment boundaries when growth has closed out future development options within containment boundaries reveals that this management technique also allows future growth to continue. Although none of the new regulatory mechanisms utilized by growth management programs actually stop future growth, the extent of interference with previous growth trends represented by the new management regulations has produced considerable difference of opinion as to the appropriate nature and degree of growth management.

Growth management literature distinguishes between growth management measures and growth-control measures. Take, for example, the following excerpts:

> The terms growth control and growth management are widely and incorrectly used to mean the same thing. . . . *Growth controls* are designed to limit significantly population growth, housing construction, and/or economic growth below levels that would otherwise be achieved in an unconstrained real estate market. . . . Rather than reducing the overall amount or rate of growth, *growth management* programs seek to redistribute growth and development in ways that minimize negative environmental, social, and fiscal impacts.[36]

> *Growth management* might be taken to mean management without any implication of limiting growth. *Growth control* carries the implication that growth is not only to be managed or guided but also limited. The term *no growth* carries the obvious implication of an intent to stop growth entirely.[37]

Such a distinction between management and control measures does not, however, stop some participants in the movement from using "the term, 'growth management' . . . to refer both to measures that aim to exert strict control (limitations) over growth and to those that seek merely to channel growth or manage its impacts."[38] The distinction is, nevertheless, significant because the degree to which any program impacts growth is apt to directly affect its likely acceptance. For many who are unable or unwilling to relinquish the growth imperative driving behavior in this country, growth management efforts remain acceptable only if they are limited to programs designed to channel growth to appropriate locations or minimize negative impacts associated with ongoing growth. As soon as programs act to limit growth, and this includes slow-growth measures that are

far removed from actual attempts to stop growth, many growth-imperative advocates condemn the programs on multiple counts.

Arguments Used to Refute Management Programs That Limit Growth

One of the central arguments that has been used to refute management programs that limit growth is based on the claim that further growth is inevitable.
Advocates of this viewpoint argue that it is irresponsible to attempt to limit inevitable future growth. As one writer has correctly observed, "Of all the current
assumptions about growth, none is more fundamental than the assumption of its
inevitability."[39] Those seeking to limit growth are told that they have "to 'deal
with' or 'cope with' growth that has both statistical and cultural momentum."[40]
As the growth management movement was forming during the latter 1960s, a
federal report addressing policies for future growth in America took the position
that continued growth was not only inevitable, but desirable.[41] A subsequent
Rockefeller task force report on land use and urban growth in the United States
released in 1973 concluded that "no growth [was] simply not a viable option for
the country in the remainder of this century."[42] Such reports established a line
of reasoning that would repeatedly surface in growth management writings. In a
later publication, the executive director of the Rockefeller task force referred to
the idea that no-growth is possible for the country as one of six myths about
land use in the United States.[43] The idea that future growth is inevitable in fact
pervades literature addressing the subject of growth management. Excerpts from
these writings illustrate the general tone of such inevitability claims:

> The United States cannot decide between a policy of growth or
> nongrowth over the next few decades, but rather must decide
> how to accommodate the growth that is certain to occur.[44]

> Growth is a fact of life. No growth is simply not an option—
> particularly in [a] metropolitan area where the continuing de-
> mand for housing and supporting facilities and services is a
> product of the new household formation rate characteristic of
> our existing population profile.[45]

Acceptance of the claim that further growth is inevitable allows proponents of
the traditional perspective on growth to dismiss management programs intended
to limit future increases. Reasoning has it that growth-control measures are irresponsible because they require the inevitable future growth to be accommodated
elsewhere, thereby serving to shift increasing burdens onto those communities
responsibly planning for the future. Under the premise advanced by this book,
that we are at a point of having to reject further growth, growth accommodation
becomes an act of irresponsibility rather than one of responsibility. As the previous chapter indicated, growth need not be viewed as an inevitable future occurrence.[46]

Another central argument that has been used to refute management programs
that attempt to limit growth focuses on the motives and consequences of such
management efforts. By advancing the viewpoint that measures intended to limit

growth are driven by socially unacceptable motives and produce undesirable social consequences, proponents of the growth imperative dismiss and condemn management programs that contain growth limitation provisions. As argued by one author, "the growth management movement has demonstrated anew that planning quite easily can become the servant of the status quo and of tendencies in the society toward elitism, regressivity, environmental irresponsibility, and social isolation."[47] This viewpoint allows a characterization of growth management in terms of its perceived "tendencies toward exclusion and inequality."[48] A land-use attorney, for example, described growth management during the early years of the movement as "the wolf of exclusionary zoning under the environmental sheepskin worn by the stop-growth movement."[49] From this perspective growth management is seen as a way of keeping out the "wrong kind" of people, whether certain income or minority groups.[50] Claims of other unacceptable motives include reference to growth controls as a form of "homeowner cartel" intended to increase the property values of existing owners,[51] and concealed "hustles" designed in "the defense of privilege."[52] In terms of undesirable social consequences stemming from such management programs, authors argue that the controls have the effect of eliminating low-priced housing, increasing housing and land prices, reducing incomes, and diverting development to other localities.[53] A recent critic argues that local growth controls contribute to metropolitan sprawl.[54] Even a quick survey of such writings can easily produce the conclusion that "[m]any authors characterize municipal growth controls as the evil stepchild of land use planning."[55]

Even though other research has provided alternative assessments of the actual effects of local growth management programs, as the work by those authors who have discounted the significance of housing cost increases attributable to growth controls,[56] negative characterizations of growth-control measures have made it easier for some to dismiss management efforts that serve to limit growth. It is in fact possible to think of these arguments as rationales for opposing growth controls and as vehicles for "cutting off debate on nongrowth in the name of social justice."[57] Social justice advocates appear committed to the idea that growth affords a means to remedy a host of social ills, which naturally puts them in the position of defending the growth imperative and opposing all measures that would serve to limit growth. Such a commitment evidences great staying power amongst social justice advocates in spite of the reality "that unchecked growth will not guarantee integration, social justice, or economic uplifting of the disadvantaged in the future anymore than it has in the past."[58] As long as these advocates remain committed to their belief that growth will serve to ameliorate social problems, they can be expected to take a stand against growth-control programs. With the possible exception of economists, perhaps no group in America can be expected to experience more difficulty in giving up on the growth imperative. As a result, the growth management movement can expect to encounter considerable friction caused by confrontations between environmental and social justice advocates. Until the latter are able to accept that growth no longer represents a possible avenue for the attainment of social justice, the transformation of the growth management movement to one of sustainability will be impeded.

Different Growth Orientations Within the Management Movement

In spite of the arguments that have been used to refute the growth management movement, it continues to both expand and evolve. Although participants in the movement hold divergent views on the position that the movement ought to espouse on the matter of growth, these different perspectives have not stopped a broad range of experimentation with management efforts exhibiting dissimilar growth orientations. Something of the nature of such dissimilar orientations toward growth has already been illustrated by the noted distinction that some make between the terms *growth management* and *growth control*. Further insights into the different growth orientations held by different participants in the movement may be revealed by way of the following definitions that have been offered for growth management:

> Managed growth . . . means the utilization by government of a variety of traditional and evolving techniques, tools, plans, and activities to purposefully *guide* local patterns of land use, including the manner, location, rate, and nature of development.[59] [italics added]

> [G]rowth management is defined as a conscious government program intended to *influence* the rate, amount, type, location, and/or quality of future development. . . . It should be noted that this definition, which in fact focuses on actively *guiding* growth, differs from the popular notion of stopping growth completely.[60] [italics added]

> Growth management is generally defined as the *regulation* of the amount, timing, location, and character of development.[61] [italics added]

> Properly defined and understood, growth management, far from being a code word for no-growth or slow-growth efforts, has as central to its meaning a commitment to *plan* carefully for the growth that comes to an area . . . [including] . . . a broadening of the term 'growth management' to include the *promotion* of economic development—the 'managing to grow' side of the equation.[62] [italics added]

> [Growth management] focuses on measures designed to *control* as well as *stimulate* growth.[63] [italics added]

As the added italics of selected words in these definitions indicate, the term growth management means different things to different people, and those different meanings in turn reflect different growth orientations. When taken together with the definitional distinctions that some have proposed between growth management and growth control, the alternative perspectives on how future growth ought to be treated indicate very real differences in how different participants in the movement view growth. The traditional perspective on growth is still alive and well for some in the movement, who see management intended to *promote* or *stimulate* growth, or efforts to *plan* for the growth that will "inevitably" occur, as appropriate. Others, who have come closer to accepting the reality of problems associated with growth, concede a need to *influence, guide, channel*, or *redistribute* growth in order to *minimize impacts*. Yet others, who have come to view growth even more critically, speak of the need to *regulate, control*, or *limit* growth. What is missing from the range of definitions provided by the literature on growth management is a definition of management activity directed at a deliberate attempt to *stop* growth entirely. Such an omission reflects the fact that the movement has simply not entertained the possibility of a no-growth focus for growth management efforts. It has instead been directed at making ongoing growth possible. Of the thousands of growth management programs that have been instituted during the last few decades by local and state governments, the overwhelming majority have in fact allowed, if not facilitated or mandated, ongoing growth accommodation. The following two sections of this chapter illustrate the extent to which growth management measures at these two levels of government have continued to support the growth imperative.

THE NATURE OF LOCAL GROWTH MANAGEMENT PROGRAMS

As noted previously, it is possible to attribute the origins of the growth management movement to the development and legalization of land-use regulations during the opening decades of this century. The development and use of these police-power regulations to manage growth provided a means of influencing growth decades before the emergence of the growth management movement during the latter 1960s. However, it was argued that these regulations were historically used to promote and facilitate growth, as opposed to the movement's more recent interest in guiding, controlling, and even limiting growth. Whatever the intent of the management activity, the association of that activity with regulatory actions tends to identify growth management activity as a local governmental function within the United States. For while the sovereign power to regulate land use for the public good is inherent to and vested in the states, all 50 states have elected to pass enabling legislation granting local units of government the power to impose land-use regulations subject to legal limitations spelled out by the enabling acts or the judiciary under litigation contesting specific regulations.[64] In the words of one analyst,

> Local governments secured their hammerlock on land controls in the 1920s, when zoning first came into wide use. Although zoning theoretically derived from a state's 'police powers,' it was routinely delegated downward, and many state constitutions protected local home rule.[65]

Local governments were, in short, entrusted with the power to regulate the use of land in this country decades ago and now implement such regulations within the framework of powers conferred on them by the individual states. As one observer has noted, "American land use controls are essentially a local matter."[66] Having the power to impose land-use controls in effect gives local units of government the power to control growth, and this represents a reality very different from that existing in most other countries: "Unlike virtually every other modern nation we seem to have adopted the position that the control of growth is primarily of concern to local rather than state or federal government."[67] We therefore have a situation in this country where local regulation of land has come to represent the primary expression of growth management activity.

The close association between land-use regulations and growth management activity has been acknowledged in the following terms: "All land use regulation is in some sense growth management and has long been recognized as a proper exercise of the police power by the highest courts of this . . . nation."[68] While growth management may encompass a broad range of nonregulatory techniques,[69] it has been conceded that "[t]he essence of the term managed growth is regulatory."[70] The real origins of the growth management movement may therefore be said to consist of efforts on the part of local governments to regulate growth in keeping with the new sentiment toward growth that had openly surfaced by the latter 1960s. It has, for example, been noted that the "history of growth management innovation is tightly attached to the idea of small communities fighting to protect their amenity and lifestyle."[71] Or as others have put it, "modern efforts to control or manage physical development and population growth first took root in several metropolitan suburbs."[72] These small local governments sought to exert a level of control over growth that was radically different from the level at which they had traditionally attempted to influence ongoing development. In attempting to expand their authority over the growth process, they quickly discovered shortcomings associated with the traditional use of land-use regulations based on the police power. Those shortcomings would eventually come to be described in the following terms: "[T]he traditional tools have generally been viewed as weak and lacking in significant ability to shape growth, control its timing, or deal with many of its impacts, particularly financial and environmental ones."[73] Local governments responded by using the traditional regulatory tools in new ways, and by revising traditional police-power mechanisms to permit them to manage growth in ways that it had not formerly been managed.

Local Efforts to Regulate the Principal Attributes of Growth

In attempting to protect themselves from the rapid growth of the 1950s and 1960s, some local governments began to experiment with new approaches toward the management of growth. Those new approaches typically reflected a different growth orientation than the accommodative nature of local regulatory activity of the past. The beginnings of the growth management movement may therefore be traced to the efforts of individual local governments to modify and expand land-use regulations in order to achieve a new level of management ability over growth. In a few instances local governments actually attempted to limit the *amount* of future growth by downzoning land, that is, by reducing the permitted intensity of use on specific parcels of land. Such actions merely used traditional tools in a new fashion, in this case by lowering density provisions contained in zoning ordinances. In the majority of cases, however, local governments continued to be more accommodating to growth, while at the same time seeking to address growth-induced problems. Some communities moved to introduce *rate* controls, attempting to gain control over the timing of future development. By reducing the rate of growth being imposed by an unencumbered development process, local governments attempted to buy time to respond to concerns about the availability, quality, and financing of public facilities and services. It was also assumed that reducing the rate of growth by such approaches as limiting the annual number of building permits would serve to slow growth sufficiently to allow it to be absorbed without destroying community character or a current way of life.

In other local communities, concerns associated with the cost of providing public infrastructure and services produced a growth management focus directed at making development permission contingent on the availability of public facilities and services. These programs typically required the development community to share in the cost of providing adequate facilities and services through an expanded system of development exactions and impact fees, and stressed the role that adequate facilities and services would play in ensuring *quality* development within any community. By the 1970s, concerns about urban sprawl, loss of open space and farmlands, and a host of environmental problems produced yet another focus for the expanding realm of land-use regulations being devised to deal with growth. An increasing number of local communities began to direct their attention to the *location* of future growth. It was assumed that containing new growth within designated growth boundaries would further a number of desired public ends, such as holding down facility and service costs, conserving resource lands such as farmlands, and protecting environmentally-sensitive lands from sprawl development. In the end, the expanded realm of land-use regulations implemented under the heading of growth management permitted local communities to manage all of the principal attributes of growth: amount, rate, location, and quality.

Some of the earliest management efforts associated with the new mood toward growth were directed at attempts to control the rate of growth within specific communities. A growth-phasing ordinance was adopted by Milford, Connecticut during the early 1950s.[74] The ordinance sought to link new development to the adequacy of a range of public facilities and services. During the mid-1950s Clarkstown, New York adopted a management ordinance that in part tried to influence the rate of growth by tying development approval to a finding that school facilities would not be overcrowded.[75] Such early efforts would not, however, have the influence of two highly publicized growth management programs that focused on rate controls during the late 1960s and early 1970s in New York and California respectively. In 1969 Ramapo, New York amended its zoning ordinance to include a development-timing component designed to control the rate of growth within the community. In 1972 Petaluma, California followed suit with an ordinance intended to limit the number of housing units built in the city on an annual basis. These two rate-control measures were widely reported and may be assumed to have played a key part in motivating the subsequent proliferation of growth management ordinances that would come to be referred to as the growth management movement.[76]

The community of Ramapo sought "to regulate the sequence and timing of residential growth in phase with the availability of municipal services and support facilities."[77] A zoning provision made it necessary to obtain a special permit for residential development on vacant land, and such permits were made dependent on the attainment of a minimum number of points awarded on the basis of proximity to existing facilities and services. The town's accompanying capital budget and improvement program was designed to ensure complete availability of public facilities and services to all properties within an 18-year time period,[78] which meant that all land would eventually qualify for development. As some observers noted,

> Ramapo merely wanted to stretch out a complete buildup of its area from the expected 'natural' period of nine years to a 'planned' period of 18 years. There never was a question of stopping growth completely. Quite to the contrary, Ramapo had a capital improvements program to provide the necessary public facilities to accommodate all growth within the 18-year period.[79]

However, some properties would not be serviced until the second or third six-year periods of an 18-year capital improvement program, and building delays of up to 18 years on specific properties made the program sufficiently controversial to produce litigation. Although a lower court overturned the ordinance, the highest court in the state of New York upheld Ramapo's rate-control program, noting that it was not designed "to freeze population at present levels, but to maximize growth by the efficient use of land."[80] An appeal to the U.S. Supreme Court was in turn dismissed for want of a substantial federal question.[81] The vehemence of the opposition that led to litigation all the way to the court of last resort is somewhat surprising considering the actual impact of rate-control ordinances. One commentator summed up that impact in the following manner: "The radical ring of the words 'controlled population growth' should be of ephemeral shock value once it is realized that not ultimate population but only the immediate rate of population growth is the subject of time control regulation."[82] Although rate-control measures therefore only serve to slow growth, and not to actually stop it, even this extent of interference with the growth imperative did not exempt this early form of growth control from being both criticized and challenged.

Petaluma's residential development control system also contained a rate-control element in the form of an annual cap on new dwelling units. Set at 500 residential units a year, this west coast experiment with rate controls resulted in the same controversy and litigation that had accompanied Ramapo's implementation of this new form of growth control. In order to decide which development proposals would be allocated the annual quota of 500 allowable units, the community instituted an annual competition among rival development plans. Ranking proposals on the basis of an elaborate two-part point system based on access to facilities and services, and such other aspects as excellence of design, the city in effect allocated development permission at a lower level than the market was prepared to build.[83] First struck down by a federal district court,[84] the rate-control ordinance was later upheld by the reviewing federal appeals court,[85] and the Supreme Court's refusal to review the appellate court decision in 1976 again validated this form of growth control in spite of another challenge carried to the highest court in the country. By the mid-1970s rate controls had therefore been established as a permissible form of growth management in spite of the controversy surrounding the use of this management technique.

Although the rate-control components of the Ramapo and Petaluma growth management programs received the most attention, both programs contained other components intended to influence other attributes of growth. The Ramapo ordinance also attempted to manage the location of future growth by restricting the provision of facilities and services to inlying areas during early years of the program, and only serving the outlying sectors of the community during the latter years of its 18-year capital improvement program. Petaluma's growth management ordinance also contained design controls intended to influence the quality of future growth. With the expansion of the growth management movement many communities instituted programs devised to manage more than one of the principal attributes of growth. Most of these programs attempted to manage the rate, location, and quality of growth. While a number of local governments attempted to regulate the amount of growth occurring annually through the imposition of rate controls, such controls only succeeded in slowing growth. With new annual growth allotments issued under rate-control programs, these management efforts effectively serve to permit growth to continue on a year-to-year basis.

Rare Local Attempts to Set Ultimate Limits to Future Growth

Any survey of growth management programs would quickly reveal how few communities have attempted to address the amount of growth by actually attempting to implement policies to stop it, and the survey would additionally disclose that these community efforts have only proposed programs intended to stop growth at some future point in time. Such a survey would also show that these efforts to set absolute limits to future growth have tended to be initiated by citizens outside formal governmental structures rather than by local elected officials. One survey of management programs reported by two investigators during the mid-1970s claimed they "could not find a single community that aimed all its ordinances and policies at stopping growth cold or holding it at some immediate level deemed optimal."[86] The same investigators went on to note that "[f]ew communities have dared to set ultimate limits on either land area or population; the more common tactic is to try to slow down the rate of development with no ultimate goal in mind."[87] The few communities that have dared to propose ultimate limits to future growth have not fared well in those efforts, and have not therefore succeeded in providing guidance to other communities that would seek to explore such new and uncharted terrain for the growth management movement.

In 1971, citizens of Boulder, Colorado collected enough signatures to have a proposed dwelling-unit cap of 40,000 put to a city vote under the state's initiative process.[88] The suggested ultimate limit to the amount of allowable future growth for the city represented only a proposed future limit, because the dwelling-unit cap would have set a "population cap" at around 100,000, or some 30,000 more than the approximately 70,000 that were already in the city as of 1971.[89] As a response, the city council put an alternative advisory measure on the same ballot with wording urging the elected officials to keep the city's growth rate "substantially below the rates experienced during the 1960s."[90] The proposed future limit to the amount of growth that could occur in the city was defeated by the voters by a six-to-four ratio, while the proposed policy regarding the rate of future growth in the city was approved by more than 70% of the voters. As a result, this early attempt to cap the permissible amount of future growth in a city was never implemented.

In 1972, the city of Boca Raton, Florida also used the ballot in pursuit of a limit to the amount of future growth that would be permitted in the community.[91] A citizens group initiated a vote on a charter referendum limiting total housing units in the city to 40,000, and the referendum passed. Based on average household size in the city, that housing-unit cap would have translated into an eventual city population of approximately 105,000 residents, versus the total of some 40,000 people at the time of the vote in 1972. In this case the attempt to place an absolute limit on the amount of future growth in a city was invalidated by a court ruling,[92] again frustrating an attempt to implement a cap on future growth. Other similar efforts would fail, as in the case of Fort Collins, Colorado, where a growth limitation initiative analogous to Boulder's was soundly defeated by that city's residents in the late 1970s.[93] It is a fact that few local governments have attempted to set absolute limits to the growth permitted within their communities, and that far fewer have actually succeeded. One is hard pressed to find examples of communities that have actually implemented absolute caps on future population. Such communities, as in the case of Sanibel Island, Florida, which succeeded in setting a cap of some 6,000 dwelling units based at least in part on development tolerances of different ecozones on the island, represent the rare exception rather than the rule in local growth management efforts.[94]

The fact that few local governments have expressed an interest in absolute limits to the amount of allowable future growth since the 1970s has been explained by some observers in terms of a forced shift in the attitude toward growth on the part of local governments by the 1980s. Those observers argue that the "new federalism" of the 1980s "debilitated the growth debate" by forcing local governments to actively pursue economic growth to make up for the withdrawal of federal aid that occurred with the fiscal retrenchment of the federal government.[95] These authors argue that under the new federalism growth became indispensable for the economic well-being of local governments, and as a consequence the growth/no-growth debate of the 1970s was displaced by the compact-versus-sprawl development debate of the 1980s and 1990s. Under this line of reasoning, stopping growth by capping the amount that any community would allow was no longer considered to be a viable option. As a result, it became fashionable to address growth-related problems through attempts to influence the other attributes of growth, with a particular focus on the location rather than the amount of future growth. Most growth management programs initiated by local governments have in fact addressed the growth attributes of rate, location, and quality, and have only incorporated measures directed at the amount of growth in the form of rate controls that impose temporary annual limits on the amount of allowable growth. This approach reveals a clear intent to continue to accommodate future growth on the part of virtually every local government involved in the growth management movement.

The Ongoing Growth Accommodation of Most Local Management Programs

Any review of growth management literature quickly illustrates the accommodative stance toward future growth on the part of most local growth management programs. One of the architects of a program in Montgomery County, Maryland conceded that that effort "was intended to *accommodate* growth, and to manage it only to the extent needed to moderate its ill effects."[96] A planner involved in putting together San Diego's program has noted that "the city hoped, neither to limit growth nor to allow it to proceed unimpeded, . . . but to *accommodate* it in a manner sensitive to the particular needs of San Diego."[97] Such postures toward growth permeate the majority of local management programs adopted during the 1980s and 1990s. Additional evidence of the fact that most local programs are accommodative of future growth appeared in published research assessing the nature of growth-control versus growth management activity in California through 1989.[98] That research indicated some cities and counties did undertake to limit growth below levels desired by the real estate market by implementing population caps, residential building permit caps, and commercial square footage limits. However, these growth-control measures only represented some 17% of the combined total of 586 growth-control and growth management measures implemented by cities and counties in California through 1989. And even these growth-control measures were typically intended to only temporarily limit the amount of growth through the imposition of annual caps on growth that would be extended to permit another round of growth allotment with each new year. Some 83% of the measures were instead directed at managing growth by geographically redistributing it through the use of such techniques as infrastructure requirements and urban limit lines.

These efforts, which have constituted the majority of programs in California, sought neither to reduce the overall amount or rate of growth, and instead reflect the belief that growth can be accommodated if it is properly planned and its negative effects properly mitigated. This belief is, in fact, characteristic of the overwhelming majority of local growth management programs implemented in the United States since the appearance of the management movement during the latter 1960s. While a small minority of local growth management efforts have attempted to redirect the management movement toward the end of at least shutting down future growth, most local management programs have instead played an active role in accommodating ongoing growth.

It should be noted that literature treating the subject of growth management in the United States has opposed local management activity directed at limiting or stopping future growth. Authors argue that local programs are apt to serve "selfish interests" of individual local jurisdictions, and in the process operate "inefficiently and unjustly."[99] It is therefore held that "[m]anaged growth decisions cannot be based solely on the wants and desires of individual jurisdictions."[100] Even if efficiency and social justice could be dealt with locally, writers assert that "policies relating to growth management cannot be adequately designed and implemented on a local basis: a regional or state outlook is required."[101] Under this line of reasoning local programs are criticized as being "extremely porous," which is to say they merely displace growth to other local jurisdictions within a metropolitan area, and are "largely irrelevant to the management of urban growth."[102] As a consequence, it is taken as a given in the literature that it is "important that growth controls be exercised from a metropolitan perspective,"[103] if not from a state or national base. Such conventional reasoning typically concludes with the claim that the appropriate local response to the current reality of ongoing growth is one of having each local government "accept its share of regional growth while still protecting its quality of life."[104]

For those who have come to accept the need to give up on the growth imperative, the aforementioned line of reasoning holds out little prospect for aiding the transition to a sustainable future. No explicit national growth policy exists in America, but the nation is implicitly wedded to the growth imperative and national policies continue to endorse and support ongoing growth.[105] It would appear that the immediate future is unlikely to yield an explicit national growth policy of any kind, let alone one directed at abandoning the growth imperative. As the next section of this chapter will illustrate, state governments are also unlikely to be sources of policies or laws intended to shut down the growth machine driving this country. Of the individual states that have formally undertaken growth management by passing statewide laws governing management activity, virtually all have mandated ongoing growth accommodation on the part of local governments. As for regional governments as potential sources of more rational growth management actions, very few have been enabled to regulate land and thereby manage growth, and of those that have, their modus operandi has been one of ongoing growth accommodation.[106] Local political jurisdictions represent the only level of government in this country that has experimented with attempts to shut down future growth, and the growth management movement has generally condemned such local efforts for previously noted reasons. The movement seems unprepared to accept the idea that "the principles of sustainable development must be implemented at the local level if preservation of viable ecosystems is to be assured."[107] It seems even less prepared to accept the reality that we have reached a point where sustainable development will only be possible under a state of no growth. The movement can therefore be criticized for impeding the efforts of local governments to make the crucial transition to a nongrowth future. As the following section will reveal, state governments are also subject to blame for the role they have played in supporting the growth imperative and blocking local attempts to implement management programs intended to stop future growth.

ENACTMENT OF STATE GROWTH MANAGEMENT LAWS

While the idea that states ought to take prime responsibility for planning and managing land within their borders has reportedly existed at least since the National Resources Planning Board was established in 1933,[108] the states have avoided that responsibility until the growth management era. The fact that all 50 states elected to pass enabling legislation granting local governments the power to impose land-use regulations reveals how willingly states relinquished the regulatory means to control land use and thereby manage growth. With the advent of the growth management movement a limited number of states acted to reclaim a certain degree of control over the use of land within their jurisdictions.

The first state to pass legislation asserting a new state role in the regulation of land and the management of growth was Hawaii.[109] With passage of a statewide law in 1961, the Hawaiian legislature divided the state into urban, rural, agricultural, and conservation districts, and made the use of land in the latter three districts subject to the regulatory control of state agencies. A tradition of strong centralized government in Hawaii may have made the Hawaiian legislation easy to dismiss at the time as a mere aberration that would not be replicated in the remaining states, but the 1970s would prove that viewpoint to be in error. Subsequent statewide growth management legislation was passed during the 1970s in Vermont (1970), Florida (1972), and Oregon (1973). These initial state laws would eventually be referred to as the "first wave of state actions" asserting a state role in growth management activity.[110]

A New State Role in the Regulation of Land Via Statewide Growth Management Laws

It has been noted by participants in the growth management movement that before the 1970s land planning and regulation had been considered primarily a concern of local governments, but that "[t]his comfortable system of local land planning and regulation began to change in the 1970s."[111] Since the power to regulate land use was conferred upon local units of government by the states, it has always been understood that it was subject to modification and recall.[112] By the 1970s the noted states began to experiment with such modification and recall activity. The statewide growth management acts contained elements that served to shift land-use control powers from local governments to regional and state entities. This aspect of these legislative enactments led some observers to conclude that "[t]his country is in the midst of a revolution in the way we regulate the use of land."[113] That revolution was described in the following terms:

> The *ancien regime* being overthrown is the feudal system under which the entire pattern of land development has been controlled by thousands of individual local governments, each seeking to maximize its tax base and minimize its social problems, and caring less what happens to all the others.[114]

A few states were acting to change this system by reclaiming a certain degree of control over the use of land, and to have states directly involved in the control of land use by the 1970s was seen as nothing less than revolutionary.

In seeking to exert some control over the use of land, states that passed statewide growth management acts regained control in one of two characteristic ways. In some instances they assumed direct regulatory control by taking over some aspect of the regulatory process, such as the issuance of mandatory permits for specified developments. Vermont, for example, instituted a system where local governments were bypassed entirely in a permitting process for development projects of greater than local impact, e.g., housing developments of 10 or more units. In other instances states elected to institute a de facto exercise of control by the state, even when the actual implementation of the controls was left to local governments. Under this form of state control the regulatory function is allowed to remain with local governments, but land-use controls are so strictly governed by state standards and criteria that local governments are in effect administering a body of state regulations. By way of illustration, Oregon adopted a statute requiring all local governments to adopt plans and land-development regulations that were consistent with state goals and policies, and empowered a state commission with the authority to issue injunctive orders requiring these plans and land-use controls to conform to the state goals and policies.

The statutory move on the part of states to reclaim a degree of authority over land-use controls continued during the 1980s. During that decade additional statewide growth management legislation was passed by Florida (1984 and 1985), New Jersey (1986), Maine (1988), Rhode Island (1988), Vermont (1988), and Georgia (1989).[115] These laws would come to be referred to as the "second wave,"[116] "second generation,"[117] or "second revolution"[118] of comprehensive growth management enactments by state legislatures. Although the laws passed during the 1980s showed a clear preference for the exercise of de facto controls rather than the direct administration of controls by state entities, states continued to assert a role for themselves in the regulation of land. By the late 1980s one report covering new state initiatives would claim that "[s]tates have continued to preempt local governmental land use control in the 1980s."[119] Another observer would similarly conclude that "the states are clearly taking more control."[120]

The quest for control over the use of land on the part of the states did not end with laws passed during the 1980s. The noted laws served to reduce the novelty of such legislation and laid the groundwork for future growth management enactments in other states. Washington state became the first state to follow suit in the 1990s with the passage of bills in 1990 and 1991, and Maryland became yet another state to adopt a form of statewide growth management with the passage of legislation in 1992.[121] Maryland's law increased the number of states with statewide enactments to 10: Hawaii, Vermont, Florida, Oregon, New Jersey, Maine, Rhode Island, Georgia, Washington, and Maryland. Although this only represents one fifth of all the states, it would appear highly probable that other states will join the movement to enact statewide growth management laws. Interest in such legislation has recently been noted in the states of California, New York, Connecticut, Massachusetts, Pennsylvania, Virginia, West Virginia, North Carolina, and South Carolina.[122] Awareness of the growing interest in statewide growth management laws has led some to conclude that "statewide growth management represents an inevitable next step in American community governance,"[123] and others to suggest "that other states will adopt such systems over the rest of the 1990s and beyond."[124] All the statewide laws to date have contained elements giving some degree of control over land-use decisions to the states, and it appears likely that future enactments will contain similar provisions. The issue of interest therefore becomes one of considering why the states have moved to assert a degree of control over local land-use decisions.

Alternative Motivations Prompting Statewide Growth Management Laws

Growth management literature contains considerable comment on the question of why states have adopted growth management laws that involve them in the control of land. During the early 1970s the so-called "quiet revolution in land-use control" was attributed to the recognition that local regulations were inadequate to cope with problems that were statewide or regionwide in scope.[125] The driving force behind early state programs was concern for the environment.[126] Environmental advocates argued that many environmental problems transcended local political boundaries, while they also criticized the environmental effects of local land-use decisions. An insensitive despoliation of land and water resources, including the destruction of dune systems along the nation's shores, the filling of wetlands, the pollution of lakes, rivers, and estuarine areas, and the cutting of woodlands all led to demands for state action to counter the behavior of local governments. As a consequence, state growth management acts in the 1970s reflected a "strong, natural systems orientation"[127] in response to the rising tide of public concern for the environment during that period.

By the 1980s statewide growth management laws reflected a response to a broader range of concerns.[128] Legislative enactments continued to reflect concern for protecting the environment by including components directed at safeguarding resource lands and environmentally-sensitive areas, as well as preserving open spaces in both rural and urban locales. Beyond the universal inclusion of environmental components in the statewide growth management enactments, these laws typically exhibited a number of other common features. A concern with development outstripping the provision of public infrastructure produced components in some of the state laws directed at ensuring concurrency, that is, the provision of infrastructure at the same time development occurs. Concern with the negative effects of sprawl resulted in many of the state laws incorporating containment components designed to achieve compact growth patterns. The concern regarding the economic well-being of local governments under declining federal revenues due to the new federalism produced components in the laws directed at promoting economic development. At the same time the laws attempted to introduce features intended to properly balance development and environmental protection. Such components of the statewide growth management laws passed during the 1980s and 1990s addressed the same concerns that many local governments had attempted to address with their own growth management programs prior to the passage of statewide laws. The new statewide enactments would, however, extend to matters not previously addressed by local growth management efforts.

Many of the statewide growth management laws would contain provisions requiring local management programs to be consistent with specified state goals and policies. These new provisions provided a form of mandated direction to local management programs that had not existed prior to the passage of the state laws. Some of the statewide acts also required local governments to regulate land in a manner consistent with previously adopted local plans, serving to grant legal status to local land-use plans and reduce the possibilities for arbitrary and capricious regulatory behavior by local governments. Some of the statewide laws additionally required local governments to plan for controversial land uses, such as affordable housing and factious public facilities such as prisons and waste disposal sites. These provisions again reinforced the position that local regulations were inadequate to deal with a number of statewide land-use issues. That fact provided additional impetus for states to assume a new level of control over at least some land-use matters. A growth management article by the early 1990s would describe this rationale for the assumption of state control in the following terms:

> Among the primary reasons for the transference of growth policy authority from local to state government has been the unwillingness or inability of local governments to deal adequately with growth issues that transcend municipal boundaries. Growth-related problems regarding environmental protection, affordable housing, or public facility siting blur the distinction between ex-

tralocal and local responsibilities. . . . Mismatches frequently appear between the common level of growth regulation—municipal—and the level of impact—regional—of many development proposals.[129]

As a result of the recognized problems associated with leaving the regulation of growth solely in the hands of local governments, some states were afforded additional motivation for drafting statewide growth management laws and assuming some control over land-use decisions and the growth process.

The noted motivations for state involvement in the control of land and the growth process are therefore seen to be varied. At the most general level one has the explanation that local controls are inadequate to deal with extralocal issues. More specifically, there is the rationale provided by public infrastructure problems, affording states a reason for intervening in the development and funding of essential facilities and services. The association of sprawl development with the loss of state resource lands, environmental damage, and inefficient infrastructure investments provided further motivation. The new federalism provided an additional inducement in the form of incentives to ensure local economic development as an assumed condition of state economic solvency. An interest in private property rights prompted the noted requirements regarding consistency with prior planning in order to avoid regulations that were arbitrary or capricious. A concern with the social problem of affordable housing provided yet further motivation for increased state control. While all these motivations have received considerable attention in the literature addressing statewide growth management laws, little comment has appeared on the possible motivation of drafting such laws in order to ensure continued pursuit of the growth imperative.

A traditional, pro-growth orientation on the part of the states has been acknowledged in growth management literature. One author has noted that "[f]or years the goals and policies of state government have revolved around the pursuit of economic growth," and that the continuation of "a pursuit-of-growth policy" is revealed by the existence of many state agencies of economic development.[130] Other authors have similarly conceded that "for a considerable period most state policy was directed toward an unfettered climate for continued development."[131] With states committed to a pro-growth stance, any local efforts to interfere with ongoing growth were destined to evoke a state response. Although only a minority of local growth management programs were directed at actually limiting future growth, another local response to growth-induced problems was impeding the growth process by the late 1960s and early 1970s.

The rapid rate of growth and its associated problems forced an increased use of moratoria on the part of local governments. While a moratorium does act to stop growth by shutting down the issuance of permits, under law it may only be instituted in response to an identified emergency, and then only for a reasonable time period to address the emergency. A local government may, for example, institute a moratorium due to an emergency stemming from an inability to service new development with sewage treatment and keep that moratorium in place until it is able to upgrade its treatment facility and service additional growth. Such temporary impediments to ongoing development played a part in giving rise to state growth management laws that would require planning for ongoing growth accommodation. These laws would in theory negate the need for future moratoria, and actually eliminate the possibility of using local growth management techniques to impede mandated growth accommodation.

A survey during the latter 1970s revealed that developers were having to contend with a number of local governmental responses to growth, but the most frequently encountered mechanism was the moratorium.[132] The use of moratoria would continue during the 1980s and 1990s. It has been noted that "Maine's developers supported a strong state role [in growth management] partly because some sixty local moratoria had been put in place over the three years preceding [the adoption of the state management law in] 1988."[133] In the two years prior to Georgia's passage of a statewide growth management act in 1989 there were more than 30 sewer moratoria around the state, "which constituted a real threat to the continued ability of the development industry to thrive."[134] It has been conceded that the same forces have been at work in other states.[135] A description of the experience in Washington state includes the following claim: "To minimize the use of moratoria and other draconian actions on the part of individual communities, those most concerned about growth turned to the legislature for a state-imposed solution."[136] The development community's interest in "timeliness and certainty in the development process"[137] produced an interest in trying "to end-run the growing ground swell of antidevelopment sentiment by beating it to the state house and securing that bastion for as long as possible."[138] By the early 1980s some observers would "argue that statewide land use programs serve the interests of a small group of liberal reformers closely associated with large development capital."[139] Supporters of the growth imperative therefore turned to the state legislatures to secure growth management laws that would reduce the prospects of local moratoria and bar local management efforts that would limit growth.

The Growth Accommodation Bias of Statewide Growth Management Laws

A review of literature treating statewide growth management acts passed to date quickly reveals the extent to which these laws promote or require ongoing growth accommodation on the part of local governments.[140] A description of Florida's statewide program references wording from the program's land-use goal directly stating the intent "to accommodate growth in an environmentally acceptable manner," and notes the requirement that local land-use plans must show that each local community "is accommodating its anticipated growth."[141] The "basic tenet" of Vermont's statewide act has been noted to be one of maintaining the state's quality of life while at the same time encouraging economic development.[142] In the state of Washington the governor initiated the process that would produce a statewide law by directing a state commission "to recommend ways to preserve the environment . . . while maintaining steady economic growth for all regions of the state."[143] The "essential purpose" of the Oregon statewide growth management program, according to one analyst, "is to plan for anticipated growth with minimal sacrifice of the environment."[144] By the 1980s all the statewide growth management laws would come to reflect such a commitment to ongoing growth accommodation.

If one looks at the legislative enactments that have to date implemented statewide growth management in 10 states, it is easy to document the clear commitment to preserving the growth imperative in those laws. The Hawaiian statute required urban districts to include "a sufficient reserve area for foreseeable urban growth."[145] Subsequent statewide laws would either encourage or mandate ongoing growth accommodation on the part of local governments. In Vermont, the enactments called on planning at all levels to provide for "reasonably expected population increase and economic growth."[146] Florida legislation required local land-use plans to indicate the previously noted "amount of land required to accommodate anticipated growth."[147] Oregon's law requires local governments to designate urban growth boundaries based on the "demonstrated need to accommodate long-range urban population growth requirements."[148] The New Jersey law called for a state plan that would identify "growth areas" in the most densely populated state in the nation, and for local plans to be consistent with such a designation.[149] Maine's legislation required local governments to prepare plans designating "growth areas . . . suitable for orderly . . . development forecast for the next ten years" and a "capital investment plan . . . to meet projected growth and development."[150] Rhode Island's law contained language stating that the intent of the act was to "establish a procedure in comprehensive planning at state and municipal levels which will accommodate future requirements."[151] In Georgia, the statewide law lists the duties of local governments, including "the development, promotion, and retention of trade, commerce, industry, and employment opportunities."[152] Legislation in the state of Washington requires local governments to designate "urban growth areas" and then to revise them at least every 10 years "to accommodate the urban growth projected to occur in . . . the succeeding twenty-year period."[153] Maryland's law mandates that all local plans contain a land development regulations element "which encourages . . . economic growth in areas designated for growth in the plan."[154]

It is clear that statewide growth management laws have to date evidenced a continuation of traditional growth-accommodation biases. As Table 2.1 illustrates, all the laws contain provisions intended to promote ongoing growth, and in 7 of the 10 states the laws actually mandate ongoing growth accommodation by local governments. The fact that statewide growth management laws were intended to further growth accommodation ends has been conceded by a number of authors who have examined these laws. One source acknowledges such a function for the laws in the following terms:

> The major vehicle for moving the concept of growth management from a close identification with no- or slow-growth efforts toward a commitment to plan carefully for growth . . . has been the series of new state initiatives that evolved during the 1980s and that are continuing into the 1990s.[155]

Another source proclaims that the "evolution of state growth policy has shown a shift . . . to . . . the incorporation of growth-accommodating economic policies into programs."[156] Yet another source argues that the different statewide growth management laws suggest "different paths to accommodating growth."[157] Clearly, statewide growth management laws have continued to support the growth imperative. While the prior treatment of local growth management programs revealed that the majority of local management measures have also served to accommodate ongoing growth, statewide laws have afforded even more sup-

Table 2.1
The Growth Orientation of Statewide Growth Management Laws

Hawaii (1961)	x[a]
Vermont (1970 and 1988)	x
Florida (1972 and 1985)	x[a]
Oregon (1973)	x[a]
New Jersey (1985)	x[b]
Maine (1988)	x[a]
Rhode Island (1988)	x[a]
Georgia (1989)	x
Washington (1990 and 1991)	x[a]
Maryland (1992)	x[a]

x   Statewide laws contain provisions intended to promote ongoing growth.

x[a]   Legislative provisions actually mandate growth-accommodation measures on the part of local governments.

x[b]   Acknowledges limits for further growth within specific locations within the state, but maintains traditional accommodative stance for the remainder of the state.

Source: The table is based on details gleaned from the statewide growth management laws in the 10 identified states that have passed such laws as of 1997.

port for the growth imperative. In the majority of states with such legislation on the books, local governments have had their management options reduced to those that provide for ongoing growth accommodation. They must accept this realm of constrained management options because under law they are required to comply with the accommodation directives spelled out in the statewide enactments.

THE CURRENT STATUS OF GROWTH MANAGEMENT IN THE UNITED STATES

As the prior portrayal of the growth management movement revealed, its origins may be traced to the efforts of a small number of local governments that sought to exert a new level of control over growth in response to a new sentiment toward continued expansion. Management efforts in states like New York, California, Colorado, and Texas were implemented without a statewide growth management law to direct the permissible nature of the local programs.[158] As a result, these local governments were free to experiment with management programs intended to limit, or even stop, future growth. In spite of having this freedom, most local programs in these state settings chose instead to exert new levels of growth management while continuing to accommodate ongoing growth. In the majority of instances that meant focusing on efforts to influence the location or quality of development. These programs sought to guide, channel, or redistribute growth to minimize its negative impacts, and often attempted to ensure infrastructure availability concurrent with new development.

A minority of local management programs addressed the timing of growth via rate controls, and thereby placed at least temporary limits on the amount of allowable growth within designated time periods. These efforts tended to incur the wrath of traditional development interests and other pro-growth advocates and produced litigation contesting such controls. Local governments also instituted moratoria to buy time to deal with growth-induced emergencies. Such moratoria and other growth-limiting measures were said to have played a part in the passage of statewide growth management laws that would make it difficult, if not impossible, for local governments subject to the requirements of those laws to impede ongoing growth. A description of the current status of local growth management efforts needs, therefore, to differentiate between those local programs subject to the requirements of statewide growth management laws and those developed in the absence of such statewide laws. As noted, the statewide laws have served to reduce management options to those that continue to accommodate growth. For the majority of local governments subjected to statewide laws this has not represented a serious constraint, because most have voluntarily limited their management efforts to those permitting continued growth accommodation. However, for the minority of local settings with an interest in actually limiting or even stopping future growth, statewide management laws serve to severely constrain, if not prohibit, such options. It is only in states without statewide growth management acts that local governments retain some latitude in their ability to experiment with management programs intended to limit or stop future growth.

Under the premise of this book, that we are at the point of having to abandon the growth imperative if we are to survive, the passage of statewide growth management laws has served to impede the needed transition to a sustainable future. These laws have acted to block local governmental experimentation with management programs that would stop future growth and thereby advance the cause of sustainability. In states with statewide laws, local governments convinced of the need to stop future growth because of local environmental constraints have been put in the position of having no option but to challenge the statewide mandates in court. One can foresee future challenges based on the argument that continued growth accommodation threatens local life-support systems to the point of endangering the public's health, safety, and general welfare. Since local governments have a legal obligation to protect the health, safety, and general welfare of their citizens, under ongoing growth some will inevitably be put in the position of having to admit that they are unable to fulfill that obligation while at the same time complying with a state mandate to continue accommodating growth.

In states without statewide management acts, local governments are still free to experiment with what would be considered radical growth management programs by most participants in the growth management movement. It has only been in the context of a limited number of such local settings that we have seen any experimentation with making the transition to a no-growth future. As has been previously illustrated, the growth management movement has tended to condemn local management programs directed at limiting or stopping growth as inefficient, unjust, and irresponsible. The movement has therefore served to impede experimentation with management efforts to slow or stop growth at the only level of government in this country where such experimentation has occurred to date. While the majority of current local management programs continue to accommodate growth, more local efforts to abandon the growth imperative will undoubtedly surface in the future. The unresolved question will be whether these local efforts will be able to overcome the numerous barriers that will be put in the way of their successful implementation, including opposition from the growth management movement itself.

Since the federal government has abstained from any deliberate national growth management effort, and few regional entities have undertaken management programs, the states remain the only other level of government where there has been significant involvement with growth management. The passage of statewide growth management laws was shown to reflect a clear endorsement of the growth imperative. Although the first statewide enactments were said to reflect a strong "natural systems orientation," even these laws contained traditional growth-accommodation provisions. By the 1980s, the statewide laws would not abandon environmental components, but they would move toward becoming "more balanced than earlier state regulatory programs in their attempt to integrate economic development . . . with environmental protection techniques."[159] As the catchword of the movement became "balance,"[160] which represented an attempt to balance the simultaneous pursuit of growth and environmental protection, the statewide acts moved to more forcefully institutionalize continued adherence to the growth imperative. A majority of the statewide laws moved beyond merely legislating growth promotion on the part of local governments, to mandating that they accommodate future growth. The current status of growth management efforts on the part of the states is therefore decidedly pro-growth. Statewide growth management laws are therefore serving to reinforce the accommodative nature of the majority of local management programs, and they represent a serious barrier to local efforts to slow or stop future growth. For those who have come to accept the current need to abandon the growth imperative, any further adoption of such statewide laws ought to be recognized as an expansion of a national movement to ensure continued growth. The growth orientation of statewide enactments would have to be reversed if growth management legislation at the state level is to play a part in bringing about an abandonment of the growth imperative in this country.

The Pro-Growth Orientation of the Growth Management Movement

The growth management movement in America has, in short, wholeheartedly endorsed management activity directed at the accommodation of further growth. The fact that current growth management efforts at both the local and state levels are overwhelmingly accommodative toward ongoing growth directly reflects the pro-growth orientation of the growth management movement. As the following excerpts from growth management literature reveal, authors writing about the movement and playing a part in shaping its future direction do not appear capable of abandoning the idea of growth as a social good:

An *enlightened* public policy . . . recognizes that it is not merely a matter of limiting growth, but rather developing strategies to *rationally accommodate* it. . . . [N]ot all growth is bad. What is needed is some form of managed growth strategy.[161] [italics added]

[L]ocalities must find ways to *accommodate reasonable growth.*[162] [italics added]

Growth management at its *best* is not an effort to stop growth, or even necessarily to slow growth. It is a calculated effort . . . to achieve a *balance* between natural systems . . . and . . . development.[163] [italics added]

Managed growth does not mean stopping change or closing the doors to new residents. *Properly* managed and implemented, a comprehensive growth management system provides a framework that enables . . . governments to *balance* and *accommodate* diverse and competing interests.[164] [italics added]

Properly defined and understood, growth management . . . has as central to its meaning a commitment to plan carefully for the growth that comes to an area.[165] [italics added]

At *worst*, growth management techniques can be used to *block legitimate growth.*[166] [italics added]

It is axiomatic that plans should be *realistic*, though many are not. To be "realistic" means that they are capable of being implemented. In practice this typically implies that development pressures are apparent and need to be *accommodated*.[167] [italics added]

The evolution of state growth policy has shown a shift from state preemptive regulatory interventions to . . . the incorporation of *growth-accommodating* economic policies into programs previously environmentally oriented. Such evolution indicates the *maturation* of state growth management.[168] [italics added]

The italics added to the selected citations from growth management literature epitomize the type of thinking driving the current growth management movement in the United States. Such reasoning argues that the *best, enlightened, realistic, mature*, and *properly defined* management programs are those that plan to *rationally accommodate reasonable* and *legitimate* growth, while at the same time balancing such competing interests as growth promotion and environmental protection. Conversely, the *worst, unenlightened, unrealistic, immature*, and *improperly defined* programs would presumably be those that sought to stop growth. Such reasoning in fact seems to pervade the growth management field. It is conceded that growth management in the current era increasingly refers to strategies that promote growth and economic development.[169] A leading spokesperson for the movement, and an acknowledged authority in the field, still argues during the 1990s that growth management systems need to balance "the equally legitimate needs of growth and the environment."[170] Any review of the literature treating the movement would quickly lead to the conclusion that the vast majority of participants agree. For most of those involved in the movement there seems to be no reasonable alternative to continued growth accommodation at present, and growth management literature evidences no willingness to entertain the prospect of management directed at stopping growth.

The current focus of the growth management movement at both local and state levels supports what the preceding chapter referred to as an obsolete ideology. Participants in the movement express a continuing belief in the legitimacy of growth in spite of mounting evidence of current limits to the expansion of the human enterprise. As the previous chapter illustrated, even the current scale of that enterprise is now being shown to represent an unsustainable assault on the planet's life-support systems. To suggest that further growth represents a legitimate social objective in the 1990s is therefore to reveal that one is either woefully uninformed or in total denial of current realities. If those who speak for the growth management movement continue to support the growth imperative, the movement risks loosing its relevance as growth-induced problems escalate under ongoing exponential growth. As evidence of our assault on the natural world mounts, it will be increasingly more difficult to rationalize the pertinence of additional growth. The country is already experiencing what one observer has identified as a "war between pro-growth and no-growth advocates."[171] The dissonance associated with that conflict seems destined to increase, because an increasing number of people appear willing to give up on the growth imperative as the century comes to a close. It remains to be seen whether the movement will be able to make the requisite transition from the traditional pro-growth position to a state of no-growth, or whether the movement will be displaced as the country struggles with the needed shift to sustainable behavior. If the growth management movement is to play a part in that transformation it will have to abandon its growth-accommodation orientation and redirect its management focus to downsizing and redesigning the human enterprise to a level and form that is sustainable. For the majority of participants in the movement such a change will not come easily, for they remain wedded to their belief in the merit of the growth imperative. Members of the planning profession have played a key role in the movement, and they have tended to be strong advocates of the movement's pro-growth position. The next chapter will illustrate the historical growth orientation of the planning profession, its role in the growth management movement, and the challenges it might be expected to face if it is to have a meaningful role in reshaping the present into a sustainable future.

3

The Role of the Planning Profession in Growth Management

The notion that growth is good, or at least inevitable, has been ingrained in much of the planning profession.

Earl Finkler[1]

The growth debate of the 1970s generated considerable vitriolic criticism of individuals and groups that continued to defend ongoing growth. Individuals who had come to accept the necessity of abandoning the growth imperative frequently lost patience with those who remained wedded to the idea of growth as the only viable option for the future. The profession of economics was especially singled out for such criticism, because few members of that profession showed the willingness or ability to think in terms other than the traditional growth model. One economist who was able to consider a future without ongoing growth has been credited with stating that "Anyone who believes exponential growth can go on forever in a finite world is either a madman or an economist."[2] As the previous chapter noted, social-justice advocates represent another group that has shown little willingness to let go of the idea of growth as a social good. These advocates tend to remain committed to the belief that growth affords a route to greater social justice in spite of mounting evidence to the contrary. One response to this naive view was put in the following words during the early years of the growth debate: "Anyone who thinks the American pattern of economic growth is a path to social justice could not have lifted [their] eyes from a textbook for years."[3]

This chapter will focus on yet another group that has evidenced little capacity for letting go of the growth imperative: members of the planning profession. As one professional planner noted during the growth debate of the 1970s, "most of the planning-and-design professions have been so long hooked to growth, so long dependent upon continued physical urban growth to justify their own professional existence that it comes hard, looking a gift-horse in the mouth."[4] The degree to which the planning profession has linked itself to the ongoing occurrence of growth will be illustrated in this chapter, as will its role in what the previous chapter revealed to be a decidedly pro-growth-oriented growth management movement. This chapter will also consider the likely nature of changes that the profession must undergo if it is to successfully take part in assisting the requisite societal transformation to a sustainable future.

ORIGINS OF THE PLANNING PROFESSION IN THE UNITED STATES

The history of planning for community development in America can be traced back to the preplanned communities that represented the norm for European colonial settlements in the New World from the latter part of the 16th century through the opening decades of the 18th century.[5] American colonial town planning was based on a European concept of the powers of municipal governments. Under this model municipal governments were granted considerable authority over the physical development of communities, including the power to own and dispose of land within communities and to set social and economic policies. This level of control was dramatically altered by the American Revolution and subsequent adoption of the Constitution in 1789. While that document spelled out the relationship between the federal government and the states, it did not address the matter of local governmental powers. American communities merely became creatures of their respective states, and the few powers they held were those specifically granted to them by state legislatures. Such powers were generally limited to those needed for maintenance of order and the provision of basic services, and local governments were given no grant of power to control or direct the development of private property. The states themselves also failed to exercise their authority in this area, and "land speculation, free of municipal control, became the dominant force shaping the American city"[6] during the 1800s. To the extent that planning occurred in this period it tended to be limited to the work of engineers platting the land of developing communities for the benefit of land sellers and builders.

As the previous historical portrayal reveals, the origins of community planning in the United States can be traced to planning that occurred for some of the earliest colonial settlements. Subsequent recordings of land subdivisions by engineers in the rapidly growing communities of a newly formed nation may also be characterized as planning activity representing other origins of planning in this country. However, while the origins of planning in America can be attributed to prior centuries, the planning agency and the planning profession are inventions of the 20th century.[7] The country's first professional planning association, the American City Planning Institute, was formed in 1917.[8] It is possible to link the origins or roots of that professional association to urban conditions existent in the 19th century. The inadequacy of what had previously passed for planning was becoming increasingly more evident by the middle of the 19th century. It would, in fact, become possible to argue that the majority of cities that evolved during the country's first 100 years did so without the influence of any real planning, and that this produced ill effects capable of being characterized in the following terms:

> Most American cities came into being without prior planning . . .
> and with only sporadic attempts to regulate their growth. *By the
> middle of the nineteenth century, therefore, the major cities were
> marked by ugliness, inefficiency, and disorder.* The provision of
> utilities and other municipal services could not keep up with the
> rapid increase in population, and the cities became overcrowded
> and congested with vast slums in which epidemics, unchecked
> crime, and political corruption were commonplace.[9] [italics added]

According to some historical assessments, the noted conditions of disorder, ugliness, and inefficiency stimulated the formation of a number of distinct interest
groups that represent the forebears of the planning profession in the United
States.[10]

Roots of the Planning Profession
in 19th Century Reform Movements

The first forebears of the contemporary planning profession in America consisted of members of a number of civic reform movements that emerged shortly
before the Civil War. Their major aim was the restoration of order in urban settings: physical order (through the demolition of slums, the construction of
model tenements, and the creation of parks), social order (through the erection of
educational and character-building facilities such as schools, libraries, and settlement houses), and political order (through the promotion of nonpolitical methods of urban decision making). These civic reformers pursued what would eventually come to be referred to as one of two distinct planning traditions in the
United States: planning for specific social reform.[11] In seeking social reform
these movements attributed many of the city problems of the day to unfettered
growth, and "[t]he means by which [the reformers] proposed to achieve the ends
[of order in its various forms] included new legislation to regulate and control
city growth."[12] The demands of housing reformers in particular produced some
of the first steps to restrict the use of private property and thereby avoid the ills
of overcrowding and congestion produced by growth.[13] While reform movements would leave their mark on the future planning profession in the form of
an ongoing tradition of planning for reform, the reform movements' position on
growth would be displaced by the growth orientation held by the other forebears
of the profession.

Architectural Roots of the Profession Dating
to the "City Beautiful" Movement

By the 1890s architects had joined social reformers as additional forebears of
the planning profession. These architects played a leading role in the "City
Beautiful" movement that occurred around the turn of the century, and their focus
was the ugliness of America's communities.[14] These forebears of the planning
profession championed the aesthetic end of beauty and proposed to counter urban
ugliness via proposals for grandiose civic centers, boulevards, monuments, and
parks.[15] The transition that would result in greater attention being paid to aesthetics than to the reformers' quest for order is described in Mel Scott's historical
treatise on city planning in the following terms:

> In the closing years of the nineteenth century, when reform groups
> had begun to celebrate some . . . initial victories . . . the civic en-
> deavors marking the beginnings of city planning were . . . mainly
> aesthetic. . . . The emphasis on aesthetics tended to negate an ear-
> lier, more humanitarian tone and was almost certain to alienate
> some . . . reformers, . . . yet without this reorientation America
> might not have entered the twentieth century with the prospect of
> evolving a new professional corps dedicated to improving the
> city.[16]

The fact that these forebears of the profession viewed growth differently than
members of the reform movements is revealed by the fact that the architects'
proposals, which principally consisted of downtown improvement schemes,
"were supported by [individuals with] downtown business and property interests,
who wanted to promote land values in these [downtown] areas and also advocated
efficiency in government to keep taxes low."[17] These new economic interests
would, to a large extent, displace the focus on aesthetics with new planning
ends, and these new ends were being championed by individuals with a clear pro-
growth bias.

Roots of the Planning Profession
in the Business Community

By 1910 the influence of architects on the evolving planning movement in
the United States had waned, and those seeking to advance economic ends were
assuming positions that would eventually have them identified as the last of the
forebears of the forthcoming planning profession. The second national conference on city planning, convened in Rochester, New York in 1910, was dominated by representatives of municipal efficiency groups and their architect-planner
collaborators.[18] Mel Scott's historical treatment of the planning movement during this period includes the following description of the change that occurred:

> The emphasis on the City Efficient or the City Functional charac-
> terizing the city planning movement by 1912 [reflected the grow-
> ing dominance of the values of efficiency and functionalism during
> that period]. . . . City planning . . . became a matter of altering
> spatial relationships to achieve the practical ends of efficiency
> and convenience. In the evolution of the city planning movement
> the City Functional was a logical phase.[19]

The influence of such alternative considerations on the planning movement and
its soon to be formed profession during the post-1910 period has also been described in the following manner:

> With the [social] reformers out of the picture, most of the support
> for planning between 1910 and World War I came from the
> Municipal Reform or Political Reform movement. With this new
> base of support came a major shift in the priorities and self-image
> of the profession. Amenity and order, which had been its explicit

objectives, were replaced by efficiency, and what had been viewed
as an 'Art' quickly became a 'Science.'[20]

Economic considerations that began to exert an increasing influence on planning
during this period were not, however, limited to a concern with efficiency.
Business people played a central role in formulating the emerging movement
that was targeting political and municipal reform,[21] and in the process "acted
more out of self-interest than their rhetoric and ideology would have us believe.
Time and time again, they took the opportunity to utilize 'liberalized' government intervention to protect the value of their property, to serve their interests."[22] In the process, the influence of these interests within the planning
movement produced a focus on governmental intervention directed at furthering
what has been referred to as the second distinct tradition of planning in the
United States: planning for general urban development.[23] Although interest in
planning for specific social reform as the other distinct tradition of planning did
not disappear, and the architects' concern with aesthetics also continued to exert
some influence within the planning movement, the focus on planning for development came to dominate the movement. The emergence of planning as a profession, in the form of the American City Planning Institute in 1917, occurred at
a time when members of the forthcoming profession had aligned themselves
with pro-growth sentiments in the country. As a profession, planning began by
embracing the societal acceptance of population, economic, and urban growth in
the United States.

THE EARLY GROWTH ORIENTATION
OF THE PLANNING PROFESSION

The newly formed planning profession began to define itself at a time when
business interests dominated the evolving planning movement in this country.
In his historical review of planning in the United States, Mel Scott refers to
planning activity of the 1920s as "City Planning in the Age of Business,"[24] and
he argues that in their attempts to change planning from an "art" to a "science"
planners in public agencies began to serve the interests of the day, which is to
say that "their planning 'science' seems to have been affected by the business optimism of the era, as was that of almost all of their fellow planning consul-
tants."[25] It was a time when planning and zoning were becoming municipal responsibilities, with civil engineers and architects filling most planning positions
because of the emphasis on land use and the provision of facilities,[26] and it was
also a time when "planners wanted to be technicians and professionals, and,
above all, to influence the development of cities."[27] One way of gaining the legitimacy and professional security that would allow them to exert such influence
was to serve the prevailing interests of the time. To do that professional planners had to subdue their interests in social reform and aesthetics and turn their attention to matters of efficiency and development.

In their quest for legitimacy and security, members of the new planning profession recognized the professional gains that could be attained by serving the
prevailing growth philosophy of the day. Scott, as part of his discussion of
planning during the 1920s, describes such a recognition in the following way:

> As long as plans promised reasonable progress . . . city planners
> could gradually win a more secure place for themselves in Amer-
> ican life. . . . To extend the city was easier than to conceive new
> forms for urban areas and to persuade people to accept them . . .
> [and] to move with the trends was less arduous than [to] crusade . . .
> [because] the rapidity of urban growth demanded 'practical'
> plans.[28]

Scott concedes that planners who chose such professional legitimacy and security
by adoption of pro-growth, business-oriented postures did so at a cost when he
notes: "The members of the profession . . . did not acknowledge, even to themselves, that they had submerged broader issues in order to concentrate on . . .
professional gains."[29] According to Alan Kravitz, "planning practitioners and
theorists alike . . . allowed their profession to be defined by its environment"[30]
rather than choosing their own direction for the profession, and as a consequence
permitted social acceptance of growth and urban development to subvert their initial concern with specific social reform. In his terms, this is expressed as the
subversion of the liberal concept of governmental intervention to achieve social
reform by the subsequent desire to serve, and thus satisfy, the wishes of an ultimately conservative ideology directed at order, stability, and economic development.[31] Such service was readily endorsed because it was seen as promoting the
quest for professional legitimacy and security.

The Pro-Growth Bias of Early Zoning Ordinances

The enthusiasm for zoning that swept the country during the early 1920s,[32]
supported both by business people and property owners as a way of protecting
and promoting property values,[33] and recognized as a tool for furthering economic development, afforded planners a vehicle for serving the dominant interests of the day. Scott describes the public view toward zoning in the early 1920s
in the following terms: "Millions of ordinary citizens could understand the need
for zoning if not for general planning."[34] He goes on to note that "the enthusiasm for zoning swept the nation and engaged the attention of some planners to
the exclusion of all else."[35] The role that this preoccupation played in associating urban planners with business interests is evident in the following citation
from Scott's work: "Popular enthusiasm for zoning threatened to overshadow
comprehensive planning and to ally the new profession with dominant business
interests."[36] As Scott puts it, in reference to what he calls unrealistic zoning ordinances of the 1920s and 1930s,

> The regulations became more varied, the legal substantiation more
> precise, but with few exceptions the allocations of the land re-
> sources of cities under these [zoning] enactments were preposter-
> ous, often providing for population densities and uses beyond any
> reasonable prospect of growth.[37]

Members of the new planning profession played an active part in creating and
implementing such "preposterous" zoning ordinances during this early period in
the profession's development. Such willingness to support pro-growth,
business-oriented interests via liberal zoning enactments intended to promote development illustrates the profession's growth orientation at this time.

The Pro-Growth Bias of Early Comprehensive Plans

While members of the planning profession devoted considerable time to zoning regulations that would make ongoing growth possible during the formative years of the profession, planners did not commit all their efforts to zoning in the 1920s. Professional planners also pursued an interest in the plan-making endeavors that were ideally intended to guide land-use regulations such as zoning. These plans also tended to reflect the business optimism of the "booming twenties," and as a result the plans were designed to permit optimistic levels of future growth. In 1926 the director of a plan for New York and its environs went on record with the view that plans had "to be elastic and capable of adjustment and readjustment to suit change and ever varying circumstances in community growth."[38] As the earlier citation from Scott revealed, the rapidity of urban growth in this era required "practical" plans that allowed for "reasonable progress" if planners were to realize their goal of achieving security for their profession in the American setting. Planners, it seems, were just as willing to employ community land-use plans as zoning ordinances to facilitate growth during the early years of the profession. As early as 1927 Lewis Mumford, who in time would establish himself as a noted urban historian, asked the profession to reject "the premise that city planning is merely a way of providing the physical means for a continuous expansion and congestion of our cities."[39]

This portrayal of the early years of the planning profession shows planners to have been actively involved in the development process that was remaking America's communities in the 1920s. Planners used the principal tools of their trade in that era, land-use regulations and plans depicting the future state of communities, to facilitate growth. Such activity indicates a decidedly pro-growth orientation by planning professionals during the profession's formative years. The subsequent section of this chapter illustrates the extent to which the profession has maintained a pro-growth position over the decades leading up to the current growth management era.

THE PROFESSION'S PRO-GROWTH LEGACY BEFORE THE GROWTH MANAGEMENT ERA

Planning has historically meant different things to different people in the United States, including different interpretations by members of the profession, who have engaged in an ongoing dialogue over what the profession actually is, or ought to be, since its formation. These different views of planning have resulted in planning being described in a number of different ways, particularly in terms of different types of planning. The view of planning as a plan-making endeavor has, for example, played a very significant role in the profession's development. The comprehensive plan-making approach has, in fact, represented the principal type of planning to characterize the profession over the course of its history. With time, this view of what planning was, or ought to be, failed to hold the loyalty of many within the profession, and the second of two dominant views of planning emerged: one which considered planning to be a rational decision-making process.

These two models of planning were in turn challenged by competing schools of thought, or so-called "partial planning models,"[40] that offered alternative suggestions as to the type of planning that ought to characterize the profession.

Over time, members of the profession have been asked to consider the merit of a number of different types of planning, including middle-range, social, advocacy, allocative, and radical planning. Brief characterizations of these different types of planning, as well as comments on the respective growth orientation of each type, are presented in subsequent sections of this chapter. The intent is one of revealing the extent to which the profession has been dominated by a pro-growth orientation over time, irrespective of the type of planning being practiced.

The Comprehensive Plan-Making View of Planning

No view of what planning is, or ought to be, has played as dominant a role in defining the profession as that which has seen planning as a comprehensive plan-making endeavor. The idea that planning ought to be directed at creating and revising what have alternatively been called general, master, or comprehensive land-use plans (depicting a community's arrangement of land uses some 20 or 30 years in the future), has represented the principal planning model from the earliest days of the profession to the present. Since the reformers, architects, and business people who represented the forebears of the profession saw their respec- tive ends as being accomplished largely through alterations in the uses of land, the relationship of such ends to plan-making produced an early interest in this type of planning. According to one source treating the nature of these early plans, "The master plan [was] essentially a technique for achieving the nine-teenth-century ends of beauty, efficiency, and order."[41] These early comprehensive plans evidenced an obvious predilection for physical planning. According to Scott's historical treatment of planning, a physical planning bias dominated the planning movement just prior to World War I, a time when the movement was "concerned principally with improving the three-dimensional environment."[42]

The fact that this physical planning bias extended well beyond the first world war may be illustrated by noting that the professional organization representing planners wrote such a bias into the statement of purposes contained in the organization's constitution in 1938.[43] That statement described the professional sphere of activity specifically as "the planning of the unified development of urban communities and their environs and of states, regions, and the nation, as expressed through determination of the comprehensive arrangement of land uses and land occupancy and the regulation thereof."[44] The influence of the view of planning contained in this statement carried on through the 1940s according to Henry Fagin, who claims that

> in the common parlance of everyday language in the 1940s, urban planning bore the limitation explicitly stated in the constitution of the American Institute of Planners: planning 'as expressed through the comprehensive arrangement of land use and land occupancy and the regulation thereof.'[45]

The continued orientation of the profession toward physical planning during the 1950s, as reflected by support for comprehensive land-use planning, has also been documented, as in the following citation from an article by Thomas Galloway and Riad Mahayni:

> Early historical events within the profession . . . tended to ho-
> mogenize the public and popular images of planning. The ap-
> proach of comprehensive land use planning, as a part of this ho-
> mogenizing influence, was accepted as a major planning symbol
> and historically has received strong support. This approach led
> the profession into the 1950s.[46]

Galloway and Mahayni offer the following description of the planning symbol,
or what they alternatively label as a model, that they credit with having led the
profession into the 1950s:

> By comprehensive land use model, we mean a model which incor-
> porates a desirable unitary end state, a portrait of the future devel-
> oped by using specific analytical and implementing tools and
> supported by a bundle of value propositions which tend to legit-
> imize as well as constrain the activity of planning to the provi-
> sion of the cities' future space and activity needs.[47]

The historical primacy of the comprehensive plan-making view of planning up
to the middle of this century has been stated in the following terms:

> From the 1920s to the 1950s a host of events, governmental ac-
> tions at all levels, theoretical developments, and methodological
> refinements extended and continuously redefined the notion of
> comprehensive land use planning. These efforts simultaneously
> sustained the consensus of the planning community.[48]

This consensus or agreement amongst members of the profession as to what
rightly constituted planning began, however, to be challenged in the 1950s.

By the 1950s a segment of the profession's membership increasingly found
fault with features of the comprehensive land-use plan, such as its emphasis on
physical planning, its portrayal of a static end state, its long-range goal-attain-
ment orientation, and its claimed representation of an apolitically derived route
for furthering the public welfare.[49] The view of planning as a plan-making endeavor would come to be challenged by changes in both society and the profession during this period. One assessment of these events concluded that
"[d]uring the decade of the 1950s this model came under increasing criticism, [in
part] because of the incongruities between the model and the political and social
phenomena of the urban area."[50] Rather than abandon the view of planning as a
plan-making activity because of shortcomings associated with comprehensive
plans, some sought to redefine the plan in order to maintain the professional influence of this type of planning. The nature of modifications that occurred in
comprehensive plans in order to maintain the profession's loyalty to this type of
planning in the post-1950s has been described in the following way:

> Given the criticism of the master or general plan as the normative
> model that held principal planning norms and activities together,
> the first phase of contemporary planning response centered on re-
> labeling the plan as a *continuing process*; the modifications to the
> plan approach emphasized *streamlining* planning activities, re-
> ducing time frames, updating and continually revising data and

forecasts, and, most importantly, continually amending the plan.[51]

For most members of the profession these changes permitted ongoing allegiance to the comprehensive plan-making approach to planning.

Continued loyalty to the physical planning embodied in comprehensive land-use plans on the part of the planning profession during the 1960s is evident in the profession's literature. The decade produced what have since become classic descriptions of these plans. In T. J. Kent's words: "The plan itself must focus on physical development; it must be long-range, comprehensive, and general."[52] A similar description of these plans by Alan Black was stated in the following terms:

> A comprehensive plan is an official public document adopted by a local government as a policy guide to decisions about the physical development of the community. . . . It is often said that the essential characteristics of the plan are that it is comprehensive, general, and long range.[53]

An example of the support that many professionals were still willing to give to this type of planning in the 1960s is vividly illustrated by the following citation from that decade:

> This [concern with the comprehensive arrangement of land uses], I submit, is something which a professional city planner has to know about, or [the individual] is not a professional city planner. . . . The product of the planning is physical. It must be stressed and restressed that city planning, as a profession, is a design profession.[54]

Looking back over the history of planning from the vantage point of 1967, Bernard Frieden acknowledged the ongoing influence exerted by the physical planning bias of the comprehensive land-use planning approach in the following words: "The physical approach had dominated city planning, providing its basic concepts as well as its methods of operation."[55] The year that Frieden made such a claim is, in fact, a benchmark for any consideration of the influence of a physical planning orientation within the profession, because it was in 1967 that the profession decided to delete from its constitution the reference to planning the "unified development" of communities "through determination of the comprehensive arrangement of land uses." In deleting that reference, the profession in effect conceded the legitimacy of planning efforts beyond those directed solely at the physical phenomenon of land-use arrangements, but the profession certainly did not abandon comprehensive land-use plans, nor the physical planning those plans have traditionally represented, with that 1967 decision.

In an article published in 1970, Kravitz was still able to claim that comprehensive land-use planning, or what he calls the classical model of planning, represented a dominant form of professional planning activity: "Contrary to much of the literature, the 'Classical Model' has not fallen from grace or power."[56] In 1974 Jerome Kaufman would similarly make the following claim: "City planning agencies appear to be as deeply involved in physical planning and land use control activities today as they were in the fifties."[57] In 1978 Melville Branch published a paper in the profession's principal journal claiming that "end-state master city plans [that] portray the proposed physical-spatial features of the community twenty or more years in the future" are "still the most common form for city planning in the United States."[58] There are, in fact, numerous contributions in the literature of planning "supporting the assertion of the historical primacy of comprehensive land use planning"[59] well into the 1970s. Since the prior chapter identified the 1970s as a period when growth management activity had already been labeled a movement, comprehensive plan-making activity clearly continued in what would come to be called the growth management era.

The comprehensive plan-making approach, as the principal type of planning to characterize the profession over time, has in reality maintained a dominant position within the profession through the 1980s and 1990s. In the last few decades, courts and state legislatures have increasingly demanded that planning be done prior to, and apart from, the enactment of land-use regulations. In such an increasing number of states, mandated plans are no longer simply advisory policy documents, they are actually the law.[60] As one commentator has noted: "The inevitable march toward a comprehensive plan as the legal equivalent of a constitution for future growth is gaining momentum."[61] Even in states without statewide growth management laws, comprehensive land-use plans are increasingly being required as preconditions for being able to regulate the use of privately held land. In states with statewide growth management laws, such plans for future growth are typically mandated. The issue of interest here is the nature of the growth orientation that such plans have evidenced over time. Plans created during the early years of the profession were said to have been "practical plans" that allowed for "reasonable progress." The question to be considered is whether comprehensive land-use plans maintained a pro-growth bias over subsequent decades.

The Historical Pro-Growth Orientation of Comprehensive Plan-Making

Any consideration of the growth orientation of comprehensive land-use plans over the course of the profession's evolution needs to acknowledge the early existence of an alternative professional conception of such plans. Not all members of the developing profession accepted the view that plans ought to be "practical" and allow for "reasonable progress" via endless growth accommodation. Another school of thought within the profession suggested that comprehensive plans had a proper role to play in helping communities develop ideal or utopian city constructs.[62] Concern with these constructs may be directly linked to the traditional concern of planners with physical planning, or their faith in "physical determinism," because these "master planners assumed that people's lives are shaped by their physical surroundings and that the ideal city could be realized by the provision of an ideal physical environment."[63] That concern with ideal or utopian ends produced characterizations of comprehensive plans as "end-state master city plans" that portray "desirable unitary end states" for communities in terms of their future space and activity needs some 20 or more years in the future. These documents would also be referred to as "static long-range master plans."[64]

This school of thought would come to be described in the following manner: "The planner's certainty about how people ought to live and how the city ought to look resulted in a nearly static plan, a Platonic vision of the city as an orderly and finished work of art."[65] For planners drawn to this form of comprehensive plan making, the salient characteristics of the plan-making approach to planning differ from those associated with "practical" plans developed to allow "reasonable progress." The focus in this case shifts to the creation of reasonable final design schemes for the future physical form of urban places that convey the "implication that disturbing overgrowth should be prevented."[66] It turned out that this version of comprehensive plans would be displaced by the "practical" plans that planners recognized as means for attaining professional legitimacy and security.

Considerable criticism would be directed at those in the profession that suggested that plan-making activity ought to be directed at producing static, unitary, end-state portrayals of ideal future designs for urban areas. Comprehensive land-use plans reflecting such an orientation were accused of representing "an old-fashioned, static ideology"[67] that is unworkable,[68] and in fact little more than a "cartoon utopia."[69] Melville Branch, a well-known spokesperson for the profession, would refer to these plans as "the grand master plan delusion,"[70] while Edgar Rose would refer to "the weakness of [the] utopian vision [with its] finite and static conceptualization of . . . utopia."[71] From the earliest days of the profession, most of its members seemed unable to seriously consider the merit of a product-oriented approach intended to produce static, utopian, end-state plans directed at preventing "disturbing overgrowth." For most professional planners, such plans seemed too rigid and inflexible to serve as tools for effectively managing change during the "booming twenties." Anything less than flexibility seem_d impractical because it was "a decade characterized by frenetic activity, runaway urban growth that seemed impossible to control."[72] The profession responded by redefining the plan-making approach, shifting the focus to one of plan-making as a continuing process of redoing the comprehensive land-use plan.

As early as 1911, Frederick Law Olmstead, Jr., a prominent figure in the early history of the planning profession, expressed the view that plans should not be considered final products:

> We must disabuse the public mind of the idea that a city plan means a fixed record . . . a plan to be completed and put on file and followed more or less faithfully and mechanically. . . . We must cultivate . . . the conception of a city plan as a device . . . for preparing and keeping constantly up to date . . . the important changes . . . in the control of the city's physical growth.[73]

Acceptance of a process-oriented view of comprehensive land-use plans grew during the first few decades of the profession, and would with time produce an acknowledgment of "the market bias of early land use planners."[74] Planners recognized the professional gains associated with "practical plans" that allowed ongoing development and continued to evolve a process-oriented view of plan-making in the decades following the 1920s. By the 1950s the profession had largely succeeded in accomplishing the relabeling of comprehensive plan-making as a "continuing process." The central feature of that relabeling exercise was the idea that it was acceptable to continually amend the comprehensive plan. Being receptive to continuous amendments conveys a different prospect for continued growth than that conveyed by a view of plans as end-state documents intended to prevent "disturbing overgrowth." The process view of plan-making won out within the profession, and with it came a "receptiveness to change" that reflected "the flexibility necessary for growth and adaptation to new conditions."[75]

According to Mel Scott, the 1950s was a time when planners were "socially rewarded for displaying short-term practicality" and "at ease adapting to well recognized trends . . . within the context of a business-dominated economy."[76] The process view of plan-making allowed planners to be practical and help communities adapt to ongoing growth. Post-1950s planning literature continued to convey a view of the superiority of the process-oriented approach to plan-making, or at the very least indicated that it was the direction in which planners were predominantly moving, in the world of both theory and professional practice. In 1967 Henry Fagin would make the following claim:

> It is part of the pervasive contemporary sense of dynamics that planners are more interested in streams of change over time, sequences of events and situations, and periodically shifting patterns than in snapshots of end states, in so-called plans of ultimate development.[77]

By 1973 David Godschalk would argue that "American planning theory is generally moving away from approaches based on a fixed 'end-state' plan to a more flexible, dynamic concept of land-use 'guidance' systems."[78] In 1974 the consequence of this new process-oriented view of plan-making was summed up by one observer in the following terms:

> Planning has come a long way in the past two decades in changing its previous utopian characteristics to more 'rational' and systematic images of the future. We now primarily turn out plans dominated by the heavy hand of the past.[79]

Under a plan-making process characterized by continuous amendments to comprehensive plans, the heavy hand of the past would continue to take communities along a path of ongoing growth, and by the early 1970s some within the profession acknowledged such a reality. As one member of the profession put it, "[g]enerally . . . urban plans are based not on what should be but on what will be. The justification for such plans is firmly anchored in projections of existing circumstances."[80] The existing circumstances that most communities were seeking to maintain was a continuation of the assumed progress traditionally associated with ongoing growth.

Another way of illustrating the pro-growth orientation of plan-making activity since the 1950s is through a brief review of the principle methods text that has been used to educate planners in the "art" or "science" of making plans. Since 1957, when F. Stuart Chapin first came out with his text titled *Urban Land Use Planning*,[81] students of the profession have almost without exception been introduced to the method of making comprehensive plans by Chapin's book. Chapin's influence on the nature of plan-making activity has continued into the 1980s and 1990s with a 1979 revision of the text, which he coauthored with Edward Kaiser. In essence, both the original and revised texts represent an accommodative planning approach that instructs students in how to calculate the prospective future demand for land in an urban setting by studies of the urban economy, employment, and population, and how then to accommodate that demand by making the necessary land and facilities available to receive the projected growth.

Even a cursory reading of the original text reveals its accommodative orientation toward ongoing growth. When discussing employment forecasts in planning studies Chapin writes of determining "a tentative estimate of the new acreage required to *accommodate* normal industrial expansion."[82] [italics added] When treating population forecasts he argues that "the use of safety factors in translating forecast data into land requirements [or making more land available than the forecast indicates] permits greater tolerance limits for error,"[83] and he also points out that "arithmetic and geometric projections assume that the same forces affecting population change in the past will continue in the future."[84] In a section on urban land studies he writes that "[t]hese studies provide information on the physical setting that *accommodates* the economic activity, and the population and their activities."[85] [italics added] As part of the same urban land studies section Chapin notes that "[t]he blighted areas map along with the land capabilities map furnish a picture of the areas where the major *growth* of the future *must be accommodated*."[86] [italics added] The vacant land study, he writes, "identifies the potentialities of vacant and open land for development."[87] In a section on location requirements for new land uses he discusses a "review of policy directions that might be followed in *accommodating growth*" and makes note of the public facilities "required to *accommodate* each of the [alternate possible] development patterns."[88] [italics added]

While the revised edition of the text coauthored with Kaiser does make concessions to the changing times of the 1970s, as in its inclusion of a section on environmental suitability analysis intended to provide information on the relative suitability of different sites for various types of development, it is nevertheless structured around the same accommodative approach portrayed above. The revised text is also based on an approach of determining demand and then carrying out the planning to receive the growth implied by that demand. Chapin and Kaiser are, in fact, quite explicit about their stance toward future growth, as the following citation from their book reveals:

> [E]ven though there are stirrings toward reexamining basic growth assumptions, it is political reality to expect that since the run-out time [for] resources is still in the future local policy on growth will continue to respond to the long-held [belief] of the business community [in economic growth]. . . . Even though traditional assumptions in economic thought can be expected to respond to questions of resource limits and bring about changed emphasis in national economic policy, these changes will only very slowly be reflected at the local level.[89]

The revised text based on such reasoning is, in effect, serving to educate a second generation of planners in a plan-making method based on ongoing accommodation of growth. It is also furthering the evolution of a process-oriented view of the plan-making approach by emphasizing the increasing importance of "the idea of a development guidance system instead of the traditional long-range land use design as the output of planning."[90]

The process-oriented view of plan-making, as it has been characterized here, consists of an acceptance of continuous amendments to comprehensive plans and a plan-making methodology based on determining a future demand for land that plans are then designed to accept. By the 1970s, this approach to plan-making was variously described as a "demand-based,"[91] "demand-activated,"[92] or "accommodative"[93] method. Under this method plan-making may be portrayed in terms of three procedural steps: 1) determination of the demand for land and facilities by the study of population and business trends, 2) calculation of the land and facilities required to meet that demand, and 3) accommodation of the demand via plans that provide for future growth, rezonings that permit more intense uses of land, and capital improvement programming expenditures that build the public facilities required to service new development. As an alternative to this pro-growth oriented approach, it is possible to characterize a plan-making method that begins with supply instead of demand determinations. This approach, which might alternatively be labeled as a "supply-based," "supply-activated," or an "allocative/carrying capacity" method, would be characterized in terms of the following procedural steps: 1) determination of the supply of available natural and institutional resources, 2) establishment of "acceptable" levels of demand that might be put on the available resources, and 3) allocation of permissible levels of use to the sources of demand.[94] On the whole, members of the planning profession showed no willingness to adopt such an alternative plan-making approach as they began to participate in what would come to be called the growth management movement, and instead continued to deploy the traditional accommodative approach in the plan-making process.

By the 1970s planning literature began to acknowledge that plan-making was essentially an accommodative undertaking based primarily on a demographic and economic analysis that amounts to little more than "a projection of future growth and the size of population to be planned for."[95] One source from that period summed up this claim in the following terms:

> Most general plans . . . in the United States are based on what might by called 'accommodative planning.' That is, they incorporated projections of population and economic increase, most of which are based on extrapolation of past trends, and plan the use of land to best accommodate these trends in terms of added housing units, added employment locations, and so on.[96]

Zoning, as the major regulatory mechanism employed to implement plans, evidenced similar accommodative tendencies during the time that members of the planning profession were initiating their involvement with the growth management movement. Mel Scott's description of the "unrealistic" or "preposterous" zoning enactments of the 1920s and 1930s would be followed in the 1960s by a foreign observer's reference to more recent practices of "vast overzoning" in response to "exuberant confidence . . . in future growth and business prosperity."[97] In 1975 such a pro-growth bias in plans and zoning ordinances could be described in the following way: "Up until recently the purpose of planning and zoning was seen as accommodating increases in population and the resultant demand for land for urban development. Local governments, in the main, responded to the operations of the market."[98] In short, as members of the planning profession entered the growth management era they evidenced little ability to think of plan-making activity in any terms other than as an accommodative exercise intended to facilitate further growth.

The 1980s and 1990s have produced no real change in the nature of the plan-making approach employed by members of the planning profession. Some insight into the holding power of the accommodative plan-making approach may be gleaned from a reading of the latest version of the principle professional text covering plan-making activity. The most recent edition of *Urban Land Use Planning*, released in 1995, and now co-authored by Kaiser, Godschalk, and Chapin,[99] suggests an expanded awareness of the need to consider environmental factors in planning for a community's future. Included within the text are treatments of such concepts as carrying capacity, land suitability, and sustainable development, but the book nevertheless maintains a demand-based approach to the creation of comprehensive plans. The work begins by identifying the management of land-use change as the fundamental rationale for the practice of land-use planning. Later in the text the planner is referred to as "a manager of urban change and growth."[100]

As was the case with earlier editions of the text, the work puts population and employment chapters that are intended to determine the future demand for land before the environment chapter which treats methods for making supply determinations. In the population-methods chapter the text notes that "population and employment growth underlie the amount of development pressure and the pace of urban development to be *accommodated*.[101] [italics added] In the land-use chapter the authors note that land use "*accommodates* the needs for growth resulting from population and economic expansion."[102] [italics added] As part of the chapter on the land-use design process, the authors treat the matter of estimating space requirements for particular land uses and note the need to "[e]stimate the amount of land needed to *accommodate* the future level of activity expected."[103] [italics added] In the land classification planning chapter they address "the designation of areas for urban growth."[104] The environment chapter clearly reveals the growth orientation of the book in the following terms: "The goal is economic growth that is socially and environmentally sustainable, balancing economy and ecology."[105] So while the text makes substantial advances in introducing environmental or supply-based considerations into the plan-making process, it still suggests the suitability of a demand-based approach to the creation of comprehensive plans. In doing so, it continues to reinforce the idea that ongoing growth is desirable if its ill effects are mitigated. The text also suggests the possibility of creating comprehensive plans that successfully balance social, market, and environmental values under ongoing growth. Overall, the new work contributes little to the development of planning directed at stopping future growth or the needed transition to a sustainable future. It instead advances the oxymoronic idea of sustainable growth.

Additional insight into the current growth orientation of plan-making activity is revealed by the legislatively mandated nature of comprehensive plans in states that have passed statewide growth management laws. As the last chapter noted, the majority of those laws mandate ongoing growth accommodation by local governments, typically doing so by requiring the creation of plans that allow for future growth. However, even in states without such laws, plan-making appears to be driven by the momentum of an historical approach that continues to design future growth potential into community plans. To the degree that planning professionals are able to influence the nature of these plans, they appear to remain content to produce plans that facilitate ongoing growth. The history of plan-making activity by planning professionals reveals that it has maintained a consistent pro-growth bias over time. Since the comprehensive plan-making approach has represented the principal type of planning to characterize the profession over time, one may conclude that the profession has exhibited a history of pro-growth activity. However, as was noted previously, there have been alternative views of what planning is, or ought to be, and those different views have resulted in planning being described in terms of different types of planning. The matter of interest here is whether the other types of planning afforded members of the profession an opportunity to exercise something other than a pro-growth orientation.

The Rational Decision-Making View of Planning

By the 1950s a group of urban theorists was sufficiently disenchanted with the ability of the plan-making view of planning to produce desired changes in communities that they rejected the sufficiency of mere modifications in the comprehensive plan. As a result, they gravitated toward what would become the second of two dominant views of planning to have played a role in shaping the history of the urban-planning profession in the United States: a view of planning as a rational decision-making process.[106] The view of planning as something other than the creation and revision of plans was advanced by members of a planning school established at the University of Chicago after the second world war, and the legacy of that school would be described in the following terms:

> The Chicagoans approached planning as a method of *rational pro-gramming*. Briefly, they argued that the essence of planning was the deliberate choice of ends and the analytic determination of the most effective means to achieve these ends—means which make optimal use of scarce resources and, when implemented, are not accompanied by undesirable consequences. . . . The . . . rational programmers owe no allegiance either to the master plan or to physical determinism.[107]

The relationship of this alternative view of planning to the previously noted move directed at redefining the plan-making approach as a continuing process of plan adaptations, and a more specific statement of the nature of the new view, were suggested in a work that appeared in the profession's principal journal:

> At the same time that . . . [modifications to the plan were being initiated in the 1950s] . . . the criticism of the master plan generated another approach, related to the above direction [of relabeling the plan-making approach as a continuing process] but further removed from the traditional master plan model. Planning was posited as independent of the object to which it was applied. This direction characterized planning as a rational decision-making process.[108]

Advocates of this view argued

> that planning is basically a methodology, a set of procedures ap-
> plicable to a variety of activities aimed at achieving selected goals
> . . . [and] . . . what makes urban planning a discipline—and its
> practice a profession—is what it does and how it does it, not where
> or to what it is done. . . . The planner should be an expert on the
> methodology by which planning is done.[109]

What planning is seen as properly doing under such a perspective is defined as
the act of applying a set of procedures for making rational decisions about the future to the process of deciding what to do and how to do it in order to attain
given ends. Rational action according to this view consists of undertaking the
five interrelated steps of what has come to be labeled the rational planning process: identifying problems/goals; designing alternative solutions or courses of
action; comparing and evaluating the alternatives and choosing or helping decision makers choose the "best" alternative; developing implementation measures;
and adjusting steps one through four based on feedback and review.[110]

The rational decision-making view of planning seemed, in the minds of
some, to represent a superior route for influencing decisions, because as observers would note, it envisioned a role for planners that linked them far more directly to the decision-making arena than the earlier plan-making view of
planning:

> This conception of planning . . . presages a change in the role of
> the planner. The city planner is no longer a nonpolitical formula-
> tor of long-range ideals, but is becoming an advisor to elected and
> appointed officials, providing them with recommendations and
> technical information on current decisions.[111]

This new role represented a very real change from the traditional comprehensive
plan-making view of planning, because the latter promoted a view of planning as
a technical, professional activity that should stay removed from politics by having lay planning commissions be the clients of plans produced by such planning. These commissions were seen as playing the role of insulating planners
from the corruptive influences of politics so that they might produce plans truly
reflective of the public interest. The new role of serving as advisors to elected
officials put planners directly into the decision-making process shaping the future of communities, and such a role carried with it clear implications for the
growth orientation of this type of planning.

The Pro-Growth Orientation
of the Rational Decision-Making View of Planning

The growth orientation of the view of planning as a rational decision-making
process may be inferred from the association of that view with a pragmatic planning approach. To be pragmatic in planning endeavors in a societal context that
has traditionally valued growth required planners to assume pro-growth planning
postures; to do otherwise would have damaged their credibility and diminished
their ability to affect change in the urban landscape. Insight into the role that

such a concern with practicality played in motivating the formulation of the rational decision-making process view of planning has been provided by Alan Kravitz:

> [The comprehensive land-use view of planning was] attacked . . . on the grounds that political and administrative reality made the model both obsolete and unworkable. [The critics] succeeded in convincing many planners that planning was a process within a decision-making environment, that this environment was not assumed under the [comprehensive land-use view], and that planning must adapt to this environment.[112]

In seeking to avoid charges that planning as it was traditionally viewed was obsolete and unworkable, many members of the profession adopted the rational decision-making view of what appropriately constitutes planning, and in the process of putting themselves in touch with political reality they assumed the noted pro-growth postures.

Part of the pragmatic adaptation suggested by the new view of planning consisted of rejecting the traditional comprehensive land-use planning contention that planners as professionals were best suited to decide the ends toward which society should be steered. As one observer noted, "[e]nds [according to the rational decision-making process view of planning], are imposed not by planning ideology or by a prior determination of the public interest, but by political and market processes and by other forms of feedback from those affected by planning."[113] Further adaptation of a pragmatic nature suggested by the new view required a rejection of the traditional orientation of the plan-making view toward the formulation of ideal or utopian communities, as such futures are subject to charges of being impractical and thereby potentially injurious to whatever degree of effectiveness planners might hope to attain in realizing professional aims. Take, for example, Norman Beckman's views on the possible shortcomings of suggesting unrealistic or utopian proposals:

> Planners, above all others, cannot afford to be called dreamers or ivory tower types. To put out proposals that clearly have little chance of acceptance and accomplishment inevitably reduces the planner's always limited supply of public confidence and makes acceptance of subsequent proposals less likely, regardless of their merit.[114]

Such adaptations accompanying a shift in views as to what rightly constitutes planning hint at the growth orientation of the rational decision-making process view of planning. Having ends imposed by political and market processes, when those processes have traditionally been wedded to the notion that growth represents progress and therefore a social good, clearly links the rational decision-making process view to a pro-growth orientation. Similarly, rejecting the idea that utopian proposals represent a legitimate planning function, while suggesting that planners need to put forth practical proposals if they are to be effective, also suggests that planners ought to serve the aim of progress with its associated pro-growth connotations.

Donald Foley, in comparing the second dominant view of planning to its pre-decessor, made the claim that the rational decision-making view of planning was "more geared to the recognition of change and growth."[115] In listing the distin-guishing characteristics of this alternative view he included mention of its fluid-ity and its latitude for experimentation, and he specifically linked the rational de-cision-making process view to a planning approach based on "the acceptance of growth."[116] To accept is by definition to approve, so such a characterization of this type of planning further suggests a pro-growth bent to this alternative view of planning. It would appear that rather than providing an alternative to the growth accommodation associated with the plan-making view of planning, the rational decision-making process view served to link professional planning activ-ity even more directly to the practice of growth accommodation.

The Pro-Growth Bias of Alternative Planning Models

The view of planning as a rational decision-making process served to greatly expand the realm of planning activity deemed legitimate by members of the pro-fession. This perceived expansion of the boundaries of what properly constitutes professional planning activity has been credited with playing a part in stimulat-ing a number of alternative views of what the focus of planning ought to be.[117] Whether thought of as alternative views, partial planning models, or sub-types of planning, these alternative formulations usually suggested refinements or ex-tensions of the two dominant views of planning. In 1956 Martin Meyerson proposed one of the first alternatives in the form of a range of intermediate func-tions between the traditional short- and long-range ones planning agencies typi-cally evidenced. He argued that these functions would serve as a "middle-range bridge" between decisions on projects and decisions on long-range comprehensive plans and thereby improve the prospects for rational decisions.[118] The five inter-related functions were directed at improving decisions both in the public and pri-vate sectors, and suggested that planners move into such new areas as market analyses for the private sector and trouble-shooting for potential problem areas in the public realm.

Meyerson left no doubt as to the growth orientation of the type of planning he was suggesting in his concept of middle-range planning. In surveying the ur-ban landscape during the mid-1950s he opined that "[m]arket decisions are more important than governmental ones in giving substance to the design and struc-ture of our urban communities [and that] [t]he political philosophy of the coun-try rests on the market as the key means to allocate resources, [including allocat-ing land uses]."[119] Taking this role for the market as a given, he suggested the market-analysis function "to aid the operations of the market."[120] The city planning agency, Meyerson suggested, should act "to *facilitate market opera-tions*, for housing, commerce, industry and other community activities through the regular issuance of market analyses" and thereby "*lubricate* the process of ur-ban *development*."[121] [italics added] By the 1960s these ideas had found their way into many planning agencies, which came to be thought of "not merely as planning organizations but as departments of planning *and* development."[122] So to the extent that this view of planning influenced the behavior of members of the profession it clearly maintained its pro-growth bias.

During the 1960s a number of articles appeared in the planning profession's main journal on the subject of social planning.[123] Increased acceptance of the view that social planning was a legitimate concern of planners produced an expansion of planning activity beyond a concern with planning the physical environment during this period. Planners felt increasingly more comfortable directing their attention to such diverse areas as employment opportunities, social services, elimination of racial discrimination, and so on.[124] This reawakened empathy for disadvantaged groups in society brought with it a readily discernible endorsement of continued economic growth. Take, for example, the following excerpts from the articles on social planning in the profession's main journal:

> [T]here are probably no more direct routes to human betterment than improvements in the educational system and *stimulation of the regional economies.*[125] [italics added]

> It is . . . increasingly recognized that . . . *economic development programs to strengthen the regional economy* . . . are of great significance to social planning.[126] [italics added]

This revival of the social-reform tradition of planning may therefore be credited with providing further support for a pro-growth bias among planning professionals, because as the previous chapter indicated, social justice advocates have remained committed to the idea that growth affords a means to remedy a host of social ills.

In 1965 Paul Davidoff introduced members of the planning profession to the concept of advocacy planning, or the notion that the "public plan" could be improved by lively political dispute over "plural plans" reflecting the interests of different groups in society, with advocate planners representing those different groups as actors in a contentious, politicized process.[127] Part of the motivation for Davidoff's proposal came from his belief that the comprehensive plan did not represent the interests of all groups. While his proposal suggested a concern with bringing all groups into the planning process, the principal focus was on gaining representation for traditionally underrepresented groups. As Davidoff put it in a subsequent publication co-authored with others: "From its beginning, the movement toward advocacy planning has stressed the need to plan with, and in the interests of, the formerly unrepresented groups in the planning process—the poor, the black, and the underprivileged."[128] The emphasis that proponents of advocacy planning tend to put on improving the status of the disadvantaged, and the credit they are inclined to give growth as the means of accomplishing that improvement, is typically expressed through a spirited defense of continued physical mobility and economic growth.[129] Once advocacy planners identified suburbs as the centers of economic growth,[130] their faith in the curative effects of such growth naturally them to oppose any growth controls that would exclude the disadvantaged from such areas.[131] As was the case with social planning, advocacy planning served to provide further support for a pro-growth orientation amongst planning professionals.

During the second half of the 1960s articles also appeared in the profession's principal journal elaborating on the view of planning as an allocative activity. One of those works offered the following comment on the allocative decisions made by planning agencies: "The most important decisions that any government planning agency is called upon to make or to recommend are decisions on how to allocate scarce governmental resources among a large number of different public needs."[132] The authors of that cited viewpoint suggested "optimal resource allocation methods" designed to achieve a distribution of resources among competing systems in such a way that they would be equally productive in each system. A subsequent article took the issue of allocation from the level of intra- to inter-community allocation decisions, and proposed a system for correcting "share imbalances" between communities in such things as jobs and low-income residences by allocating future development based on a metropolitan plan.[133] However, irrespective of the nature of such allocation decisions or the scale at which they are considered, the growth orientation of allocative planning is suggested by its close ties to economic reasoning and its traditional growth fixation. The noted works do not suggest the possibility of allocation decisions within a nongrowing economy, and the growth bias of the works is clearly presented in the articles. In one of the cited articles, the authors argue that the objective of providing a minimum standard of living for the economically and socially immobile "requires examining programs designed to *stimulate economic activities and employment.*"[134] [italics added] In the work on metropolitan allocation decisions, which discusses an incentives scheme for achieving the cooperation of local governments in accommodating future regional development allocations, the author suggests: "If local governments have accepted targets for development, they will receive substantial grants to enable them to build the community *facilities, and* to offer the *services necessary to attract growth.*"[135] [italics added] The view of planning as an allocative activity clearly served to once again reinforce the profession's pro-growth mindset.

Of the alternative views of planning that surfaced before the planning profession's active involvement in the growth management movement, only formulations of so-called radical planning during the early 1970s offered members of the profession an option to the continued support of growth. As proposed, radical planning was fundamentally different from the previously surveyed types of planning in that it represented more than a refinement or extension of the two dominant views that portray planning as either plan-making or a rational decision-making process. These formulations of radical planning were linked both to extensions of advocacy planning directed at radical action and participant democracy, and to broader treatments of the process of system transformation and societal change.[136] Radical planners made a case for the need to reconstruct existing institutions, and their proposed solution tended to "attack the institutional problem with the exhortation to decentralize, transfer power, and alter institutional structure in the direction of 'grass roots' control."[137] A single article in the profession's central journal suggested the nature of changes the planning profession would have to undergo to realize radical planning: "Not only the goals of planning, but its internal structure as well needs changing. At present, it perpetuates elitist, centralized, and change-resistant tendencies."[138] The same authors portrayed their vision of a future associated with radical planning by way of the following description: "A new paradigm rising to challenge the 'rational-comprehensive' [or rational decision-making] model of modern planning is based on systems change and the realization of a decentralized communal society that facilitates human development in the context of an ecological ethic by evolutionary social experimentation."[139] More than two decades after the introduction

of this option, these precepts have found little, or no, expression in planning literature, nor have they gained a following among members of the planning profession.

The growth orientation suggested by radical-planning formulations was obviously very different from the traditional pro-growth perspectives associated with
the earlier types of planning generated by the profession prior to the growth
management era. Radical planning proposed that people ought to be freed from a
"constrained, bounded, technological way of thinking" that reflects, among other
things, a preoccupation with "maximum material productivity."[140] Radical
planning suggested that people's well-being was based on something other than
materialistic and technological foundations, and questioned the worth of unending
economic growth in a manner illustrated by the following citation:

> Human development consists of social and economic development
> and should be contrasted to the present emphasis on economic
> growth. . . . This desire for growth, sold to the people by the
> promise of economic well-being, has proven a hollow victory: the
> emphasis on economic growth has resulted in the alienation of in-
> dividuals from themselves and from each other . . . and from their
> environment. . . . Some level of economic well-being is necessary
> for people to exercise choice between survival and risk, but once
> attained, continued economic growth seems only to prevent fur-
> ther development of the individual.[141]

As the growth management era gained momentum during the early 1970s, the
planning profession seemed unable to consider such an alternative perspective on
growth. It was even unable to consider a far less radical proposal contained in a
limited number of publications coauthored by members of the profession, which
merely suggested that planners ought to give serious consideration to "nongrowth" as an alternative to some development proposals.[142] In those publications, Earl Finkler and his associates made it clear that the term nongrowth was
"not meant to imply that communities want to stop any and all future
growth."[143] Instead they made a case for the view that growth was "a variable to
be influenced in pursuit of a desirable quality of life,"[144] and that communities
"should elect certain types of growth on the basis of identifiable need."[145] As
one of those publications put it: "Unlike the unfounded previous assumption
that 'all growth is good,' the argument for nongrowth rests on the modified assumption that 'some growth is good, some growth is not good.'"[146] As the
growth management era began, the profession showed no willingness to examine
even such a partial reformulation of the proper stance toward growth and instead
remained committed to an unconditional pro-growth stance.

If the planning profession was able to ignore the call for radical planning and
its implied rejection of the growth imperative during the early 1970s, the other
partial-planning models had to varying degrees influenced the behavior of members of the profession. The pro-growth orientation of those alternative types of
planning served to reinforce the profession's support for ongoing growth. Just
as the plan-making and rational decision-making process views of planning had
come to be associated with a pro-growth orientation, the extensions and refinements of those dominant views by the partial-planning models contributed to the
historical pro-growth posture of the profession before the advent of the growth

management movement. Whether members of the profession were engaging in comprehensive plan-making, attempting to influence rational decision making, taking part in middle-range planning functions, championing social planning ends, practicing advocacy planning, or participating in decisions regarding resource allocations, professional behavior tended to support ongoing growth prior to the growth management era. As Henry Fagin put it in 1970, "The truth is that for half a century our profession has specialized predominantly in advocacy planning for the business community."[147] Even if the focus was on something else, such as advocating the interests of the underrepresented, growth was still seen as the route to achieving these other ends.

The profession's support for growth during this period exhibited some of what had been referred to as "growthmania" in the opening chapter of this book. In 1968 a book by Constantinos Doxiadis argued the inevitability of a continuous settlement of some 35 billion people covering the inhabitable earth by 2100, which he considered to be desirable because it would create a global community and permit the exploitation of resources for the benefit of all people.[148] In 1973 a book by Marion Clawson and Peter Hall rejected the objective of no-growth, stating "that no-growth would create more problems than it would solve," and it suggested a future where many families would own a second, a third, or even a fourth home in different locations for different purposes.[149] While some members of the profession would have considered these extreme viewpoints at that time, most supported ongoing growth. As the profession embarked on a future of participation in the growth management movement, it in fact exhibited a decidedly pro-growth posture.

THE PROFESSION'S GROWTH ORIENTATION DURING THE GROWTH MANAGEMENT ERA

Little has appeared in the literature of the planning profession during the growth management era to indicate a change in the profession's historical pro-growth orientation. In the late 1970s the profession's principal society, the American Institute of Planners, adopted a policies document with wording indicating a continued endorsement of future growth:

> While growth has become a controversial subject, it must be accepted that some *growth is inevitable* simply as a result of the *need to accommodate* this nation's reduced, but still very substantial prospective population increase. Furthermore, if living standards of the underprivileged groups in our society are to be lifted without concomitant reductions in those of the middle class, some economic *growth is essential.* . . . Growth need not be associated with the kind of negative effects that have engendered the current widespread resistance. It is precisely the task of planning to find ways in which . . . communities can satisfy legitimate societal objectives with minimum negative impact. . . . Many basic problems in housing, education, health, personal safety and transportation are related to levels of income, employment and productivity. Without improvement in these areas, little can be done in other areas. Economic stability and a measure of *growth* are *fundamental to the future of the nation and of its component jurisdictions.*[150] [italics added]

Such a pro-growth bias has continued to appear in the profession's principal journal over the course of the growth management era. Take, for example, the following excerpts from works that appeared in that publication during the 1980s and 1990s:

> [A] . . . vision of growth management is emerging in local plan-
> ning practice . . . and it is free from the enticements, self-decep-
> tions, and pitfalls that are attendant on the population-limitation
> approach. . . . Having no influence on aggregate numbers of peo-
> ple, growth management can have a great deal of influence on the
> demands that people put on systems of life-support. . . . It is the
> articulation of the human presence, not the fact of human pres-
> ence, that requires regulation.[151]

> [With respect to growth management] . . . the hard choices—those
> by which localities must find ways to accommodate reasonable
> growth—will still be essentially political ones.[152]

> Under the new federalism [with its withdrawal of federal aid]
> growth has become indispensable for the economic well-being of
> regions and cities. . . . [The challenge is one of developing pol-
> icy] . . . aimed at solving the urgent problem of how to continue to
> grow in an environmentally responsible manner.[153]

> The last decade of the twentieth century will present the planning
> profession with a variety of challenges. Chief among them will
> be the refinement of workable strategies to deal with growth and
> its various byproducts. . . . [C]ommunities interested in growth
> management are communities seeking to balance the benefits of
> growth . . . [while] . . . mitigating the negative effects that invari-
> ably accompany growth.[154]

> States and localities have enacted growth management laws be-
> cause they are coping with the strains of high growth rates. These
> places are meeting a national need to accommodate the country's
> growth.[155]

As the selected citations reveal, the planning profession has, on the whole, maintained its traditional support for growth during the growth management era in spite of the nature of current problems associated with ongoing growth.

If the profession has made any concession to the problems accompanying growth in the present period, it has appeared to accept the idea of pro-growth advocates that it is possible to achieve a "balance" between "the equally legitimate needs of economic development and environmental protection."[156] That viewpoint, reflected in some of the cited journal excerpts, concedes the existence of problems associated with growth, especially environmental ones, but asserts the possibility of continuing to reap the benefits of ongoing growth if it is properly planned and its negative effects adequately mitigated. As one member of the profession has put it, "The hallmark of growth management is its *balance* among competing objectives."[157] With the focus of growth management efforts increasingly directed at the "concept of balance,"[158] planners have been able to participate in the movement without abandoning their traditional support for growth. They have been able to define their role in the movement in terms of a professional obligation "to address the issue of balancing the needs of the environment with the need to accommodate growth in a responsible way."[159]

By the 1990s this faith in "balanced growth"[160] produced the following characterization of growth management programs: "Central to all growth management programs, regardless of location, is the belief that land development and population increases can be balanced with the conservation of open space and natural, historical, and/or cultural resources."[161] With acceptance of a belief in the possibility of achieving such a balance, it has been possible for planners to maintain their historical pro-growth stance. Members of the profession have continued to ignore the call for even a partial reformulation of the profession's stance toward growth called for in the previously noted works on nongrowth that appeared in the 1970s. As a result, planners have continued to endorse the merit of ongoing growth in even the most populated areas of the country. The 1990's version of the profession's principal methods text on land-use planning continues to advance the oxymoronic idea of sustainable growth.[162] In 1994 a survey of planners' attitudes toward growth in southern California revealed "that planners [there] hold a more positive attitude toward growth than the general population does."[163] It seems that as the 20th century comes to a close, the planning profession remains as committed to a pro-growth orientation as it was during the profession's formative years.

Members of the planning profession are key actors in the development process that brings ongoing growth to communities. They do not control that process, but they are able to influence it by taking part in structuring the policy agenda that addresses growth in America's communities.[164] Planners are able to influence development policy through the key roles they play in creating the comprehensive plans and associated development regulations that spell out the prospects for future growth. To date those professional tools have been used principally to facilitate growth. Even under growth management, those plans and regulations have been directed at a "managing to grow"[165] option, rather than toward real efforts to control or limit future growth. As one observer has noted, "Urban planners have traditionally conceived of themselves as accommodating to growth rather than planning to control it."[166] This orientation has not changed with the profession's involvement in the growth management movement. As the last chapter revealed, most local management programs have played an active role in accommodating ongoing growth, and members of the planning profession have been active participants in developing such programs. Even during the growth management era, "planners have aligned themselves with the forces of growth and development."[167]

CHALLENGES ASSOCIATED WITH A SHIFT
TO A NO-GROWTH PLANNING ORIENTATION

Accepting the premise of this book, that our species has arrived at a point where its survival depends upon a rejection of the growth imperative, would challenge the planning profession in a number of significant ways. Obviously, the most serious challenge would come from having to abandon the profession's historical pro-growth orientation. Supporting no-growth instead of serving to promote growth would not come easily to the profession, because it would require significant changes in the way its members have traditionally thought and behaved. Having endorsed much of the logic employed by society-at-large to support continued adherence to pro-growth perspectives, and having reflected its support for further growth in its plan-making and implementation activities, the profession would have to concede that its past growth orientation and associated behavior was inappropriate under current circumstances. It has been conceded that "most development and planning theory is based on growth,"[168] so the profession would have to develop an entirely new theoretical base to guide the practice of its members. In abandoning the growth imperative, the profession would have to find an alternative to the development facilitation activity that has characterized the profession since its inception. It is a sad reality that most members of the profession appear unable to consider planning as anything other than the practice of facilitating growth.

In addition to the basic challenge presented by the need to accept the current limits to ongoing growth, the planning profession would be confronted by other challenges associated with the shift to planning for a sustainable future. The plan-making and implementation activities that represent the core of professional planning would have to be altered to advance the primary end of ecological sustainability. Plan-making would no longer follow a demand-based method designed to determine the amount of ongoing growth to be accommodated, but would instead employ a supply-based approach intended to discover the capacity of natural systems to indefinitely sustain the demands placed on them. A recognized need to maintain ecosystem integrity by limiting development to levels within the bounds of ecosystem regeneration and self-renewal would force planners to reconsider the traditional idea of end-state plans.

Plans of an ideal end-state for communities would represent an acceptance of limits to physical growth. They would not, however, represent static portrayals of a final future state. While ceasing to grow, such communities would continue to evolve to ever more refined states of sustainability. Overseeing that evolution would represent the new day to day focus of the profession. This transformation would require the prior acceptance of ideal end-state plans depicting limits to growth and a professional willingness to undergo an about-face regarding the profession's characterization of such plans as "cartoon utopias" and "master plan delusions." With comprehensive community plans no longer directed at the accommodation of growth, implementation tools such as zoning regulations could then be directed toward transforming communities into sustainable entities.

Other aspects of conventional planning thought would also have to be abandoned if the profession were to reject the growth imperative. The profession would, for example, have to reconsider the widely asserted view in planning publications that a single public interest is rarely, if ever, identifiable,[169] because a rejection of future growth on grounds that it violates the principle of ecological sustainability identifies such a public interest. If everyone's future is finally acknowledged to be dependent on the maintenance of a state of ecological sustainability, then such a state certainly represents a vital public interest capable of guiding planning for the benefit of all members of the community of life.

Acceptance of the need for a no-growth position would also require planners to reassess their faith in the notion of relativism,[170] which finds expression in planning literature in the view that it is wrong for planners to impose their ideas on others under the declaration that there are no right or wrong decisions or solutions.[171] Regarding questions of growth, the notion of relativism produces opinions among planners along the following lines: "A large and wealthy society like America's is quite capable of accommodating a multiplicity of lifestyles and the simultaneous pursuit of many different interests."[172] Under a recognition that we have already encountered limits to growth, lifestyles based on a continued pursuit of growth would no longer be condoned. With the current scale of the human enterprise already implicated in the destruction of life on a scale characterized as "biological meltdown," and that extinction process linked to associated implications for the ability of ecosystems to provide vital life-support systems essential to all life, members of the profession would have to be willing to declare lifestyles based on growth to be wrong.

Acceptance of a no-growth position in the context of a society still driven by pro-growth influences would additionally necessitate the abandonment of the profession's prevailing skepticism about the influence it is capable of exerting on social events, including its view that growth is uncontrollable.[173] As the 1970s came to a close, a recognized spokesperson for the profession offered an alternative view in the following terms: "It has been possible for years to limit growth in cities by not extending utilities to serve new structures, by zoning, building codes, health regulations, or some other form of restriction."[174] If the planning profession can first come to think in terms of a no-growth future and take the leading role in helping the rest of society to think in no-growth terms, it will likely discover that the major tools of the profession, that is, comprehensive plans and a range of implementation mechanisms, may be as effectively employed to prevent growth as they have been historically used to facilitate growth. To employ tools of the trade for a no-growth end would also require planners to relinquish the profession's historical preference for large urban places. As the first chapter noted, such centers have traditionally been thought of as the best settings for economic growth, but planners have also supported them on the grounds that they have been believed to afford the widest range of choice and opportunity for people.[175] Under an acceptance of the need to give up on the growth imperative due to ecological limits, the profession would additionally have to acknowledge that large metropolitan agglomerations represent the antithesis of a sustainable settlement pattern because they have far outgrown the capacity of bioregions to support them.

As these examples show, the planning profession would encounter a number of challenges associated with a rejection of the growth imperative and a corresponding adoption of a no-growth orientation. Whatever the difficulties, it will become increasingly more evident that the profession must face such challenges, because it is currently assisting society in the pursuit of an unsustainable end. Even the current scale of the human enterprise is now being shown to have exceeded the capacity of the planet's natural life-support systems in ways identified in the opening chapter of this book. Faced with that reality, the profession has yet to realize that it has a societal responsibility to help people recognize that growth must end, and that the focus of society must now shift to a concerted effort to make progress in realizing the needed transition to a sustainable future.

At present, the planning profession continues to support the prevalent growth management view that economic development and environmental protection represent equally legitimate societal needs, and that a balance can be achieved between these needs. While conceding that ongoing growth infers associated environmental problems, the profession has accepted the conventional wisdom that such problems can be successfully mitigated. Even though current environmental realities, such as the fact of "biological meltdown," are demonstrating the fallacious nature of this viewpoint, the planning profession doggedly holds on to such outdated reasoning. Rather than conceding the arrival of limits to growth, the profession appears intent on advancing the growth management idea that planning for "balanced growth" represents "responsible" planning behavior. As each year of ongoing exponential growth presents mounting evidence of an unsustainable assault on the planet's life-support systems, such "responsible" growth facilitation will in actuality be revealed to represent the height of irresponsibility. To assist communities in realizing ongoing growth will increasingly be recognized as destructive activity that further dismantles what remains of the natural world, advances an unsustainable end, and hinders the imperative transition to a sustainable future. A member of the profession has argued that planners have an ethical obligation to state what they think ought to be.[176] The profession has yet to acknowledge that what ought to be includes an outright rejection of the growth imperative. Relinquishing a legacy of pro-growth ideas and behavior will not come easily, but the alternative is one of defending an obsolete ideology and continuing to base professional theory and behavior on the oxymoronic idea of sustainable growth. If the planning profession is to play a meaningful role in reshaping the present into a sustainable future, it will have to begin by letting go of the growth imperative.

4

The Role of the Courts in Shaping Growth Management Efforts

> The legal situation is not an automatic dead end or an insurmountable obstacle for nongrowth.
>
> Earl Finkler[1]

As the previous treatment of the evolution of the growth management movement in this country revealed, the essence of the movement has been its regulatory nature. In response to a changing national perspective toward growth, many local governments began to accept the need for new land-use regulations. The resultant expansion in the regulation of land came to represent the primary expression of growth management activity. Local units of government started to use traditional land-use regulations, such as zoning and subdivision ordinances, in new ways. Some communities went further and experimented with novel police-power regulations to impose a new level of control on growth during the course of the management process. This expanded realm of regulatory activity permitted local governments to manage all of the principal attributes of growth: amount, rate, location, and quality.

The regulatory nature of most growth management activity has produced nearly all of the controversy associated with the management movement since its inception. While the prior portrayal of the growth management movement revealed that the majority of management programs have continued to maintain an accommodative stance toward future growth, they have nevertheless imposed additional police-power regulations on the use of land. Even when communities implemented no change in the overall *amount* of growth they intended to assimilate, their management programs often included regulations affecting the permissible *location* of future development. These efforts to direct development to a particular *location*, such as urban containment zones, typically served to limit the *amount* of development that landowners and developers could place in locations outside designated urban growth boundaries. Attempts to conserve resource lands and protect environmentally-sensitive areas also served to disappoint private development interests, often impeding the *amount* of development permitted at a particular *location*. Management programs seeking to assure *quality* development, by making development permission contingent on the availability of facilities and services, also served to thwart the *amount* of development allowable at a specific *location*. In a minority of growth management programs, local governments have sought to regulate the *rate* of growth below that being imposed by an unencumbered development process. These *rate* controls represent further possible frustrations to private development interests by imposing limits on the *amount* of growth permitted in a specified time period. So while all of these regulatory responses to the management of growth allow continued growth, they uniformly represent increased regulatory interference with the use of private land.

New regulatory activity with respect to land generates inevitable conflict in the American context. In the words of one observer, "A natural tension exists between the government's interest in land-use regulation and the private property owner's interests in land development."[2] As described by another author, "The rights of the community under the police power and the rights of the property owner under constitutional and other safeguards push in opposite directions."[3] These differences in public and private interests in the use of land, and in perceived rights concerning its permissible uses, have produced innumerable land-use regulations designed to mediate a balance between these competing interests and rights. The common thread running through these innumerable land-use regulations has been their placement of limits upon the use of private property.[4] Advocates of private property rights have often contested those limits in the courts, creating a situation where "intense pressure is placed on the judicial system to define the limits of governmental regulation, the boundaries of the police power."[5] With growth management programs typically extending the boundaries of land-use regulation, management efforts have frequently been litigated by individuals seeking to curb new restrictions on the use of private land.

Since growth management programs usually represent an expanded realm of police-power regulations governing the use of private land, and since the courts are often called upon to decide the legality of such new regulations, the courts obviously play a pivotal role in shaping management efforts. In order to illustrate the role of the legal system in setting permissible boundaries to growth management, this chapter first considers private property rights in America and the standards employed by courts in protecting those rights. Following the description of standards used by courts to decide the legality of land-use regulations, the chapter provides general conclusions on the legality of growth management regulations that have been attempted to date. The chapter then addresses the growth orientation evidenced by courts in some of the legal opinions that have decided the fate of contested management programs. Since this book is based on an acceptance of the necessity to reject the growth imperative due to current ecological limits, the chapter concludes with consideration of possible legal obstacles to growth management programs that would be designed to stop growth.

PRIVATE PROPERTY RIGHTS IN THE UNITED STATES

Any consideration of land-use rights in America must acknowledge the British legacy that shaped perceptions toward land in this country, specifically "the inherited English notion of absolute property rights."[6] In reality, public controls on the private use of land have origins extending back virtually to the beginnings of civilization,[7] and the British were not exempt from governmental regulation of the use of private property. In the English context, "[l]and use regulation, even if it forbade 'landowners' any development of their property, did not appear to have offended the medieval sense of justice."[8] So while English citizens engaged in colonization of what would come to be America brought with them a sense of "victory of property rights over the royal prerogative of seizure," they "also inherited . . . a concept of property which permitted extensive regulation of the use of that property for the public benefit."[9]

The fact that land was extensively regulated in the colonies did not inhibit development of "an American fable or myth" that people are entitled to use their land as they wish regardless of the impact on neighbors or the community at large.[10] This myth developed in spite of a long history of so-called nuisance law. In the 12th century, English courts recognized that one individual's exercise of absolute freedom in the use of land might restrict another individual's similar right, and in the process began to develop the doctrine of nuisance. That doctrine made every landowner subject to restrictions so that all would have a reasonable degree of choice in the use of land. For the next seven centuries the English, and later the American, courts worked out rules regarding what might be considered a form of enforced "neighborliness" during the course of deciding cases based on an evolving set of nuisance-law standards.[11] Part of this common law development of the doctrine of nuisance included decisions regarding the control of public nuisances, which represented cases where landowners were imposing noxious effects on the public at large. The evolution of this aspect of nuisance law led to the right of government to protect the public interest by suing private individuals responsible for public nuisances. In 1846 Chief Justice Shaw enunciated such private and public nuisance-law principles in a judicial opinion in the following words:

> All property is acquired and held under the tacit condition that it shall not be used so as to injure the equal rights of others, or to destroy or greatly impair the public rights and interests of the community; under the maxim of the common law, *Sic utere tuo ut alienum non laedas* [one must so use their property as not to injure that of another].[12]

These nuisance-law principles effectively reduced the realm of property rights and in the process clearly established the mythical nature of the notion of absolute property rights.

In the late 1800s local governments began to impose new limitations on the rights of property owners' freedom to use their land in a more direct manner than that represented by civil lawsuits based on nuisance-law violations. Horrific tenement conditions in major cities produced housing and construction laws to control some of the worst features of such buildings. Many of these initial laws prohibited nuisance-like conditions or activities. As extensions of the recognized governmental power to abate nuisances, these controls made all private property subject to regulations under the police-power authority to regulate private behavior, including the use of private land, in order to protect the health, safety, and general welfare of the public. These land-use regulations further circumscribed the rights of land owners to do as they wished with their lands, this time limiting their rights based on the demands of the public interest.

During the 1900s the scope of property rights has been further reduced by new police-power regulations that have gone beyond merely stopping activity deemed to be harmful. Communities have also employed land-use regulations to promote and enhance the general welfare during this century, and this increase in justifiable objectives for the exercise of police-power regulations additionally eroded private property rights.[13] In 1926 the highest court in this country upheld the general constitutionality of comprehensive zoning ordinances based on the police power. As part of that legal opinion the Court conceded that the scope of the police power "varies with circumstances and conditions," and specifically anticipated an expanding realm of police-power regulations: "[W]ith the great increase and concentration of population, problems have developed, and constantly are developing, which require, and will continue to require, additional restrictions in respect of the use and occupation of private lands."[14] This wording acknowledged that the police power was not static, and that newly perceived general welfare objectives would, over time, provide justification for novel regulations to avoid current problems and advance contemporary ends. During the 1970s, for example, new regulations were devised to promote several pressing general welfare objectives: environmental protection, energy conservation, historic preservation, and the retention of community character. By the 1980s a land-use attorney would describe the increased scope of police-power regulations in the following terms: "The police power [regulation of land] has been steadily expanding during this century to meet the growing needs of an increasing populace in occupying and utilizing land."[15]

Emergence of the growth management movement contributed significantly to an expansion of police-power regulations as communities began to employ a new set of land-use regulations to address management objectives. Some local governments designated urban growth boundaries and instituted regulations to contain growth within them. Others implemented concurrency programs and used regulations to limit development to areas with adequate facilities and services. Yet others adopted rate controls to limit the amount of development that could occur in designated time periods. These and other related management regulations expanded the range of land-use regulations beyond those that existed prior to the growth management era. In the process, these new regulations additionally eroded the rights of land owners to do as they wished with their lands, and in doing so further refuted the claim of absolute property rights in this country.

As noted, the police power is not static, and it has in fact expanded in response to changing circumstances and conditions. The permissible bounds of this expanded realm of police-power regulations have been adjusted over time by both legislatures and courts as new problems offered justification for augmenting existing regulations. In the same way that the police power is not static, property rights are also not static. Such rights, which consist of powers held by owners of land, are also subject to adjustment over time by legislatures and courts. Rights associated with private property are, in reality, not absolute, but rather created by the laws of the land. As Walter Lippman put it decades ago,

> Private property is, in fact, the creation of the laws of the land. . . It is a primitive, naive, and false view of private property to urge that it is not subject to the laws which express the national purpose and the national conscience.[16]

While rights associated with private property ownership are not absolute, there are limits to the degree that police-power regulations may circumscribe the rights of owners to use their land. These limits are determined by statutory, constitutional, and case-law standards which delineate the permissible parameters of any new land-use regulations based on the police power. Courts ultimately determine what constitutes "property rights" and permissible extensions of the police power, and they employ the noted statutory, constitutional, and case-law standards to make such determinations. As private property owners are subjected to new levels of land-use regulation, they frequently contest the extensions of the police power in the courts. New regulations associated with growth management efforts have not been exempted from such legal challenges. Standards used by the courts in deciding the legality of land-use regulations utilized to achieve growth management objectives are of interest to the present inquiry, because such standards finally determine whether specific management regulations are likely to survive litigation seeking to invalidate them. The following section examines the nature of the standards that courts have used in deciding the legality of any land-use regulation based on the police power. These standards are reviewed in order to provide a framework for subsequent inquiry into the legality of both current and prospective land-use regulations used in growth management programs.

STANDARDS USED TO DETERMINE THE LEGALITY OF LAND-USE REGULATIONS

As indicated in the prior section, there are no absolute property rights conferring unlimited use options on property owners in this country. Over time an expanding set of nuisance-law principles and police-power rationales increasingly circumscribed the rights of property owners to do as they wished with their land. The most significant constraints on property rights have come from the expanded use of the police power over the course of this century. Local governments have implemented additional land-use regulations based on the police power in response to new problems and evolving goals. Those regulations have been intended both to protect, and enhance, the health, safety, and general welfare of communities. The resulting erosion in the right to use private property produced litigation, and involved the courts in setting limits to the degree of permissible interference with private property rights. Courts have used statutory, constitutional, and case-law standards to decide how far police-power regulations of land may go before they are found to be beyond the law.

Statutory Law Standards Limiting the Regulation of Private Property

Perceived excesses in the use of the police power to regulate private property may be challenged on the basis of claims that a land-use regulation is not in compliance with state statutory requirements.[17] Under conservative reasoning, local governments are said to be creatures of the states, possessing only limited powers that have been specifically granted to them by state legislatures. The traditional rule governing local regulatory authority, known as Dillon's Rule, is that local governments only possess the powers delegated to them by specific state enabling acts and those associated powers that are necessarily implied by such acts.[18] Under a strict interpretation of Dillon's Rule communities could only adopt land-use regulations specifically authorized by enabling acts. Most local governments in America are not, however, constrained by this narrow view of local authority.

When landowners have contested the legality of land-use regulations based on compliance with state statutory requirements, some courts have been willing to interpret enabling acts in a broad, liberal fashion.[19] The landmark court case contesting the legality of rate controls to regulate the timing of development in Ramapo, New York, for example, was litigated on the basis of a claim that such a form of land-use regulation was not authorized by the state's enabling legislation. Although there were no specific provisions for rate controls in the state statute, the court upheld the new form of regulation on the basis of the claim that it was consistent with the overall stated purpose of the enabling legislation, and therefore permissible.[20] The absence of specific provisions for new forms of land-use regulation in enabling acts authorizing such general forms of control as zoning and subdivision regulations may not therefore bar adoption of novel regulations. Although local governments may not violate specific stated requirements spelled out in state enabling acts, such laws may be construed to permit a reasonable degree of experimentation with new regulations if the new controls adhere to the stated intent of the state statutes.

The constraints of Dillon's Rule (which allows communities only such powers as are expressly granted, or as are necessarily implied, in enabling acts) have been further eroded by increased acceptance over time of the concept of "home rule" (which allows local governments to exercise all powers and functions not prohibited by general laws). Some states have clauses in their state constitutions permitting local governments to adopt any regulations necessary for the protection of health, safety, and the general welfare, as long as the regulations do not violate existing state laws.[21] These so-called home-rule provisions in state constitutions give local governments considerable latitude in adopting regulations beyond those specifically authorized by state statutes. Other states have granted home-rule authority to a broad class of local governments by legislative enactments. These enactments similarly move designated local governments beyond the constraints imposed by Dillon's Rule, allowing them to adopt needed regulations as long as they do not violate existing state laws, constitutional provisions, or case-law precedents on a particular legal matter.

As the prior observations reveal, statutory law does not necessarily provide definitive standards for judging the legality of new land-use regulations. The existence of home-rule powers gives many local governments a certain degree of latitude to experiment with regulations not specifically identified in state enabling acts. Even those communities without home-rule powers may be able to safely go beyond specific stated provisions of individual state statutes, if their actions remain consistent with the overall purpose of the statutes. However, some standards for assessing the legality of regulations are afforded by statutory law. As noted, local government may not violate specific requirements, either procedural or substantive, of individual enabling acts. In one particular respect, this fact may present a serious obstacle to efforts to limit or stop growth in those states that have passed statewide growth management acts that actually mandate ongoing growth accommodation by all local governments. The concluding section of this chapter will provide further comment on this point. For purposes of the present review, however, statutory standards need not be viewed as necessarily presenting insurmountable obstacles to the implementation of new land-use regulations, as long as the regulations do not violate the categories of existing general laws (statutory, constitutional, or case laws).

Constitutional Law Standards Limiting the Regulation of Private Property

Many legal challenges to land-use regulations come in the form of allegations that federal and state constitutional limitations on the imposition of land-use controls have been exceeded by the implementation of the regulations. Claimed violations of constitutional limitations arising from land-use regulations are most frequently based on due process, equal protection, and taking arguments. The due process and equal protection clauses of the Fourteenth Amendment, and the taking or just compensation clause of the Fifth Amendment, all provide certain federal protections to private property rights. The Fourteenth Amendment to the U.S. Constitution prohibits any governmental action that deprives "any person of . . . liberty or property, without due process of law," and also provides that no state "shall deny to any person within its jurisdiction the equal protection of the laws." The taking clause of the Fifth Amendment provides additional protection in the form of wording stating "nor shall private property be taken for public use, without just compensation." Initially the Fifth Amendment barred only the federal government from taking private property for public use without just compensation, but a U.S. Supreme Court ruling in 1897 applied the taking limitation to the states and their political subdivisions.[22] State constitutions replicated the wording of the due process, equal protection, and taking clauses of the federal constitution, reinforcing the protections afforded private property rights by such clauses. And over time, the courts have spelled out the nature of those protections, identifying the standards that would be used to judge whether specific land-use regulations violated due process, equal protection, or taking provisions of federal or state constitutions.

Substantive Due Process Standards Governing the Legality of Land-Use Regulations. A U.S. Supreme Court opinion in the 1894 case of *Lawton v. Steele* [23] first set out the standards for judging the legality of land-use regulations under the due process clause. In that case the Court identified components of what would come to be know as the "reasonableness" test in the following terms:

> To justify the State in . . . interposing its authority in behalf of
> the public, it must appear, first that the interests of the public . . .

> require such interference; and second, that the means are reason-
> ably necessary for the accomplishment of the purpose, and not
> unduly oppressive upon individuals.[24]

By 1976 the U.S. Court of Appeals of New York would offer a more elaborate restatement of the reasonableness test used in assessing the legality of land-use regulations under substantive due process challenges:

> A zoning ordinance is unreasonable, under traditional police
> power and due process analysis, if it encroaches on the exercise of
> private property rights without substantial relation to a legitimate
> governmental purpose, . . . if it is arbitrary, that is, if there is no
> reasonable relation between the end sought to be achieved by the
> regulation and the means used to achieve that end, . . . [and] if it
> frustrates the owner in the use of . . . property, that is, if it renders
> the property unsuitable for any reasonable income productive or
> other private use for which it is adapted and thus destroys its eco-
> nomic value, or all but a bare residue of its value.[25]

The three noted prongs of the reasonableness test require that any land-use regulation must advance a legitimate governmental purpose, employ means that are reasonably necessary for the accomplishment of that purpose, and not be unduly oppressive on the individual property owner.[26]

Under the first prong of the test a regulation could be challenged as having an improper purpose or objective. A legitimate purpose or objective would be one that protected, furthered, or promoted the public health, safety, morals, or general welfare. A regulation would be unreasonable under traditional substantive due process analysis if it encroached on the exercise of private property rights without substantial relation to a legitimate governmental purpose. Courts have traditionally applied a "presumption of constitutionality" or "presumption of validity" in reviewing the legitimacy of stated purposes when they consider substantive due process challenges to land-use regulations, meaning that a court will accept the legitimacy of a stated governmental purpose if it is reasonably debatable.[27] During the growth management era local governments have had little difficulty getting courts to accept the legitimacy of such new regulatory purposes as environmental protection, historic preservation, and growth management itself. As new problems and conditions called for new regulations based on legitimate purposes, the courts have sanctioned an expanding application of the police power even though it represented increased interference with private property rights. If future problems call for even more regulation, it appears that this component of the reasonableness test will present little in the way of obstacles to future land-use regulations.

The second prong of the substantive due process reasonableness test assesses whether regulations represent means unrelated to an otherwise proper objective. This component of the analysis addresses the issue of arbitrariness, by requiring that there be a reasonable relationship between the regulation's legitimate objective and the means or regulations selected to accomplish that objective. Out of recognition of the separation of powers principle, and an assumed expertise on the part of legislative bodies in deciding matters of public policy, "the courts are extremely reluctant to strike down legislative determinations of means for accomplishing a given end."[28] The courts only require that a regulation appears to have a reasonable relation to the stated objective, leaving fairly debatable questions as to wisdom and propriety to local legislative bodies. Again, this component of the reasonableness test presents no serious barriers to new land-use regulations intended to further legitimate public purposes.

The third prong of the reasonableness test addresses potential legal challenges claiming that regulations, although employing means related to a proper end, are unreasonable to accomplish that end. In requiring that regulations not be "unduly oppressive," this component of the test has come to be interpreted as a prohibition against controls that are "confiscatory." In the area of land-use controls this has meant that regulations would be deemed unreasonable if they rendered property unsuitable for any use to which it was adapted, and thus destroyed all, or virtually all, of its value. As the wording associated with this element of the test implies, "it would take a substantial amount of injury before the court would invalidate a regulation on this ground,"[29] because it is assumed that some injury accompanies any legitimate regulation, and the courts are reluctant to usurp the legislative role in making determinations regarding the need for particular regulations. Since few land-use regulations attempt to legislate away all use and value, this standard has in fact served to impede few attempts to implement new regulations over time.

Although the confiscation component of the substantive due process challenge may not present serious limits to the regulation of private property, it is significant in that it acknowledges that excessive police-power land-use controls may effectively serve to "take" private property. In such an instance, an owner may argue that the regulation goes so far, and destroys the value of property to such an extent, that it has the same effect as a taking by eminent domain. By the 1990s, both land-use law textbooks and court opinions would be referring to law suits against confiscatory regulations based on a "substantive due process taking claim."[30] From a private property rights perspective, the shortcoming of such a suit stems from the remedy or relief available under such a fourteenth amendment "due process takings claim." Whereas a fifth amendment "just compensation claim" would have monetary compensation available as a remedy, a "due process taking claim" only affords the remedy of invalidation of the application of the regulation. As a land-use attorney has put it, "for a violation of one, compensation is required, while a violation of the other results in invalidation since compensation is unauthorized."[31] It is this difference in the relief possible under the two claims that has produced dissatisfaction with the due process claims avenue for seeking relief from excessive land-use regulations.

Property owners have long been interested in the possibility of being able to litigate onerous regulations under the taking clause, because to be allowed to do so would expand possible legal relief from mere invalidation to compensation for regulations found to effect a taking. In 1987 the U.S. Supreme Court in its *First English* ruling finally resolved the question of whether takings accomplished by regulation were compensable, deciding for the first time that the compensation provision of the takings clause did apply to the regulation of private property.[32] The standards used to make regulatory taking determinations for compensation under the fifth amendment are presented following the identification of standards associated with equal protection challenges to land-use regulations.

Equal Protection Standards Governing the Legality of Land-Use Regulations. Challenges to land-use regulations based on claims of equal protection violations represent an additional basis for questioning the reasonableness of particular land-use ordinances. The equal protection standard requires that any distinctions or classifications made by regulations between groups or individuals must give similar treatment to persons similarly situated with respect to the purpose of the law. A component of the "reasonableness test" in the arena of land-use regulations therefore requires that similarly situated properties be treated similarly. If regulations pass this test they are declared reasonable and satisfy the equal protection clause. However, this general description of the basis for judging regulations under claimed violations of the equal protection clause only conveys part of the legal complexity associated with these claims. The actual standards used in assessing claims of equal protection violations depend on which of two tests a court uses: the rational basis test or the compelling state interest test.[33]

In order to apply either of these equal protection tests, a court must first determine that a legal classification differentiating among citizens exists, and that it is the result of governmental action. If those two conditions are met, then the court must decide which equal protection test to apply based on the affect of the challenged land-use regulation. In those instances when only economic interests in property are affected, the court applies the rational basis test.[34] To survive a challenge under that test, classifications must serve permissible state objectives (i.e., those that serve the public health, safety, and general welfare), be rationally related to such permissible state objectives, and be applied in a nondiscriminatory manner. Most land-use regulations are capable of meeting these requirements, and "application of the rational basis test nearly always means that the classification will be approved by the courts."[35] In those cases where a classification affects a fundamental constitutional right (such as the right to travel and settle) or is based on suspect criteria (such as race) the courts will apply the strict scrutiny judicial review represented by the compelling state interest test. To survive review under this test the regulating body must show that a compelling state interest justifies the classification, and that the classification is necessary to accomplish the compelling state interest. In practice, "[t]he courts almost never find that the governmental interest advanced is compelling."[36] In the growth management context, exclusionary efforts that place burdens on interstate travel could be expected to force litigation under the compelling state interest test. The likelihood of growth-control measures intended to stop growth surviving legal challenges based on the compelling state interest test will be addressed in the concluding section of this chapter. However, since most land-use regulations challenged under claimed violations of the equal protection clause are litigated under the rational basis test, the standards associated with that test present no serious challenges to the implementation of new regulations.

Taking Standards Governing the Legality of Land-Use Regulations. Of all the constitutional standards that have been used to judge the legality of land-use regulations, none have been as controversial as those associated with the "taking" issue. Most of the standards employed to decide if a regulation has "taken" property have come from U.S. Supreme Court opinions issued during the growth management era of the 1970s, 1980s, and 1990s. However, some standards come from the Court's earlier opinions, and those standards may be associated with two schools of thought regarding "regulatory takings." These earlier standards still play a role in deciding the legality of land-use regulations, so they are identified and described as part of a preface to the presentation of more recent standards.

One school of thought regarding regulatory takings maintained that land-use regulations based on the police power should not constitute a compensable taking. Advocates of this viewpoint argued that there is "no evidence that the founding fathers ever conceived that the taking clause could establish any sort of restriction on the power to regulate the use of land,"[37] and that there is "no indication that [they] ever conceived the possibility that a regulation of the use of land could be considered a taking."[38] According to this perspective, "[t]he idea that too extensive regulation of the use of land could constitute a taking was [in fact] an invention of the early Twentieth Century."[39] A view of the concept of regulatory taking as "a judicial fiction of the early 1900's"[40] produced the commitment to maintaining a separation of the taking and due process clauses in litigation associated with land-use regulations. Proponents of this position argued that the clauses provide protection from different governmental powers: the power of eminent domain and the police power.[41] Under the former power, which derives from the fifth amendment, a government has a *duty* to pay compensation if land is seized for public use, while under the latter, which derives from the sovereign power of the state, it has a *right* to regulate use as long as the regulation is reasonable.[42] Relief from the former, it was argued, comes from the taking clause, while relief from excessive use of the police power comes from the due process clause. Those who made these distinctions denied the possibility of compensation for excessive land-use regulations on the basis of the claim that the due process clause does not authorize compensation.

The argument that land-use regulations based on the police power ought not to constitute a compensable taking was also based on the so-called *Mugler* "nuisance exception" to a compensation claim. In 1887 the U.S. Supreme Court's opinion in *Mugler v. Kansas*[43] contained Justice Harlan's assertion that "prohibiting . . . use . . . of . . . property as will be prejudicial to the . . . public . . . cannot be burdened with the condition that the State must compensate."[44] A simple prohibition of certain uses legislatively judged to be injurious to the public could not, according to the Court, in any sense be deemed a taking requiring compensation. Under this reasoning "if government is merely preventing a private property owner from creating a nuisance, then compensation is not required, regardless of the impact on the property owner."[45] In the words of another legal expert, "The essence of this idea is that one has no right to use property in a harmful or noxious fashion, and therefore no property right is 'taken' when such use is prohibited."[46] A compensation requirement in instances where the public is merely seeking to prevent a use that is prejudicial to the public interest is therefore opposed on the grounds that "it would often make regulation unworkable, if only because of the transaction costs, [and] it would also reward, and hence encourage, antisocial behavior[47] Based on this reasoning, "The [*Mugler*] Court took the stance that a regulation, if reasonably related to a valid public purpose, could never constitute a taking."[48] As noted previously, the Supreme Court's opinion in the 1987 *First English* case would negate that position, ruling that the compensation provision of the taking clause did apply to the regulation of private property. However, as will be shown, in another decision during the 1980s the Court also restated the *Mugler* exception from takings scrutiny for police-power prohibitions of nuisances. Such a *nuisance exception* to a compensation claim therefore continues to represent a current *standard* for judging the legality of land-use regulations under the taking clause. In short, regulations that prohibit *true* nuisances are still exempt from takings scrutiny.

Advocates of a second school of thought concerning regulatory takings were unwilling to accept the distinction that restrictions are placed on the power of eminent domain by the taking clause, while restrictions are placed on the police power by the due process clause. Proponents of private property rights were especially troubled by the associated conclusion that police-power regulations could therefore never constitute a compensable action since the due process clause does not authorize compensation. They were rather inclined to argue "that the improper use of [the] police power is an implied exercise of eminent domain and requires the payment of just compensation."[49] Support for this view appeared to gain some support in the form of a 1922 Supreme Court opinion in the case of *Pennsylvania Coal*.[50] It was in that case that "the regulatory taking doctrine was born."[51] In that opinion Justice Holmes, writing for the Court, stated: "The general rule at least is, that while property may be regulated to a certain extent, if regulation goes too far it will be recognized as a taking."[52] The actual meaning associated with the usage of the word "taking" in that citation produced a heated debate. Some argued that Holmes used the word not in the literal fifth amendment sense, but rather as a metaphor for actions having the same effect as a taking by eminent domain. Under this latter view, overly restrictive regulations are not seen as triggering an award of compensation, but rather as an invalid means of accomplishing what constitutionally can be accomplished only through the exercise of eminent domain.[53] Resolution of whether excessive land-use regulations could be directly litigated under the fifth amendment's taking clause would not be resolved until the 1980s, but in the intervening years property owners found an alternate route for pursuing regulatory taking claims.

In the absence of legal authority to directly challenge excessive land-use regulations as violations of the taking clause, property owners sought relief under an evolving body of law that addressed cases where government actions served to take property without formal condemnation procedures. In these instances "the doctrine of inverse condemnation provide[d] [possible] compensation on suit brought by the private owner."[54] The phrase "inverse condemnation," as the term would suggest, describes an action that is the "inverse" or "reverse" of a condemnation proceeding, in that the taking precedes the affirmative action required of formal eminent domain acquisitions. The doctrine therefore acknowledges that there are other forms of taking than the classic eminent domain action, which formally accomplishes the transfer of title from a private property owner to the government with the accompanying required compensation.

Inverse condemnation actions may be brought against governments for different kinds of "takings." Historically, only physical seizures or invasions were considered compensable under the fifth amendment, but over time the law evolved to permit compensation claims for "nontrespassory" invasions as well.[55] In addition to "physical takings," the doctrine of inverse condemnation expanded to encompass both "title takings"[56] and "economic takings."[57] While title takings involve *legal* interests, economic takings involve interference with *economic* interests by imposing economic loss on property owners.[58] These "[e]conomic takings [claims] comprise the vast majority of regulatory taking cases."[59] Efforts to seek compensation under the doctrine of inverse condemnation for takings that impose economic loss have been less than satisfactory on at least two counts. First, the courts have been less inclined to find a taking when economic harm is imposed by a regulation limiting the use of land than under "physical" or "title" taking claims.[60] Second, even if a regulation is judged to affect a taking there has been no guarantee of compensation under such taking claims, because "the right to compensation in inverse condemnation never has been held to be absolute" and courts have also granted "nominal, equitable, or declaratory relief."[61]

The fact that courts have had difficulty making taking determinations under the doctrine of inverse condemnation for those regulatory actions that impose economic loss may in large part be attributed to the nature of the standards that were available to make such determinations. The courts have employed three major standards to distinguish between permissible regulations for which compensation need not be paid and those representing a taking requiring compensation[62]: one approach has been based on a *harm/benefit* distinction (regulations preventing a harm were said to not be compensable, while regulations imposed to achieve a public benefit were); another standard has focused on the financial loss consequences of regulation (*diminution of value* that amounts to a practical confiscation or that leaves no reasonable use [usually meaning no economically profitable use] represents a taking); and the third standard has employed a *balancing test* (the importance of the public end furthered by the regulation against the degree of intrusion into private property rights, with takings being found when the intrusion is out of proportion to any needed furtherance of a specific public end). None of these standards provided definitive guidelines for making a taking determination—most regulations could be linked to both the prevention of a harm and the furtherance of a public benefit, no set diminution of value had been identified as the point at which regulations became unreasonable, and the balancing test certainly provided little in the way of a standard for deciding whether courts are apt to approve or disallow a certain degree of intrusion into property rights to further a specific public end.

In spite of the shortcomings associated with these standards for making regulatory taking determinations, two of the three standards continue to play a role in deciding the legality of current land-use regulations under takings challenges. The Supreme Court would eventually reject the "harm-based" analysis of regulatory takings under the reasoning that an ever expanding harm-prevention rationale for exemptions from takings scrutiny could in effect negate the prohibition against regulations that go "too far."[63] As will shortly be illustrated, the Court has, on the other hand, retained and expanded upon the balancing test standard initially introduced in the 1922 *Pennsylvania Coal* decision,[64] maintaining the practice of weighing public interests served against the degree of intrusion into private property rights as a method for making taking determinations. The consideration of intrusion into property rights has continued to include an assessment of the costs to individual property owners, maintaining a role for the diminution in value standard in current assessments of taking claims. As noted, while the courts have been willing to declare a taking in physical and title taking claims, they have not evidenced a similar willingness to so rule when regulations have been challenged under the category of economic takings. In reality, claims filed under the doctrine of inverse condemnation and reviewed under the noted standards have not tended to provide satisfaction to property owners in the form of compensation for economic loss. As a result, taking claims based on economic loss have historically presented little in the way of a potential barrier to new land-use regulations prior to the growth management era. Proponents of property rights recognized this and continued to argue for the option of directly litigating excessive regulations under the fifth amendment, in hopes that taking claims and associated compensation awards would fare better under that avenue than under the doctrine of inverse condemnation.

The ability to litigate excessive land-use regulations as violations of the fifth amendment's taking clause would eventually be sanctioned by the U.S. Supreme Court, but the Court did not make a definitive ruling to that effect until the 1980s during the growth management era. Justice Brennan's dissent in the 1981 *San Diego Gas* case,[65] became the majority opinion in the Court's 1987 *First English* ruling.[66] In *First English* the Court finally ruled that the just compensation clause of the fifth amendment requires compensation for a taking of property effected by regulatory action. In that opinion, and in a number of other regulatory taking rulings during the 1970s, 1980s, and 1990s, the Court provided a refined and expanded set of standards for judging regulatory taking claims.

Although the Court did not abandon the balancing test for making regulatory taking determinations during the growth management era, one legal observer has noted that since the 1980s the Court has appeared to evidence a "growing preference for categorical answers over balancing tests."[67] Such *categorical* or *per se takings* represent categories of action that are automatically takings irrespective of whether they achieve important public purposes or have only minimal economic impact on an owner of property. In the 1982 *Loretto* opinion the Court announced a categorical taking rule by holding that "a permanent physical occupation is a government action of such a unique character that it is a taking without regard to other factors that a court might consider."[68] The 1987 *Nollan* opinion from the Supreme Court expanded the categorical taking rule by characterizing an easement exaction which allowed the public on private land as an equivalent "occupation."[69] Justice Scalia's opinion likened the public right to pass and repass, in effect a right to invade at will, to the "permanent physical occupation" that had been labeled a categorical or per se taking in *Loretto*.[70] The Court's 1992 *Lucas* decision announced yet another categorical taking rule.[71] *Lucas* declared such a categorical standard where regulations deny "all economically beneficial or productive use of land."[72] As the Court put it, this created another "categor[y] of regulatory action as compensable without case-specific inquiry into the public interest advanced in support of the restraint."[73] This categorical rule based on so-called "total takings" represents a variation of the categorical rule first stated in the Court's 1980 *Agins* case,[74] where the Court declared a denial of "economically viable use" to be a taking regardless of the government's intent.[75] In a similar vein, the 1987 *First English* ruling, which established the "remedy standard" of compensation for regulations judged to be takings, declared the required remedy for a denial of "all use" to be compensation.[76] Whatever the wording, the Court's opinions clearly declared a denial of "all use," "economically viable use," or "all economically beneficial or productive use" to be illegal.

The significance of such *categorical rules* as limitations to regulatory activity is somewhat tempered by the fact that the Court has identified *exceptions* to such rules. In the *Nollan* case the Court conceded that a permanent physical occupation might be justified and excused from a takings claim if the occupation was legally realized through the imposition of a required condition for the issuance of a land-use permit.[77] Under this line of reasoning, even permanent physical occupations and interference with the right to exclude may not represent takings if development conditions satisfy two legal requirements: the exaction sought by the permit condition must evidence an "essential nexus" to a legitimate state interest,[78] and, as the Court held in the 1994 *Dolan* case, the degree of exactions demanded by the permit condition must bear a "rough proportionality" to any projected impacts stemming from the proposed development.[79] The *Lucas* Court similarly announced an exception to categorical takings associated with regulations that effect "total takings." During the course of the *Lucas* opinion the Court held that regulations that deny projects that would be prohibited under existing state property or nuisance laws would be exempt from taking claims, even if such denial resulted in the depravation of "all economically beneficial or productive use of land."[80] Such exceptions aside, the categorical taking rules do not in fact serve to constrain typical land-use regulations, because such controls have not imposed permanent physical occupations nor deprived owners of "all economically beneficial or productive use."

On the matter of exceptions to takings claims, the Supreme Court's 1987 *Keystone* opinion reaffirmed a categorical exception from takings scrutiny for regulations that prohibit harmful or noxious uses of property, even if such prohibitions severely diminished or destroyed the value of property.[81] Such an absolute excuse, or defense, from taking claims based on nuisance arguments was, however, substantially narrowed by the 1992 *Lucas* opinion. In that case the Court announced that there was only a finite range of nuisances that would be tolerated as exceptions to the compensation mandate embodied in the fifth amendment. According to the Court those exceptions would have to be based on existing state nuisance-law limitations rather than being newly legislated or decreed.[82] In setting this guideline, the Court effectively reduced the possibility of exceptions from takings scrutiny for a broad range of nuisance-like activities, and limited the nuisance exception to nuisances already proscribed by state nuisance law. For purposes of land-use regulation, this means that harm-preventing regulatory activity may not automatically be considered exempt from takings scrutiny.

For regulatory taking claims not decided on the basis of categorical taking rules or exceptions, taking determinations continue to be made on the basis of the formerly noted "balancing test," that is, the practice of weighing public interests served against the degree of intrusion into private property rights. To have a regulation evaluated under this balancing test, it must first pass the so-called "legitimacy review" established by the *Agins* case. That case stated that a regulation applied to a particular property would effect a taking if it did not substantially advance a legitimate state interest,[83] that is, the purpose of the regulation must be a legitimate state interest and the means chosen must substantially advance the intended purpose. If a contested regulation passes this *substantially advancing test* it is then evaluated under the *balancing test*. In the 1978 *Penn Central* case[84] the Court introduced a more elaborate formulation of the balancing test than the one that had come out of the 1922 *Pennsylvania Coal* case, in effect establishing the criteria to be used in assessing whether a regulation has gone "too far." Emphasizing the importance of weighing several factors in the constitutional balance, the Court identified the *relevant factors* as including: *the character of the governmental action*; the *economic impact* of the regulation; and the extent to which the regulation has interfered with *distinct investment-backed expectations.*[85] These factors, when taken together, have been labeled "a multi-factor balancing test" for determining if a particular regulation has gone "too far" and therefore represents a taking.

With respect to the character of the governmental action consideration, the Court has identified certain regulatory actions as likely takings, for example, those that may be characterized as a physical invasion by government, those that confer a benefit on the public, and those that achieve acquisition of land for uniquely public functions. With regard to the "economic impact" consideration, which may be thought of as the diminution in value test, the Court has provided less in the way of usable standards for assessing taking claims. In *Penn Central* the Court said its prior opinions "uniformly reject the proposition that diminution in property value, standing alone, can establish a 'taking'"[86] when regulations are reasonably related to the promotion of the general welfare, "and the 'taking' issue in these contexts is resolved by focusing on the uses the regulations permit."[87] In addition to considering diminution in value, the multi-factor balancing test added an assessment of whether a regulation has unreasonably interfered with distinct investment-backed expectations to the economic impact review. This concept has, however, proven to be a troublesome one for the courts, because they "have not traditionally looked with favor on things identified merely as 'expectations.'"[88] In the absence of specific guidelines on this matter there has appeared to be a continuation of the traditional focus on the extent of diminution in value.[89] A bias in favor of the "mere diminution rule," "has given rise to a common notion that a regulation must restrict *all* reasonable economic use before it can be recognized as a taking."[90] As a result, taking claims decided on the basis of the balancing test have continued to conclude that no taking has occurred.[91] As was the case with the formerly noted taking standards, the standards embodied in the balancing test do not appear to present serious barriers to the implementation of typical land-use regulations.

The *Penn Central* case was also significant in that it adopted what has come to be known as the *whole parcel rule* for making determinations of interference with economic interests, that is, a landowner's entire parcel of property was to be considered as the unit of land against which interference was to be assessed.[92] Courts do not, in other words, divide a single parcel into discrete segments and attempt to determine if rights in a particular segment have been taken. Land-use regulations may, therefore, legally deny *all* use to a portion of a landholding, as long as some reasonable use remains for the entire property. This rule allows regulators to keep development off environmentally-sensitive portions of individual landholdings without risking taking claims, and further reduces the threat that taking standards present to land-use regulations.

Any potential threat that the new taking standards may present to land-use regulations is also decreased by the fact that the new standards established significant *ripeness barriers* to bringing taking claims. In its 1986 *McDonald* ruling the Court stated that it could not determine if a regulation had gone "too far" under the balancing test unless it knew how far a regulation actually went.[93] To make that determination, the Court has emphasized the need for a "final decision" regarding the use of property, and in the process has established associated standards for deciding whether a case is "ripe" for litigation under "as applied" challenges to specific regulations.[94] The 1980 *Agins* case established the basic requirement of having to file an application for a specific use. The 1985 *Williamson*[95] decision added the need to apply for a variance from any initial denial of an application and to obtain a "final" determination of actual permitted uses. *McDonald* extended the ripeness requirements by holding that denial of an application for maximum permitted use would have to be followed up by a proposal for some less intensive use in order to determine what actual use would be allowed. Such ripeness barriers to bringing an "as applied" regulatory taking claim were somewhat reduced by the noted 1992 *Lucas* decision. That opinion established a "futility exception" to the prior enunciated ripeness requirements, with the Court expressing doubts about requiring an application, and rejecting the jurisdictional barrier to its consideration of cases that had not obtained a final decision, in cases where either action could be shown to be futile. Nevertheless, the ripeness standards do serve to block frivolous taking claims, requiring property owners to make a case for an actual taking based on development applications and the previously noted categorical and balancing test standards.

Comment on the standards that have been developed by the U.S. Supreme Court for making taking determinations may be concluded by noting particular types of regulatory impact that the Court formally decided to *exempt* from taking claims. As part of its *Agins* opinion the Court announced that "[m]ere fluctuations in value during the process of governmental decisionmaking, absent extraordinary delay, are 'incidents of ownership' . . . [that] . . . cannot be considered a 'taking' in the constitutional sense."[96] In the *First English* opinion the Court noted that its holding did not pertain to "normal delays in obtaining permits, changes in zoning ordinances, variances and the like."[97]

As was the case with substantive due process and equal protection standards governing the legality of land-use regulations, taking standards present few serious obstacles to the implementation of new regulations that can be reasonably linked to furtherance of the public health, safety, and general welfare. As noted, the categorical or per se taking rules address forms of regulatory activity rarely encountered in the realm of land-use regulations. Very few regulations have ever attempted to impose permanent physical occupation. Correspondingly, few regulations have attempted to deny "all use," "economically viable use," or "all economically beneficial or productive use."[98] Consequently, one would expect few court rulings based on the *Lucas* categorical "total taking" rule to yield taking holdings requiring compensation. For regulations that do not deny all beneficial or reasonable use (that is, less than total diminution in value cases) the courts have had to return to assessing claims on the basis of the *Penn Central* multi-factor balancing test. While "total taking" claims are now clearly compensable under the taking clause, such "partial taking" claims face a rough road because they are litigated under what has been called "the Bermuda Triangle of the Court's balancing approach."[99] Private property owners have, to date, had little success in obtaining taking rulings under that approach.

Case-Law Standards Limiting the Regulation of Private Property

In the same way that state statutes and constitutional provisions place limits on regulation of private property, judicial rulings also establish legal precedents that limit regulatory activity. These case-law rulings by the courts, or what are alternatively referred to as judicial-law decisions, set standards for determining the legality of land-use regulations beyond standards specifically established by statutory and constitutional law. While standards instituted by case-law opinions are typically based on an expanded interpretation of specific statutes or constitutional provisions, they nevertheless establish law beyond that explicitly contained in statutes and constitutions. Under the separation of powers doctrine the courts are not viewed as the appropriate source of such law-making activity, but in the absence of legislative enactments addressing specific problem issues some courts have been willing to fashion new laws.

An example of the manner in which case-law rulings have established new standards for judging the legality of land-use regulations is provided by those court decisions in a limited number of states that have redefined the concept of the general welfare. Under the due process clause land-use regulations must further the health, safety, and general welfare of the community. Traditionally, local governments have only had to consider the general welfare of residents within their own jurisdictions. During the growth management era a few state courts have declared that the general welfare was to be measured on the basis of a regional standard.[100] This declaration of a "regional-welfare standard" for judging the legality of land-use regulations appears to have been principally motivated by a view of housing as a basic and fundamental right, leading to the belief that the provision of adequate housing for people of all income levels across a region is absolutely essential to the promotion of the general welfare. This perspective produced skepticism in these courts of any regulatory actions that involved total exclusion of certain residential uses (for example, apartments and mobile homes) and in some cases a stated requirement that local governments accommodate growth in furtherance of the general welfare.[101] Such a requirement stemming from the idea that the regional welfare would be furthered by ongoing growth would obviously present a serious obstacle to growth management efforts intended to slow or stop growth. However, to date only a handful of state courts have institutionalized ongoing growth through case-law rulings, and the impact nationally remains dependent on the number of states that will eventually adopt a regional-welfare standard based on growth accommodation.

Another example of case-law rulings establishing a new limitation on land-use regulations is provided by those court opinions that have made the exclusion of mobile homes illegal. The 1962 state supreme court ruling in a New Jersey case upheld the total exclusion of mobile homes, but the same court in a subsequent 1983 ruling declared such total bans to be impermissible.[102] In 1978 a state supreme court opinion in the state of Washington similarly made the total exclusion of mobile homes illegal.[103] These rulings illustrate examples of courts establishing law not specifically found in state statutes or constitutional provisions that then serve to limit a particular form of regulatory activity. Since most state courts are reluctant to make law due to the separation of powers doctrine, such imposed limits on local regulation of land are not widespread. They do, however, represent a potential source of limits to new regulations as courts react to increasing regulation of private property to achieve new growth management ends.

Statutory, Constitutional, and Case-Law Standards Limiting the Regulation of Private Property

When viewed together, statutory, constitutional, and case-law standards present no serious challenges to the implementation of an expanding realm of land-use regulations based on the police power. Courts have generally given liberal interpretations to state statutes governing land-use regulation as long as new regulations were consistent with the overall stated purpose of the enabling acts, and the constraints imposed by these enabling acts have been further eroded by increased acceptance of the concept of "home rule." As a result of these factors, local governments have had considerable latitude in adopting new regulations as long as they have not violated existing laws. With respect to constitutional law constraints, the due process clause does represent a prohibition against "confiscatory" regulations, but this seems to present minimal obstacles to new regulations because few have pushed the level of regulation to the point of destroying all, or virtually all, value. With regard to equal protection challenges, few regulations have actually been based on suspect criteria or affected the fundamental right to travel, and they have not therefore been subject to the strict scrutiny represented by the compelling state interest test. They have instead been reviewed under the rational basis test, and this standard of review also seems to present little in the way of obstacles to new land-use regulations. With regard to regulatory taking challenges, regulations rarely attempt to legislate away "all" use and therefore do not represent the "total takings" prohibited by law. They instead effect "partial takings," and the courts have to date allowed the imposition of such economic loss without requiring compensation. As for case-law rulings constraining regulatory activity, the reluctance of the courts to engage in such "law making" activity has minimized the limits to new regulations stemming from this type of law.

If statutory, constitutional, and case-law standards have not yet impeded the adoption of an expanding set of land-use regulations, that does not mean that these standards will permit an unlimited degree of interference with private property rights. As noted, the standards do afford protection for such rights, and the question becomes one of determining how far new regulations may go before the courts invalidate them based on these standards. Since the primary expression of growth management activity has been the local regulation of land, growth management programs have played a part in using traditional regulations in new ways and in introducing new regulations, which have both tested the permissible bounds of regulation. The next section comments on the legality of regulatory techniques commonly associated with growth management programs.

THE LEGALITY OF COMMON GROWTH MANAGEMENT TECHNIQUES

A number of specific regulatory techniques have been associated with many current growth management programs: moratoria and interim development regulations; rate of growth regulations; containment regulations; concurrency regulations; and resource conservation and environmental protection regulations. The courts have ruled on the legality of these regulatory techniques based on the statutory, constitutional, and case-law standards identified above, and subsequent comment illustrates the current legal status of the noted techniques.

Moratoria and Interim Development Regulations

During the course of implementing growth management programs, many communities resort to utilizing moratoria and interim development controls in order to buy time for needed planning and regulatory responses to growth-related problems. Moratoria represent the more extreme form of growth control because they halt development activity. If they can be shown to only stop development for a reasonable and generally specified period of time needed to respond to an immediate emergency, then the courts are not apt to find such measures to be illegal. Because moratoria impose such a severe limitation on the right to use property, they are most likely to be challenged on the basis of a regulatory taking claim. However, as land-use lawyers have recently noted, "Moratorium ordinances are generally upheld as not constituting a taking."[104] Such moratoria are capable of being characterized as the "normal delays" that the *First English* ruling exempted from taking claims.

Short of enacting moratoria, communities may adopt interim development controls that allow some forms of development but postpone those forms that are creating a particular problem. These deferrals of development allow communities to respond by studying solutions and enacting needed regulations, and again only represent temporary suspension of development rights that under the *Agins* and *First English* standards are not compensable takings.[105] As noted by the same lawyers who are cited for the prior claim generally exempting moratoria from the category of compensable takings, "[i]n many cases, this technique has also avoided the taking label."[106] *First English*, which established the compensation remedy for regulatory takings, it should be noted, involved an interim development ordinance that deferred development for five years and on remand was found not to be a taking. It would appear, therefore, that the new regulatory taking standards have not placed obstacles in the way of using either moratoria or interim development controls as part of growth management efforts, if the techniques can be shown to allow reasonable use over a reasonable period of time.

Rate of Growth Regulations

Current growth management programs have also evidenced an interest in attempts to control the rate of growth. While few local governments have had either the interest or the courage to embark on management efforts limiting the amount of future growth, a number have employed rate controls. This approach is based on the belief that many of the ill effects of growth can be overcome if local regulatory bodies merely have the time to address them. In essence, a focus on rate controls assumes that quantity and quality are both attainable if communities have the ability to accommodate growth over a reasonable time frame. Since these rate controls may interfere with individual property owner's desires to use land under market-driven time frames, rate controls have been contested in the courts.

As noted in the treatment of limits placed on land-use regulations by statutory law, the landmark court case contesting the legality of rate controls in

Ramapo, New York was litigated on the basis of a claim that this form of land-use regulation was not authorized by the state's enabling legislation. The opinion in that case upheld the rate controls in spite of the fact that there were no specific provisions for such regulations in the state statute, ruling that rate controls were consistent with the overall stated purpose of the enabling legislation and therefore permissible. The fact that rate controls limited residential subdivision activity for up to 18 years in some parts of Ramapo also lead to litigation of the controls as an unconstitutional taking. In ruling that the rate control ordinance did not constitute a taking, the court in effect permitted a time element to enter the land-use/taking equation, and the legality of rate controls was increasingly accepted by the courts: "Beginning with *Golden v. Planning Board of Ramapo* and continuing through current decisions, both state and federal courts have uniformly upheld growth-timing planning techniques against taking challenges."[107] Litigation of rate controls has produced a standard for judging whether timing regulations represent a taking: "The standard for these cases, and the standard required of a regulation in order to avoid a taking claim, is 'reasonable use over a reasonable period of time' as measured by the comprehensive plan."[108] Reasonable timing controls would therefore not be judged to effect a taking because property would not be permanently deprived of use or value, that is, it would be allowed a use within a reasonable period of time as measured by what the comprehensive plan indicated as acceptable uses for the property. One caveat needs to be added, however, and that pertains to those rate controls based on the adequacy of public facilities:

> When a community seeks to time and phase growth on the basis of adequacy of public facilities, courts will enforce an obligation on the part of the government to build the facilities within a reasonable period of time, i.e., evidence is required that the governing body is making a good faith effort to comply with a comprehensive plan.[109]

As this requirement implies, the courts are more likely to uphold rate controls against taking claims if communities implementing the controls can show that they are "accepting full population and employment growth through timed and sequenced development."[110]

In Petaluma, California rate controls were litigated on the basis of a claimed interference with the fundamental right to travel, and a district court assessing the claim on the basis of the compelling state interest standard agreed, invalidating the ordinance.[111] The finding that no compelling state interest existed to justify interference with the fundamental right to travel was dismissed by a court of appeals on the grounds that the plaintiffs lacked standing to sue on the behalf of potential residents. Following the Petaluma case the courts have been reluctant to apply the compelling state interest test to land-use regulations allegedly violating the right to travel.[112] Since rate controls only slow, and do not permanently impede, the right to travel, courts have not been forced to address the issue of whether growth management may violate the constitutional right to travel. As long as growth management programs continue the practice of accommodating ongoing growth, the courts will not be pressed to decide whether communities can justify interference with the right to travel based on rationales that constitute compelling state interests. Due in large part to the fact that rate controls do allow ongoing growth accommodation, these controls have not been invalidated on the basis of statutory, constitutional, or case-law standards. The courts have instead endorsed the legality of rate controls as a growth management technique.

Containment Regulations

Another common feature of many current growth management programs consists of efforts to contain development within designated boundaries or so-called urban growth areas. These containment programs are based on a number of justifications, including the provision of cost-effective services and facilities, the conservation of resource lands, and the protection of environmentally-sensitive lands in outlying areas. To achieve containment under the pressures of ongoing growth, communities usually increase allowable densities within identified urban growth areas and decrease permissible densities outside those designated growth zones. The need to decrease densities outside designated growth areas by downzoning actions stems from the widespread overzoning and excessive platting of outlying areas prior to the growth management era. Property owners in these outlying locations, who have their properties reclassified to less intensive uses by downzoning actions, might be expected to legally contest the resultant decline in the market value of their properties. The legality of downzoning private property might, therefore, be expected to represent the primary legal issue associated with containment regulations.

Before the growth management era and the concurrent development of regulatory takings law most downzonings were contested on substantive due process grounds. Under those suits landowners had to show that the downzoning actions deprived them of *all* uses to which their properties were reasonably adapted, and were therefore confiscatory. As put by one attorney, "Since most downzoning measures merely diminish the economic value of the subject property rather than destroy it, the landowner's attempt to prove confiscatory action by the community is generally unsuccessful."[113] Short of proving confiscation, landowners could also attempt to have downzonings invalidated on the basis of other components of the due process or "reasonableness" test, for example, claiming that no legitimate public purpose supported the restriction. As noted earlier, these attacks have not generally proven successful because courts have given communities the presumption of validity in evaluating contested regulations under that test. Landowners could also attempt to show that the rezoned intensity was incompatible with that of surrounding properties or the existing land-use pattern, or that under some state law constructs the action did not meet the legal requirements for a rezoning of being supported by a substantial change in conditions or a mistake in the original zoning.[114] The most likely challenges have, however, tended to be based on taking claims.

Beyond the potential avenue of contesting downzonings as violations of the substantive due process standard covering confiscatory land-use regulations, property owners could also bring inverse condemnation actions in hopes of attaining compensation awards. When one legal analyst assessed this option in 1980 he came to the following conclusion:

> In the absence of physical invasion or harm, the landowner is not
> entitled to compensation for mere diminution in market value. In

accord with this principle, the courts have consistently denied compensation in cases in which communities have downzoned property.[115]

A case may be made for the claim that the Supreme Court's regulatory taking rulings during the 1980s and 1990s have not increased the likelihood of obtaining compensation for downzoning actions. As long as downzonings comply with the *Agins* requirement of not denying landowners economically viable use, and the *Lucas* requirement of not depriving them of all economically beneficial or productive use, the downzonings will not represent the "total takings" that require compensation. Downzonings that impose lesser economic impacts would be legally evaluated under the "balancing test," and the traditional focus on diminution in value in that test has not tended to produce compensation awards. Unless the courts undergo a shift in the consideration that they are willing to give to landowner's expectations in so-called "partial taking" claims (effectively placing the focus on "the extent of interference with reasonable investment-backed expectations" component of the *Penn Central* balancing test, rather than on the "diminution in value" component), it would appear that downzonings will continue to be relatively immune to successful taking claims. The current taking standards have not, therefore, served to impede the realization of containment policies pursued through downzoning actions.

Concurrency Regulations

An attempt to have services and facilities available at the time that developments are available for occupancy and use represents another common feature of many of today's growth management programs. Programs directed at having associated facilities and services available coincident with the occupancy and use of development represent so-called concurrency requirements. The potential regulatory issue arises from the typical attempt to have the private sector contribute to the cost of providing facilities and services through regulatory exaction programs. Those programs condition development permission on a range of possible exactions, including dedications, impact fees, and other conditions that are necessary to meet the facility and service needs created by growth. As local governments have attempted to shift a greater proportion of the facility and service requirements associated with growth to new development, a phenomenon that has developed parallel with the growth management movement, the increased exaction demands have come to represent a fertile source of taking claims. Private property owners have reacted to the cost implications of concurrency requirements by claiming that the exactions impose economic losses that represent takings.

Both of the Supreme Court's opinions in the previously noted *Nollan* and *Dolan* decisions involved taking claims stemming from exaction programs that imposed conditions on the issuance of development permits. Those two decisions did not question the general legality of exaction programs. As one legal authority noted following the *Nollan* opinion, "The Supreme Court appears to have given its collective blessing to impact fees, dedications, exactions, and other conditions on land development in *Nollan v. California Coastal Commission*."[116] The subsequent *Dolan* decision did nothing to alter the basic legality of these measures, it merely provided further detail to the standards that would govern the constitutionality of exaction programs. Following the *Dolan* decision, regulating bodies knew that exactions would have to meet two legal requirements: any exactions sought through a conditioned permit system would have to evidence an "essential nexus" to a legitimate state interest, and the degree of exactions demanded by the permit condition would have to bear a "rough proportionality" to any projected impacts stemming from a proposed development. For exactions fulfilling the two requirements, the Court made it clear that legal exaction systems could even survive challenges based on categorical taking rules, if the exaction provided an alternative to outright denial of development permission.

One particular type of exaction activity does, however, seem extremely vulnerable based on the standards set forth by the *Nollan* and *Dolan* cases, the so-called "linkage programs." These programs "link" development approvals to the provision of some identified public need, like affordable housing, basing the issuance of a permit on the requirement that the development contributes to the solution of an identified public problem. Under this rationale, permits to construct office buildings have been conditioned on developers directly providing, or donating funds for, low-income housing, child-care centers, and public transportation facilities. One land-use attorney argues that in some cases "the only 'linkage' between the proposed project and the demanded tribute is that the developer needs a permit and the government wants to fund an otherwise unfunded public program."[117] In those instances where there is clearly no rational relationship between a proposed development and the public program to which it is "linked" (no relationship between the exaction demanded and a development's impact or contribution to an identified public problem), one can expect linkage programs to be declared illegal if contested in the courts. As stated by one land-use lawyer, "After *Nollan*, the bare 'linkage' program is in all likelihood, not only indefensible, but unconstitutional as well."[118] Most exaction programs intended to fulfill concurrency objectives under growth management could, however, be designed to meet the current "nexus" and "proportionality" requirements. Consequently, the regulatory mechanism employed to achieve concurrency appears likely to continue to be sanctioned by the courts.

Resource Conservation and Environmental Protection Regulations

Many current growth management programs also contain resource conservation and environmental protection elements. In many locales governments have become increasingly concerned with the loss of productive resource lands, particularly agricultural and forest, to nonresource-based uses. As a result, land-use regulations have been used to prohibit the conversion of resource lands, and where prior regulatory activity had already allowed such uses as residential subdivisions on these lands, regulatory bodies have had to downzone resource lands to maintain the desired uses. Similarly, many governments have moved to protect environmental resources within their political jurisdictions during the growth management era. These efforts have typically been to protect environmentally-sensitive lands, like aquifer recharge areas, floodplains and wetlands, and wildlife habitats. As with productive resource lands, governments have adopted regulations to prohibit any intensity of use that would damage such sensitive lands, and again, when former regulations had already made inappropriate intensities possible, actions have been taken to downzone properties to levels commensurable with specific environmental protection ends. In both of these cases regulations have been used to suppress allowable intensities of use, giving rise to potential regulatory taking claims.

Since both resource conservation and environmental protection have a well-established history of being considered legitimate police-power purposes, regulations intended to achieve these ends would have little trouble passing the "legitimacy review" component of the taking inquiry. With state laws pertaining to agricultural preservation and environmental protection, it has been easy to argue that the purpose of preservation and protection regulations represents legitimate state interests and that the regulations substantially advance those interests. The taking inquiries have, therefore, centered on the economic impact of conservation and environmental protection regulations, and the courts have tended to permit severe limitations on use without handing down a taking ruling. In a 1983 Idaho case, for example, a court upheld agricultural zoning with an 80-acre minimum lot size, while in a 1981 ruling in Pennsylvania a court upheld similar zoning with minimum lot size requirements of 160 acres in agricultural zones.[119] Similarly, in the often cited 1972 *Just v. Marinette County* opinion[120] the Wisconsin supreme court upheld the principle of allowing considerable use limitations to protect environmentally-sensitive wetlands, declaring that it was permissible to use the police power "to prevent harm to public rights by limiting the use of private property to its natural uses."[121] As the justices in that case put it,

> An owner of land has no absolute and unlimited right to change the essential natural character of . . . land so as to use it for a purpose for which it was unsuited in its natural state and which injures the rights of others.[122]

This ruling would appear to permit extreme limitations on use if the natural character of land did not lend itself to traditional developmental uses. However, the new regulatory taking standards established by the U.S. Supreme Court during the growth management era have set limits on the degree to which regulations may constrain the use of private property in order to achieve public purpose ends such as conservation and environmental protection. Unless certain proscribed uses are barred by background principles of state nuisance and property law, the *Lucas* decision made it clear that regulations could not deprive landowners of all economically beneficial or productive uses of land. To do so would represent a categorical or so-called total taking requiring compensation under the fifth amendment.

Where regulations fall short of effecting a total taking, property owners are faced with the difficulty of attempting to obtain so-called "partial taking" rulings. As noted previously, unless courts shift their traditional emphasis from tolerating significant diminutions in value for the furtherance of legitimate public purposes to a new focus on the significance of landowners' expectations in less than total taking claims, these claims will continue to have little chance of success. It would appear that the real threat to conservation and environmental protection efforts from the new regulatory taking standards stems not from what the Supreme Court has already established as taking standards, but from what the

Lucas ruling portends in terms of future standards. Legal commentators have made note of the majority opinion's disdain in that ruling for regulations that seriously damage use rights of private property in the name of resource conservation and environmental protection[123] and of the fact that the Court cited two state decisions, "both of which held that the protection of the environment could not, by itself, justify overreaching regulations."[124] Two footnotes in the *Lucas* case indicate that both "partial takings"[125] and the "whole parcel rule"[126] appear likely to be on the Court's future agenda. If the Court rules that partial takings are in fact compensable, and that property may be segmented for purposes of assessing the effects of regulations on portions of a property holding, then the regulatory implications could in fact be severe. Many essential conservation and environmental protection regulations would in all likelihood never be enacted if governments were forced to pay out damages for any diminution in value that may occur as a result of these regulations. Current regulatory taking standards do not impede needed regulations in this manner.

At present, regulating bodies do, however, need to understand the economic impact of conservation and environmental protection regulations, knowing that they may not regulate to the point where land no longer possesses economically beneficial use. With respect to conservation regulations, the new taking standards place new demands on regulating entities to understand the economics of forestry or agricultural operations in order to avoid regulations that make economically viable use impossible. Regulations intended to protect environmentally-sensitive lands would similarly have to leave landowners some economically viable use. But in both instances regulating bodies are able to take advantage of the current "whole parcel rule" used by the courts in making taking determinations, that is, the courts look at an entire parcel of property in assessing the degree of interference. That rule makes it possible to prohibit *all* uses on some portion of a property holding as long as some reasonable use is permitted on the remainder. It is in instances of total prohibitions on the use of a portion of property on conservation or environmental grounds that the effects of the Lucas decision and the new taking standards mentality may be observed.

In spite of the existence of the whole parcel rule and its function in exempting total use prohibitions on portions of land holdings from taking decisions, the new concern that severe limitations may represent takings has produced a reluctance to impose complete use limitations on even a portion of private land holdings. To accomplish the same end of prohibiting all use of a part of an entire parcel, such as a wetland, regulators have evidenced a striking interest in so-called transferable development rights. This technique allows the allocation of development rights to those portions of land denied all use, and the subsequent transfer of those rights to another portion of the property deemed suitable for use. Rather than risking a possible taking claim, this approach grants development permission where taking standards would not require such permission, and then makes possible more intense uses of remaining portions of a parcel than would otherwise be allowed under existing regulations. In effect, these allocations represent a compensation payment where none was actually required under current regulatory taking standards. In spite of this tendency, under the current taking standards, regulations furthering resource conservation and environmental protection continue to appear capable of surviving legal challenges even when they impose severe use limitations, as long as they permit economically viable use of a whole parcel of land.

The Legality of Common Growth Management Regulations

As the prior examples illustrate, most police-power regulations that have commonly been employed while attempting to manage growth have survived legal challenges based on statutory, constitutional, or case-law standards. The fact that the surveyed regulatory techniques used to manage growth have survived legal challenges based on such standards is in large part explained by the fact that the overwhelming majority of growth management programs employing these techniques have allowed growth to continue. While the programs have uniformly increased regulatory interference with the use of private land, they have not stopped the utilization of land over time. Although regulations have interfered with individual landowner's desires to use land in specific ways at particular times and locations, the regulations have not attempted to stop growth. Under ongoing growth some use options continue and the more extreme challenges to private property rights are avoided. If communities were to extend management efforts to actual attempts to stop growth, the implications for property rights would obviously be more severe. Since courts play a key role in protecting property rights one might expect them to be critical of regulatory attempts to stop growth, and a reading of legal opinions reflects this predisposition. The following excerpts from cases that have litigated growth management programs exhibit the extent to which courts may reveal a pro-growth bias.

THE PRO-GROWTH ORIENTATION OF THE COURTS

If rejecting the conventional wisdom that further growth represents a social good has been difficult for society at large, it has been no less difficult for members of the legal profession who have been called on to judge the legality of growth management programs reflecting the new stance toward growth. A number of highly publicized cases litigating efforts to control the amount and/or rate of growth during the early years of the growth management movement clearly reflect reluctance on the part of the judiciary to sanction efforts to impede continuing growth.

In 1966 the Pennsylvania supreme court invalidated a community's effort to limit the amount of growth it would have to absorb through large-lot zoning in the *National Land* case,[127] and in the process evidenced its pro-growth bias in the following terms:

> Zoning is a tool in the hands of governmental bodies which enables them to more effectively meet the demands of evolving and growing communities. It must not and can not be used by those officials as an instrument by which they may shirk their responsibilities. *Zoning is a means by which a government body can plan for the future—it may not be used as a means to deny the future. . . . Zoning* provisions *may not be used . . . to avoid* the increasing responsibilities and economic burdens which time and *natural growth* invariably bring. . . . *The question posed is whether the*

> township can stand in the way of the natural forces which send our
> growing population into hitherto undeveloped areas in search of a
> comfortable place to live. We have concluded not.[128] [italics
> added]

In its 1970 *Appeal of Girsh* decision[129] the same court rescinded an ordinance
barring apartment houses in a community seeking to avoid the impacts associated with significant population increases, noting:

> Nether Province Township may not permissibly choose to only
> take as many people as can live in single-family housing, in effect
> freezing the population at near present levels. Obviously if every
> municipality took that view population spread would be com-
> pletely frustrated. . . . [A]s long as we allow zoning to be done
> community by community, it is intolerable to allow one munici-
> pality (or many municipalities) to close its [their] doors at the ex-
> pense of surrounding communities and the central city.[130] [italics
> added]

The same court in its 1970 *Kit-Mar Builders* decision[131] again voided a minimum lot-size requirement intended to limit future population growth, repeating
its stance:

> The implications of our decision in *National Land* is that *commu-
> nities must deal with the problems of population growth. They
> may not refuse to confront the future by adopting zoning regula-
> tions that effectively restrict population to near present levels*. It
> is not for any given township to say who may or may not live
> within its confines, while disregarding the interests of the entire
> area.[132] [italics added]

The sentiments expressed in these opinions have been paralleled by courts in
a number of other states. In 1971 a New Jersey court invalidated a zoning ordinance requiring large minimum lot sizes and limiting the number of muti-fam-
ily units in its *Madison* decision,[133] noting that housing needs require the general welfare to be assessed in regional terms, and stating that *"a municipality
must not ignore . . . its fair proportion of the obligation to meet the housing
needs of its own population and that of the region. . . .* The general welfare does
not stop at each municipal boundary."[134] [italics added] In 1975 New Jersey's
supreme court dealt with an ordinance excluding multi-family units in the widely
reported *Mt. Laurel* case,[135] and in the process reaffirmed the *Madison* decision
and clearly evidenced its position on growth in the following terms:

> As *a developing municipality*, Mount Laurel *must, by its land use
> regulations, make realistically possible the opportunity for an
> appropriate variety and choice of housing for all categories of
> people who may desire to live there*, of course including those of
> low and moderate income. It must permit multi-family housing. . .
> [We] feel that *every municipality must bear its fair share of the
> regional burden*.[136] [italics added]

A few years later a New York court declared a zoning ordinance to be unconstitutional for failure to make adequate provision for multi-family housing, and in that *Berenson* decision[137] revealed its stance on growth:

> As a court of law, we cannot provide any lasting solution for the complex problems posed by cases such as this, but *we can and must in appropriate cases require a developing municipality* such as the Town of New Castle *to cease its policy of immunizing itself from the ordinary incidents of growth* and 'confront the challenge of population growth with open doors.'[138] [italics added]

In the previous cases traditional pro-growth views were evoked by local attempts to regulate the *amount* of future growth by such techniques as large-lot zoning and limitations on multi-family zoning. Attempts to limit the *rate* of future growth also produced court opinions reflective of a conventional pro-growth view. In the landmark 1972 *Ramapo* case,[139] a New York court of appeals upheld rate controls in spite of the fact that they potentially withheld development rights for up to 18 years in outlying areas of the community, but in the process revealed the court's bias on growth:

> [The] exercise [of zoning] assumes that development shall not stop at the community's threshold, but only that whatever growth there may be shall proceed along a predetermined course. It is inextricably bound in the dynamics of community life and [the] *function* [of zoning] *is to guide, not to isolate or facilitate efforts at avoiding the ordinary incidents of growth. . . .* What we will not countenance, then, under any guise, is community efforts at immunization or exclusion. But, far from being exclusionary, the *present amendments . . . represent a bona fide effort to maximize population density consistent with orderly growth. . . .* They [community officials] *seek not to freeze population at present levels but to maximize growth by the efficient use of land,* and in so doing testify to this community's continued role in population assimilation.[140] [italics added]

Another early rate control ordinance was initially invalidated by a U.S. district court, in part because the court considered it to represent unconstitutional interference with the fundamental right to travel. As part of its opinion in that 1975 *Petaluma* case,[141] which would be reversed on appeal, the court stated its stance on growth:

> [T]he *issue: may a municipality capable of supporting a natural population expansion limit growth simply because it does not prefer to grow at the rate which would be dictated by prevailing market demand. It is our opinion that it may not.*[142] [italics added]

In 1978 New Hampshire's supreme court upheld a "slow growth" ordinance in its *Beck* decision,[143] but in the process made its position on growth clear in the following words:

> *Zoning is a legislative tool that enables governmental bodies to meet more effectively the demands of evolving and growing com-*

> *mur.ities. . . .* Growth controls must . . . be reasonable and nondiscriminatory. They should be the products of careful study and should be reexamined constantly with a view toward relaxing or ending them. . . . *Towns may not refuse to confront the future by building a moat around themselves and pulling up the drawbridge.* They must develop plans to insure that municipal services, which normal growth will require, will be provided for in an orderly and rational manner. *Any limitations on expansion must not unreasonably restrict normal growth.* . . . At this time under the circumstances of this case we uphold the validity of this zoning measure only as a <u>temporary</u> emergency measure to allow the town two years at most to develop a master or comprehensive plan for phasing in growth and providing therefor.[144] [italics added]

As these citations reveal, the courts appeared as troubled by early efforts to control the rate of growth as by controls directed at limiting the amount of future growth, but they seemed more inclined to permit rate controls. In both instances, however, the excerpts reveal the extent to which the courts were challenged by some of these initial moves to limit the amount or rate of future growth. Legal opinions from those cases indicate a pro-growth posture in their repeated reference to *natural* and *normal* growth, and in their stated or implied belief that ongoing growth furthers the general welfare in spite of its associated problems.

Evidence that pro-growth perspectives continue to affect legal opinions on litigated growth management programs beyond the 1960s and 1970s appears in more recent court rulings deciding the fate of these efforts. In a 1980 ruling New Hampshire's supreme court reaffirmed its decision in the previously noted *Beck* case, but its opinion in the *Convey* case[145] upholding a "slow growth" ordinance again revealed the court's conditioned approval of the measure:

> *Towns may . . . adopt reasonable time controls on population growth.* . . . The *ordinance* in the instant case . . . *provides for normal growth in an orderly and rational manner.* . . . The ordinance is also effective for only one year and will be subject to revision by the town. . . . At this time and under these circumstances, *we uphold* the validity of this zoning ordinance *only as a temporary measure.*[146] [italics added]

Four years later the same court invalidated an ordinance in the 1984 *Stoney-Brook* case[147] that sought to limit the number of annual building permits to 3% of the number of dwellings in the town at the start of the calendar year, and in the process again revealed its growth orientation:

> [T]he *appropriateness of any particular growth restriction is premised on a determination of the normal growth rate.* . . . It is unrealistic to suggest that limiting its growth indefinitely to 3% per year is guiding the town's growth, as expressed by its community plan, in 'a reasonable, responsible and conscientious manner' when, by its own figures, the average growth in the seven abutting towns is almost double that growth rate. . . . *Growth control ordinances are intended to regulate and control the <u>timing</u> of develop-*

ment, see RSA 31:62-a (Supp. 1983), *not the prevention of development.*[148] [italics added]

In 1986 New Hampshire's supreme court ruled against another attempt to enforce a 3% annual growth rate in the *Rancourt* case,[149] once again expressing its pro-growth bias:

> *We have stated in the past that growth controls cannot be permanent or unreasonable.* They must be carefully studied and continually reexamined in order to relax or eliminate them. . . . Put simply, to date we have held that *a growth control ordinance is valid only if it restricts projected growth no more than is necessary to allow for an orderly and good faith development of municipal services.*[150]

Even in California, where the courts have upheld numerous growth management programs, the persistence of pro-growth sentiments continued to influence growth management litigation. In the *Livermore* case,[151] which established a regional welfare standard for judging disputes, the state's supreme court upheld an ordinance that prohibited the issuance of residential building permits until local facilities complied with specified standards. That regional welfare standard required courts to identify the competing interests affected by restrictions (described by the judges as the conflict between the environmental protectionists and the egalitarian humanists) and to determine "whether the ordinance, in light of its probable impact, represents a reasonable accommodation of the competing interests."[152] In the 1981 *Arnel* decision[153] a state court of appeal invalidated an ordinance that restrictively rezoned property that owners sought to develop for apartment use based on a regional welfare assessment. That opinion acknowledged such adverse effects as "added traffic fumes, congestion, and noise" that would result from more intense development, but decided against the ordinance when it balanced those concerns against "the interests of the landowners and developers whose economic interests are adversely affected and of moderate income persons who are being deprived of the opportunity to live within the area affected."[154] During its consideration of competing interests, the court revealed a continued faith in the view that further growth represents a social good, as in its stated belief that continued development would contribute to the availability of affordable housing.[155]

A similar faith in the merits of further growth surfaced in the 1982 *Del Mar* ruling,[156] where a state court of appeal upheld the approval of a new community of some 40,000 by the city of San Diego that had been challenged by the city of Del Mar based on numerous adverse environmental impacts. As the following excerpts from the case reveal, when the court considered the "accommodation of competing interests" in making its ruling based on the regional welfare standard, it was influenced by the pro-growth perspective of the judges who were being called upon to decide the matter:

> This *appeal* by the City of Del Mar *describes the negative, almost frightening, physical, social and financial costs imposed upon society by* the *further urbanization* of the City of San Diego in its creation of the new community called North City West. . . . As we

shall explain, although it is *undisputed the project will have numerous adverse environmental impacts on the region,* we *nevertheless* conclude that San Diego did not abuse its discretion in approving the steps at issue here as *a rational accommodation of the social, economic and environmental interests* with which the city must concern itself. . . . [T]he North City West approvals are inclusionary in nature. San Diego has attempted to provide for its share of regional new housing needs. . . . [A]pprovals by the City of San Diego *promote the general welfare* of the region . . . in that . . . they *provide needed housing* in the region . . . and serve to satisfy housing demand . . . [and] . . . *provide employment opportunities* in the region and generally benefit the economy of the region. . . . San Diego views itself as *merely planning for the inevitable population growth* of the north city region . . . and in view of the demonstrated need for new housing, the North City West *approvals* at this stage *constitute a reasonable accommodation of* these *interests.*[157] [italics added]

In making its ruling, the court not only accepted the inevitability of further growth in the San Diego region, it reaffirmed the traditional pro-growth view that further growth represents a net benefit in spite of serious accompanying negative externalities. While the court acknowledged that the San Diego air basin was a nonattainment area for all pollutants except sulfur and conceded that any population growth would contribute to difficulties in attaining regional ambient air quality standards required by state and federal law,[158] it nevertheless endorsed further growth after enumerating its assumed benefits.

Perhaps the most striking aspect of growth management litigation in the current era has been the tendency of courts to uphold these efforts in spite of their challenges to traditional pro-growth perspectives. In contrast to the noted rulings in New Hampshire and California that struck down attempts to impede growth, many court decisions have upheld growth management ordinances while reaffirming a pro-growth position. While these ordinances continued to represent obvious challenges to pro-growth orientations within the American judiciary, justices with such orientations have been willing to approve management ordinances if they could be shown to represent reasonable efforts to confront problems brought on by growth. Citing language from the *Mt. Laurel* decision, a superior court in New Jersey upheld a rezoning that reduced densities on environmental grounds in the 1984 *Albano* case,[159] while at the same time restating the pro-growth position enunciated in *Mt. Laurel:*

> *Land use regulations should take into account ecological and environmental concerns. Mount Laurel I, supra,* 67 N.J. at 186-187, 366 A.2d 713. *Yet the regulations adopted cannot be used to thwart growth. Id.* at 187, 366 A.2d 713. *They must be only those reasonably necessary for public protection of a vital interest. Ibid.* Here the record supports a finding that the zoning restrictions are not overly burdensome and are necessary to protect Lake George.[160] [italics added]

In its 1980 *Sturges* opinion[161] the supreme judicial court in Massachusetts upheld a "rate of development bylaw" that limited the number of annual building permits. In doing so the court evidenced a pro-growth posture while upholding time controls on development, and also conceded that at least in some circumstances preserving the environment may outweigh undesirable economic and social consequences associated with impeding growth:

> *A Massachusetts city or town has the authority to adopt zoning measures which control orderly growth.* We *hold that a municipality may impose reasonable time limitations on development,* at least where those restrictions are temporary and adopted to provide controlled development while the municipality engages in comprehensive planning studies. . . . Thus, in a rural, as opposed to a suburban, setting, where no showing has been made of regional demand for primary housing, *the public interest in preserving the environment and protecting a way of life may outweigh whatever the undesirable economic and social consequences inhere in partly 'closing the doors'* to affluent outsiders primarily seeking vacation homes.[162] [italics added]

Another rate-control bylaw was upheld in Massachusetts by the 1982 *Giuliano* opinion,[163] in which a U.S. district court allowed the measure in response to water supply contamination problems. In the course of upholding the bylaw the court revealed its reluctance to abandon a positive view of further growth when it credited the town with taking a less restrictive position on growth than it might have taken: "*After careful study, the town chose to adopt* [bylaw] 11.1, *a limitation on* the *timing* of subdivision development, *rather than a more restrictive control such as a growth moratorium.*"[164] [italics added]

As the prior examples illustrate, even courts with a clear pro-growth bias have been willing to uphold growth controls directed both at the amount and rate of growth, controlling the former via reduced density allowances and the latter by timing regulations. Other cases may be cited to illustrate this predisposition. For example, in addition to the noted *Albano* case in New Jersey, which upheld reduced densities on environmental grounds, the 1980 *La Salle* opinion[165] from the appellate court of Illinois upheld density restrictions noting a "governmental body may reasonably restrict increased population density as necessary for its health, safety, and welfare."[166] As was the case with the previously noted opinions upholding rate controls, in the 1985 *Tisei* case[167] the supreme judicial court of Maine upheld a public sewer usage limitations ordinance, citing a ruling it had handed down in its former *Begin* opinion,[168] where the court stated that a "town had authority to adopt a slow growth ordinance provided it was otherwise constitutional."[169] The *Tisei* ruling included the following wording: "*This court has held that municipalities possess the power to regulate their growth and development by enacting 'slow growth' ordinances, Begin v. Town of Sabattus. . . We accord any such grow-controlling ordinance a presumption of constitutionality.*"[170] Any review of litigation addressing growth management programs would quickly confirm that many courts have been willing to uphold growth controls in spite of the challenges they present to traditional pro-growth perspectives. As the previous section on the legality of common growth management regulations revealed, most of these controls are capable of surviving legal challenges. When litigated, the courts have confirmed the general legality of most growth controls attempted to date by upholding the majority of challenged management efforts.[171] This willingness on the part of the courts to sanction growth management programs may in large part be attributed to the fact that the overwhelming majority of these programs have continued to provide for ongoing growth. While some communities have attempted to reduce the amount of future growth with their management programs, the previous treatment of the evolution of the management movement showed that most programs have been limited to attempts to influence the location, rate, or quality of development. If communities decided to go beyond these concerns to more aggressive attempts to impact the amount of future growth, including attempts to actually stop it, one might expect their efforts to evoke even more controversy and litigation than that associated with past programs. The remaining portion of this chapter addresses the matter of whether these more "extreme" management programs might survive legal challenges in light of the pro-growth orientation evidenced by most courts.

LEGAL OBSTACLES TO GROWTH MANAGEMENT PROGRAMS SEEKING TO STOP GROWTH

As the introductory paragraphs to this chapter noted, there are differences in public and private interests and rights in the use of land. An elaborate set of regulations has evolved over time to mediate a balance between these competing interests and rights, and the regulations have uniformly represented increased interference with the use of private land. Many of the regulations placing limits on use have been contested in the courts, which have been called upon to define the permissible limits of governmental regulation. The courts have historically permitted even severe limitations on use and associated diminutions in value when justified by a legitimate public purpose.[172] As one legal observer has noted, the U.S. Supreme Court has "repeatedly upheld regulations that destroyed or adversely affected real property interests, provided that the state's interest in the regulation was . . . strong enough."[173] The ability to utilize regulations for the public good has not however been unlimited, for as this chapter has shown an elaborate set of statutory, constitutional, and case-law standards have evolved over time to limit the permissible degree of public interference with the legal rights of individuals, especially those associated with private property. The courts have been active over time in setting the standards governing such interference, and in spelling out the extent to which private property rights (use rights) and associated interests (economic interests) would be protected when regulations were litigated.

Police-power regulations that limit use obviously affect the value of land, and growth management regulations have typically imposed new levels of restriction on allowable use during the course of attempting to manage the amount, rate, location, and quality of development. Courts in this country have historically defended the right to make use of private property, so they could be expected to be skeptical of the new limitations on use imposed by growth management. It is not difficult to understand why this skepticism would naturally be associated with a pro-growth bias on the part of the courts: ongoing growth would be considered to facilitate increased use options, while growth controls would reduce these options, potentially to an illegal extent. The fact that judges are members of a larger community that has historically endorsed the growth imperative because of its assumed association with a host of benefits would additionally explain why most courts might be expected to hold a pro-growth bias. In spite of that bias, and for whatever reasons such a bias may exist, the courts have evidenced a willingness to uphold most growth management regulations in spite of their impediments to growth. It would be possible, however, to argue that the courts have only tolerated these management regulations because they have continued to provide for ongoing growth in spite of their increased interference with private property rights. The issue of interest in the remaining portion of this chapter is whether the courts would continue to uphold growth management programs if they actually attempted to stop further growth.

Those seeking to argue that governmental attempts to stop growth would be illegal could base their claim on a number of different rationales. For purposes of illustrating that claims of illegality might be contested with opposing legal arguments, four rationales that might be used to assert the unlawful nature of no-growth programs will be critiqued. While it must be conceded that rationales underlying the presumed illegality of management regulations directed at stopping growth do present legal obstacles to management efforts, a case will be made for the fact that they do not represent insurmountable barriers. The rationales that one might expect opponents of no-growth efforts to use in impugning their legality would almost certainly include presumed violations of the categorical "total taking" rule and the fundamental right to travel. In a minority of state contexts, other rationales would in all likelihood include claimed violations of the regional welfare standard and statewide growth management enactments that mandate ongoing growth accommodation.

No-Growth Programs as Claimed Violations of the Categorical "Total Taking" Rule

Advocates of private property rights could be expected to defend the growth imperative because ongoing growth would assure increased use options for land. Conversely, they would likely argue that stopping growth would stop vacant land from being put to use in violation of the prohibition against a denial of "all use," "economically viable use," or "all economically beneficial or productive use" that has been established by the Supreme Court. Such restrictions on use, according to this line of reasoning, would be assumed to represent the categorical "total takings" that the Court declared to be unconstitutional. Communities imposing such use limitations in order to stop growth, it would be argued, would have to compensate all landowners who had not yet exercised their use rights on vacant land. That requirement would, it might be claimed, bankrupt public treasuries as a logical outcome of attempting to implement such an unconstitutional measure.

As a counter argument to the prior noted line of reasoning, no-growth advocates could argue that there are other "economically viable" uses of privately held land than the commercial and industrial uses that generate growth through expanding employment opportunities, or the residential uses that serve to house a growing population base. There are, for example, a host of income-producing agricultural and recreational uses that are capable of representing an "economically beneficial or productive use" of land that could be undertaken without forcing growth on a community. Private property owners desiring more intense uses associated with residential, commercial, or industrial uses may not be happy with these use limitations, but such use restrictions are capable of surviving regulatory taking challenges. Local governments accustomed to increased tax revenues associated with more intense uses may in turn not like the reduced revenue potential of less intense uses, but there is legal precedent in the case of agricultural preservation efforts for reducing property taxes on agricultural lands (that is, taxing them on current use rather than the potential use assessments usually associated with the taxing principle of "highest and best use") in order to increase the prospects for economically viable agricultural operations. While the standards associated with regulatory taking law do not allow a denial of all use, there are, in short, allowable uses that may be permitted without generating further growth.

It must also be remembered that the "whole parcel" rule under regulatory taking law permits regulations to legally deny *all* use to a portion of a landholding in order to protect the public interest, as long as some reasonable use remains for the entire property. If communities have the political will, they may therefore legally deny all use on environmentally-sensitive portions of private landholdings, for example, wetlands, floodplains, geologically-unstable lands, steep slopes, aquifer recharge areas, wildlife habitats, and so forth. Taking these lands out of use consideration would reduce the amount of land for which regulations would have to be devised that would permit reasonable remaining uses while furthering a no-growth end. This objective would require regulating bodies to creatively explore the economic viability of a broad range of agricultural and recreational use options, so as to ensure the "reasonableness" of remaining permitted uses. While these actions would be legally challenging, stopping growth is theoretically possible without violating the categorical "total taking" rule governing regulatory activity. As the treatment of regulatory takings standards noted, most taking claims are resolved by focusing on the remaining uses that regulations permit. That fact would challenge regulatory bodies to provide remaining uses that were both economically viable and no-growth oriented.

No-Growth Programs as Claimed Violations of the Fundamental Right to Travel

Defenders of the growth imperative could also be expected to argue that attempts to stop growth with land-use regulations would be unconstitutional based upon their interference with the fundamental right to travel. They could claim that the courts have decided that the "constitutional right to travel encompasses transient passage from state to state as well as interstate migration and settlement."[174] They could also assert that federal courts have held that the right to travel includes intrastate travel as well,[175] and go on to claim that the right infers a corresponding right to settle in any community. They might additionally argue that this fundamental personal liberty is protected from infringement under the compelling state interest test used in equal protection analyses,[176] and that land-use regulations have little hope of surviving challenges under that test because they would be unable to devise the compelling state interest arguments needed to justify regulatory interference with the right to travel.

Proponents of no-growth could counter by pointing out that the Supreme Court has ruled that the right to travel is not absolute, but rather subject to reasonable limitations.[177] They could also note that during the course of litigation addressing low-income housing and single-family zoning[178] the federal courts have rejected the idea that the intrastate right to travel includes the right to settle in any community. It would also be possible for them to point out that a rigorous requirement regarding "standing to sue" makes such litigation unlikely, because parties such as developers or landowners cannot assert the rights of others in order to obtain relief for themselves. If the standing requirement is overcome, there would still be the obstacle presented by the fact that the courts have been reluctant to apply the rigorous compelling state interest test in cases alleging interference with the right to travel.[179] For example, the California state supreme court in its *Livermore* ruling[180] decreed that land-use ordinances that substantially limit immigration into a community need not be sustained by a compelling state interest test, but are constitutional if they are reasonably related to the welfare of the region affected by the ordinance. Even if the courts were to apply the compelling state interest test, one might assume that some current environmental rationales might suffice as compelling state interest arguments justifying interference with the right to travel and settle, for example, an inability to provide sustainable groundwater supplies for the current population base let alone an expanding one. At present, it appears that the fundamental right to travel and settle need not be considered an insurmountable barrier to growth controls directed at stopping growth.

No-Growth Programs as Claimed Violations of the Regional Welfare Standard

In a limited number of states (Pennsylvania, New Jersey, Michigan, New York, California, and Washington) the courts have established a regional welfare standard for judging the legality of land-use regulations. A few other states, such as Massachusetts, appear to have at least partially adopted the same standard.[181] As noted in the treatment of such a standard earlier in this chapter, in a few of these states (Pennsylvania, New Jersey, Michigan, New York) the regional welfare standard has translated into a stated requirement that local governments must accommodate growth in furtherance of the general welfare. In these cases the courts have viewed housing opportunities for all income groups as essential to promotion of the general welfare and have endorsed the idea of ongoing growth accommodation as furthering the likelihood of increased housing opportunities. Proponents of ongoing growth in these states would likely argue that the regional welfare standard established by case-law rulings prohibits growth management efforts intended to stop growth. Citing language from those cases they could point to the fact that courts adopting the regional welfare standard have said that land-use regulations may not be used to avoid natural or normal growth. Those courts have, it could be argued, imposed a legal requirement to confront growth with "open doors."

Those seeking to stop growth with land-use regulations in states with a regional welfare standard could counter the former claim by citing language from court opinions establishing such a standard that indicates that the growth accommodation requirement associated with the standard may be waived in certain circumstances. Even in New Jersey, which seems to have gone further than any of the other states in requiring affirmative action to accommodate future growth in furtherance of the general welfare, the previously noted *Albano* opinion allowed reasonable interference with ongoing growth based on environmental concerns.[182] That opinion restated the general rule that regulations "cannot be used to thwart growth," but conditioned that rule by permitting regulatory interference with growth when "reasonably necessary for public protection of a vital interest." Similarly, in the noted *Sturges* opinion the supreme court in Massachusetts conceded that at least in some circumstances "the public interest in preserving the environment . . . may outweigh whatever the undesirable economic and social consequences inhere in partly 'closing the door.'" Again, it appears that while the regional welfare standard may seriously impede attempts to stop growth in those states where courts have adopted such a case-law standard, it need not be considered an insuperable roadblock to growth controls directed at stopping growth if the imposed limits are based on compelling and vital public interests.

No-Growth Programs as Claimed Violations of Statewide Growth Management Statutes

As the chapter on the evolution of the growth management movement in the United States revealed, the majority of statewide growth management statutes passed to date actually mandate ongoing growth accommodation by local governments. Advocates of the growth imperative in these states could argue that management efforts directed at stopping growth would be illegal, because under law communities are required to comply with the accommodation directives spelled out in the statewide growth management enactments.

Proponents of stopping growth might respond to the claim that statutory law in the form of statewide growth management laws legally mandates continued growth accommodation by pointing out that legally the issue is complicated by the existence of other state laws. These other state statutes may, in fact, legally require local actions quite different from, and potentially in conflict with, continued growth accommodation. Many state environmental laws, for example, direct local governments to protect the environment. California's Environmental Quality Act, to illustrate the point, declares that "it is the policy of the state to . . . [e]nsure that the long-term protection of the environment, consistent with the provision of a . . . suitable living environment for every Californian, shall be the guiding criterion in public decisions."[183] If ongoing growth accommodation would threaten the ability of a local government to fulfill other state legislated requirements, the courts would have to resolve the conflict between state laws. One might hope that in spite of traditional pro-growth perspectives some courts might be willing to exempt specific local settings from further growth on environmental grounds, even if statewide management laws mandate continued development.

On a more general level, it has also been noted that local governments have a legal obligation to protect the health, safety, and general welfare of their citizens, and no-growth advocates have little trouble arguing that at least in some local settings it has become impossible for communities to fulfill that obligation while at the same time complying with a state mandate to continue accommodating growth. There may, therefore, be a legal out even from a state statutory requirement forcing continued growth on local communities. This, however, raises the awkward prospect of local governments having to take legal action against states that have imposed statewide growth accommodation mandates in order to stop growth. Statewide growth mandates do, therefore, represent very real obstacles to shutting down further growth, but the kind of obstacles that might nevertheless be overcome.

The Legality of Using Land-Use Regulations to Stop Growth

As the former examples show, legal rationales may be used to argue the illegality of stopping growth with land-use regulations at the local governmental level. While the noted rationales, and additional legal arguments, may be used to question the legality of achieving a no-growth state with local police-power regulations, the prior examples illustrate that counter legal arguments may in fact be asserted to support the legality of such an end. There are, unfortunately, few court opinions available to shed light on the matter. Few communities, as the chapter on the evolution of the management movement revealed, have attempted to shut down growth, so the courts have not yet been faced with resolving the matter. Those that have attempted such an end have only sought to stop growth at some future level through the adoption of a cap designating an ultimate limit for growth. Litigation associated with these cases appears to have conditionally endorsed the legality of such programs.

In the highly publicized 1979 *Boca Raton* case[184] a district court of appeal upheld a lower court's invalidation of a cap on the maximum number of dwelling units that would be allowed within the city. The court opinion in that case included the following note:

> The *trial judge held that the City had the power to establish a 'cap' or maximum number of dwelling units allowable within the city boundaries*. However, he opined that, as with any zoning restriction, the 'cap' must bear a rational relationship to a permissible municipal purpose, i.e., it must promote the public health, morals, safety or welfare.[185] [italics added]

While the community did not succeed in convincing the court of such a relationship in that instance, the door was left open for another community to satisfy a court of the rational relationship of a proposed cap to a legitimate public purpose. One of the city's major justifications for the cap was rooted in a so-called "water crop" theory, which sought to limit population by a budget of rainwater falling within city limits, but the court labeled the action an "unnecessarily drastic solution" to a local water resource issue when alternative water resources were available to Boca Raton through regional water-management bodies. That court was not yet prepared to accept the progressive idea that a community ought to limit itself to a level capable of being supported by the sustainable use of local resources, and instead endorsed the traditional pro-growth stance of parasitically relying on external resources in order to maintain ongoing growth. Perhaps a future court will be capable of declaring the former objective a legitimate public purpose and of concluding that regulations designed to achieve it are reasonably necessary for the accomplishment of that legitimate end.

By 1983 the same Florida district court of appeal was willing to uphold a cap in its *Hollywood* decision.[186] Referring to the denial of a cap in its *Boca Raton* ruling the court contrasted that former attempt to the one implemented in Hollywood and explained why it was willing to uphold such a regulatory approach in the instant case:

> We cannot conclude the subject of a unit cap without addressing this court's recent decision in *City of Boca Raton v. Boca Villas Corp.*, 371 So.2d 154 . . . wherein we upheld the trial court's conclusion that a 40,000 unit cap for the entire city '[did] not contribute substantially to the public health, safety, morals, and welfare [and was therefore] arbitrary and unreasonable.' However, the facts in that *Boca Raton* case reveal that the cap was established by public referendum, the City planning department was never even consulted and when examined, the Boca Raton City Planning Director knew of no compelling reason for imposing this fixed limitation. In the case before us now, the City did not adopt any such Alice-in-Wonderland approach. The record is replete with comprehensive plans, studies, reports, public meetings and actual discussions with the developer over a period of years. Unlike the *Boca Raton* case, the City of Hollywood did not present its community purpose in the abstract, but *presented a more than adequate case for the proposition that the proposed cap would contribute substantially to the public health, morals, safety and welfare of its citizens.*[187]

The approval of an absolute cap on future growth in the Hollywood case may be viewed as signaling the arrival of a new landmark in growth management litigation, for in that case the court acknowledged a community's right to set an absolute growth limit if it was justifiable on public welfare grounds. While a number of legal arguments may be employed to contest the legality of setting such limits, a case has been made here that the legal situation, to draw on the words of Earl Finkler in the opening citation to this chapter, need not be considered an insurmountable obstacle to stopping growth. Perhaps the larger challenge will consist of mustering the social and political courage to undertake such a radical course of action. If local governments are able to summon sufficient courage for this radical new step in the management of growth, it will undoubtedly come from an increasing awareness of and concern for ecological sustainability. The concluding chapter addresses ecological sustainability as the new central focus for future growth management efforts.

5

Ecological Sustainability as the New Growth Management Focus

> It is development that can have the attribute of sustainability, not growth.
>
> Herman E. Daly[1]

The opening chapter of this book makes a case for the existence of current limits to further physical growth of the human enterprise on this planet. Even the present scale of the human enterprise is shown to be exerting unsustainable pressures on the natural world. With respect to the consumption of renewable resources, it is noted that our species is already consuming the capital of the natural resource base rather than living off its renewable income.[2] As for global pollution levels, reference is made to research concluding that the "generation of many kinds of pollutants [has] already surpassed rates that are physically sustainable."[3] On the matter of meeting the food needs of our species, a study is cited claiming that the demands of an additional 90 million people each year for grain and seafood are only being satisfied by reducing consumption among those already here.[4] With regard to the planet's biodiversity, it is shown that even the current level of the human enterprise is producing a loss of other species that is being described as an "ecocatastrophe of biological meltdown"[5] that is "unraveling the fragile, resplendent web of life on this planet."[6] These and other indicators have produced the view that "[t]he human world is beyond its limits"[7] in terms of maintaining a sustainable relationship with the natural world. For those who accept this viewpoint, nothing seems more pressing than the need to abandon the growth imperative that is driving today's worldwide cultural network and in the process dismantling the natural world.

As the first chapter also reveals, a case for the existence of current limits to further growth is ultimately being made in terms of present threats to the planet's life-sustaining ecology. Ecologists have helped popularize the understanding that the earth's ecosystems constitute humanity's life-support apparatus. These ecosystems provide such essential life-support services as maintaining a benign mix of atmospheric gases, regulating the hydrologic cycle, purifying air and water, generating and maintaining fertile soils, disposing of wastes, recycling nutrients, providing pest control and pollination services, supplying forest products and food from the oceans, and creating and maintaining biodiversity.[8] Ecologists state the obvious when they tell us that the human enterprise is supported by these ecosystem services and that civilization cannot persist without them.[9] Human life "is enmeshed in the circuits of the [global] ecosystem"[10] and in the numerous ecosystems that comprise its functioning parts. A sound economy, for example, is utterly dependent on sound ecosystems for its support[11]; "[i]f those ecosystems collapse, the human economy will collapse as well." [12]

As our total dependence on the earth's ecosystems has come to be more widely understood, we are being confronted by accumulating evidence "of the increasingly troubled relationship between us . . . and the natural systems and resources on which we depend."[13] Ecosystems and the services they provide are under assault because the expanding scale of human activities is displacing the natural landscapes that make up ecosystems. They are also "being degraded as myriads of their living components are exterminated."[14] By eliminating other life forms we are simplifying ecosystems and thereby compromising the essential life-support services they provide. Some of those who have studied the "mounting pressures on our life-support systems" have recently concluded that "for the first time, growing human demand is crossing the sustainable threshold of global ecosystems."[15] Others have similarly concluded that "the capacity of Earth's life-support systems to maintain civilization is already being severely compromised."[16] These perspectives have lead some to claim that the "ecology of the planet is already coming undone,"[17] and that our dogged pursuit of the growth imperative has "brought the world to the brink of ecological disaster."[18]

A belief in the existence of a global ecological crisis stemming from a dismantling of natural ecosystems produces an understandable interest in an ecologically sustainable future.[19] For those who attribute the current ecological crisis to the present scale of the human enterprise that has been generated by ongoing growth, the central challenge facing our species is one of making the transition from "growthism" to sustainability.[20] If current indicators increasingly reveal the existence of an unsustainable present, then we are clearly faced with having to implement changes that would make a sustainable future possible. Based on the line of reasoning presented here, there is an obvious and urgent need to base the quest for a sustainable future on the primacy of ecological sustainability. This chapter is intended to reveal the extent to which the idea of ecological sustainability has found its way into the growth management movement. In order to achieve that end, the chapter will first review the range of traditional growth management goals to illustrate the role that environmental considerations have played in the growth management movement to date. Following the review of growth management goals the chapter portrays the nature of both environmental and sustainable development concerns that have found their way into growth management, and concludes with consideration of ecological sustainability as a new and primary growth management focus.

TRADITIONAL GROWTH MANAGEMENT GOALS

In the chapter treating the evolution of the growth management movement in the United States, it was noted that "environmental concerns sparked much of the early development of growth management systems."[21] Passage of the "first wave" of statewide growth management laws during the 1970s reinforced this environmental focus due to the "strong, natural systems orientation"[22] of those initial statutes. During this early period of the growth management movement, local governments in many states, including those without statewide growth management laws, typically included environmental components in their growth management programs. Those components supported a number of environmental ends: preventing further environmental deterioration of air and water quality, minimizing a range of negative environmental impacts, protecting environmentally-sensitive lands, conserving resource lands, and avoiding the loss of open spaces. However, as was noted, a few other principal concerns also provided an impetus for interest in growth management.

Communities experiencing the large-scale change associated with post-war suburbanization saw growth management as a way of protecting community character and an existing way of life. Another motivating force behind the development of the growth management movement was said to have come from a concern over the impacts of growth on community facilities and services. In many locales governments saw growth management as a way of reducing facility and service deficiencies associated with prior growth, and as a means of holding down the costs associated with providing future facilities and services. As these examples illustrate, even during the early years of the growth management movement competing ends served to dilute the initial environmental focus of many management programs. Over time, growth management programs would come to be directed at achieving a number of additional anthropocentric goals, which would further erode the support that had been originally given to environmental ends.

As the growth management movement evolved it came to be associated with an expanding range of objectives and techniques. Many management programs undertook efforts to contain what was increasingly coming to be seen as costly and destructive sprawl. While the focus on controlling sprawl was at times motivated by environmental considerations, such as reducing development threats to environmentally-sensitive lands in outlying areas, it was even more likely to be justified on the grounds of holding down facility and services costs. Many growth management programs would emphasize techniques for the efficient provision of public facilities and services, including various approaches for ensuring that the development community would take part in funding the cost of these public improvements. In some instances local programs directly linked the timely provision of these facilities and services to a community's quality of life. In other local settings management programs included design-control measures to ensure the quality of future development. Other communities emphasized rate controls in order to buy time to respond to facility and service requirements, and to allow time to absorb growth without destroying community character or a way of life. In other jurisdictions management programs began to address the matter of ensuring housing choices, with particular attention being given to affordable housing. These and other objectives and techniques associated with the growth management movement diverted attention from the initial environmental focus of the movement and from other possible environmental goals being suggested by those advocating the interests of the natural world.

The earlier portrayal of the "second wave" of statewide growth management laws enacted during the 1980s and 1990s revealed the extent to which those laws reinforced the management movement's shift from environmental considerations to other concerns.[23] While this second generation of state laws exhibited a universal inclusion of environmental components, they were directed at advancing a far broader agenda. In many instances the state statutes merely reinforced what many local governments were already attempting to do with local growth management laws. Some of the statewide laws addressed the problem of development outstripping the provision of public infrastructure via "concurrency" components intended to ensure that infrastructure would keep pace with development. Other statewide enactments reflected a concern with the negative effects of sprawl via "containment" components designed to achieve compact growth patterns. In some cases the statewide management bills included provisions to advance the cause of affordable housing. In these respects the laws addressed many of the concerns that local governments had sought to address with local management programs prior to the passage of statewide growth management laws. However, the statewide laws also extended to matters not previously addressed by local management programs. Some statewide laws contained "consistency" provisions requiring local programs to be consistent with specified state goals and policies, and in some cases additionally required local land-use regulations to be consistent with previously adopted local plans. Other statewide laws required local governments to plan for such controversial land uses as prisons and waste-disposal sites. Additionally, all the statewide laws contained provisions requiring local jurisdictions to promote ongoing growth, and most of the laws actually mandated continued growth accommodation by all local governments.[24]

This range of compulsory new objectives for growth management invariably reduced the attention local management programs might give to environmental concerns. As local governments were required by state legislative enactments to address an expanding range of concerns in their local growth management programs, pursuit of an increased number of objectives undoubtedly came at the expense of environmental considerations. However, acknowledging a reduced role for environmental concerns in current growth management programs says nothing about the nature of environmental considerations presently addressed by the management movement. It also sheds no light on whether these current environmental considerations address the critical matter of ecological sustainability. Some insight into both of these environmental issues may be gained from an examination of what has passed for environmental planning when environmental concerns have been subsumed under the rubric of growth management.

ENVIRONMENTAL PLANNING CONSIDERATIONS UNDER GROWTH MANAGEMENT

Environmental concerns and a perceived need for environmental planning obviously predate the growth management era in this country, extending back in time to the 19th century. As early as 1864, George Perkins Marsh's book, *Man and Nature: or, Physical Geography as Modified by Human Action*, detailed evidence of the growing impact of human action on the earth, and made a case for a form of environmental land-use planning that would both conserve natural re-sources and restore degraded resources.[25] In 1878, John Wesley Powell's *Report on the Lands of the Arid Region of the United States* translated Marsh's ideas into proposed policy.[26] Powell suggested a public land policy based on *capabilities* of the land, whereby land would be classified according to its *suitability* for different uses and actual uses would reflect capabilities. The conservation and city planning movements have also been credited with contributing to the development of environmental land-use planning during the 1800s.[27] Notable planners and landscape architects such as Frederick Law Olmstead, H.W.S. Cleveland, and Ebenezer Howard put forth designs for parks, cities, and new towns that reflected an increasing emphasis on natural principles of land use. During the last decade of the century, the national concern over conservation produced the schism between those like Gifford Pinchot who defined conservation as the "wise use" or planned development of resources and those like John Muir who opted for the preservationist interpretation of conservation.[28] These examples illustrate that the 1800s generated considerable interest in environmental considerations, and the noted environmental concerns had already produced different views regarding the nature of appropriate environmental planning responses, that is, those programs devised for addressing particular environmental concerns.

The 1900s produced a continuing interest in environmental issues and planning responses to those issues. An ongoing effort by a national conservation movement continued to advance the cause of establishing forest preserves and national parks. The County Life Movement during the early years of this century drew considerable attention to environmental issues such as soil erosion and depletion, landscape preservation, and conservation of forests.[29] A 1917 book by Thomas Adams, titled *Rural Planning and Development*, again raised the issue of classifying lands according to their *suitability* for various uses.[30] Two early texts on rural planning by Frank A. Waugh, *Rural Improvement* (1914) and *Country Planning* (1924), addressed a variety of environmental issues, including the importance of respecting natural contours during the course of development, landscape preservation, and soil erosion and depletion.[31]

During Franklin D. Roosevelt's administration a number of planning initiatives furthered consideration of environmental land-use planning. The Soil Conservation Service of the U.S. Department of Agriculture (USDA) was, for example, created during the Depression Era, and addressed major environmental problems of the period—erosion, flooding, sedimentation, and aridification—through some 3000 local soil and water conservation districts. Roosevelt's administration also utilized the USDA and its Bureau of Agricultural Economics to establish planning committees in 2,400 counties to deal with such environmental problems as flooding, runoff, and water quality. These local efforts were complemented by the work of Roosevelt's National Resources Planning Board, which focused on national resource issues, but also sponsored state planning boards and regional planning agencies across the nation to address environmental concerns.[32]

Although World War II brought an end to many of the initiatives of Roosevelt's administration, the period produced a remarkable book by Edward H. Graham, titled *Natural Principles of Land Use* (1944).[33] The publication contained a methodological framework for integrating ecological principles into land-use planning that would represent a form of environmental land-use planning in following decades, bringing together the work of soil scientists, hydrologists, geologists, biologists, and botanists to help shape sound land-use decisions. Graham proposed a land-classification system that would "serve as a basis for the most intensive *sustained use* consistent with preservation of the land as a permanent productive resource."[34] [italics added] These and other influences from the 19th and 20th centuries would all play a part in laying the groundwork for the environmental-protection era that emerged during the 1960s in the United States. That era would produce three major environmental planning responses to perceived environmental concerns of the day: planning based on impact assessments, planning based on land-suitability analyses, and planning based on the carrying capacities of natural systems.

Environmental Planning Based on Impact Assessments

In 1969 the U.S. Congress passed the National Environmental Policy Act (NEPA), "which established a new national policy on environmental protection"[35] and ushered in the age of environmental impact statements (EIS). As one author on the subject of environmental planning suggested, "[t]he objective of the environmental planning process is to find ways to do things with the least natural systems damage as possible."[36] The preparation of environmental impact statements appeared to directly serve this desired end. A widespread national practice of requiring impact statements for all development proposals judged to have significant impacts was widely perceived to afford a means for minimizing natural systems damage. Environmental impact statements require a set of standard considerations before the issuance of development permission: a description of pr⁻sent conditions, an identification of alternative means of accomplishing the desired development objective, an enumeration of the probable impacts of each alternative, identification of the preferred alternative, a description of the impacts of the selected alternative, and a list of possible actions to minimize the negative impacts of the selected development alternative.[37] With the objective of protecting the environment by minimizing natural systems damage associated with any specific development proposal, impact statements naturally tend to focus on the latter of the noted considerations. As the authors of a recent book on environmental assessment opined, the EIS process "should not be used, nor was it intended to be used, simply to stop unwanted projects." [38] The process was rather considered to be a way of minimizing negative environmental impacts, so the principal interest in such a process has been on *mitigation* measures, that is, "means taken to minimize damage that would otherwise occur."[39] If "all reasonable mitigation measures" are taken, then the letter and the spirit of the EIS process are assumed to have been fulfilled,[40] even if that means going ahead with a particular development proposal in spite of serious environmental impacts that cannot reasonably be mitigated.

The EIS process may be criticized on a number of counts. Environmental impact assessment is generally used to evaluate a specific development proposal at a specific location. Such a narrow focus on the impacts of a particular land use at a specific site, and on associated actions to mitigate negative consequences, tends to constrain the nature of the environmental inquiry in a number of ways, the most obvious being geographic. In addition, while these impact assessments may conclude that a specific use will have only a negligible effect on the environment, they do not lend themselves to identifying cumulative impacts associated with a series of similar activities. However, from the perspective advanced here, the most serious shortcoming associated with this form of environmental planning is its implied acceptance of ongoing growth. Such an environmental impact and mitigation focus infers an accepted faith in the ability to have quantity with quality if the negative effects of ongoing growth are merely mitigated. In this sense, this form of environmental planning is antithetical to ecological sustainability. If even the current scale of the human enterprise is destroying the ecosystems upon which we depend, then merely minimizing the future damage via mitigation efforts must be recognized to represent an insufficient response. The principal failing of the impact-assessment approach to environmental planning is therefore one of denying that further growth must be rejected.

Environmental Planning Based on Land-Suitability Analyses

The objective of protecting the environment by minimizing natural systems damage may also be pursued by basing environmental planning on land-suitability analyses. These *"suitability analyses* can be used to determine the fitness of a specific place for a variety of land uses based on thorough ecological inventories."[41] As an environmental planning approach, such analyses are based on the "central assumption . . . that a location's natural environmental characteristics render [any specific] site inherently more suitable for some land uses than for others."[42] Specific methodologies employed under this form of environmental planning "are generally used to produce maps depicting the appropriateness of land areas to various land uses."[43] Such appropriateness or *suitability* is assumed to be based on the natural *capabilities* of different sites to absorb different types of uses without serious environmental effects. As an alternative form of environmental planning, this approach has only been popularized during the period of the environmental protection era that began in the late 1960s. However, as the preceding comments on the history of environmental concerns and associated planning responses in this country revealed, a focus on determining suitable uses for land based on the natural capabilities of different sites for different uses reflects a century-old tradition dating back to Marsh and the subsequent contributions of others such as Powell, Adams, and Graham.

While the idea of basing environmental planning on suitability analyses has a considerable history, the approach attained currency with the publication in 1969 of Ian McHarg's *Design With Nature*.[44] In that work McHarg provided a methodology for carrying out suitability analyses based on an "overlay technique." His "ecological method"[45] consists of creating individual maps of specific physiographic factors within a study area (for example, soils, slopes, vegetation, water resources, critical habitats, and so forth) in order to determine "the degree to which these are permissive or prohibitive to certain land uses."[46] Each map reveals the "intrinsic opportunities and constraints to human use"[47] at different locations within a designated study area based on a single physiographic factor. The individual maps in transparent form are then superimposed on one another to identify the collective set of opportunities and constraints associated with all the mapped physiographic factors. Such an exercise based on map overlays is assumed to show "that certain areas are intrinsically suitable for certain uses while others are less so."[48] A belief that each area has an "intrinsic suitability" for certain land uses led McHarg to conclude that development decisions based on suitability determinations would make it possible to keep growing without compromising the "natural processes" that support our civilization and the rest of the planet's life community.[49] The challenge as he saw it was simply one of employing "physiographic determinism" to reveal the optimum pattern of development.[50]

As portrayed here, environmental planning based on suitability analyses evidences a number of advances over that based on traditional impact assessments embodied in the EIS process. Whereas environmental impact assessments tend to focus on particular land uses at specific locations, suitability analyses tend to be undertaken on a communitywide basis and evaluate the fitness of each location in a jurisdiction for various possible uses. Suitability analyses also tend to incorporate more biophysical or ecological information than has traditionally been considered in the EIS process. However, the methodology exhibits the same basic flaw as the impact assessment approach, in that it proposes an out to growth-related problems that is assumed to permit continued growth. McHarg's book clearly exhibits a willingness to accept further growth if it is limited to suitably identified sites on the landscape. The work makes reference to "the abundance of land available for metropolitan growth,"[51] argues that "[d]evelopment is inevitable and must be accommodated,"[52] asserts that "[w]hile growth and development are thus inevitable, if controlled they need not be destructive,"[53] and claims that "the objective . . . is not to oppose inevitable change, but rather . . . [one of] . . . ensuring optimum development." [54] As advanced by McHarg, suitability analyses suggest that ongoing growth can be made acceptable if land is merely put to suitable uses as indicated by an assessment of its natural capabilities. As in the case of impact assessments, the method ignores the possibility that the cumulative effect of doing the "right things" at a number of specific sites may overload some aspect of a local or regional ecosystem, and by presenting an option for ongoing growth it ignores the mounting evidence in support of the view that further growth is not ecologically sustainable. This environmental planning approach therefore also exhibits the shortcoming of denying the fact that further growth must be rejected on ecological grounds.

Environmental Planning Based on the Carrying Capacities of Natural Systems

Environmental planning based on the concept of natural carrying capacities affords an alternative to planning based on impact assessments or suitability analyses. The concept of natural carrying capacities has its origins in the natural sciences, where wildlife biologists and other renewable resource managers concerned themselves with the concepts of population carrying capacity and maximum sustainable yield. In such contexts it has been credited with being "an established scientific method for the management of renewable resources such as agricultural land, forests, watersheds, and wildlife."[55] With a theoretical base for environmental carrying capacity drawn largely from ecology and from the natural sciences, it is not surprising that it developed "a strong emphasis upon the integrity of natural systems."[56] This emphasis is revealed by some of the definitions that have been advanced for the concept of natural carrying capacities. In the area of ecosystem management it has been defined "as the maximum population density for a given species in an environment which could be supported without degradation of that environment."[57] When the concept has been applied outside the area of ecosystem management it has tended to maintain its focus on the integrity of natural systems. One such definition similarly suggests that it "means the ability of the natural . . . systems of an area to support the demands of various uses . . . without resulting in instability, degradation, or irreversible damage."[58] Another source defines the concept in terms of the demands that can be placed on a region "without doing irreparable damage to the natural processes upon which we depend for life."[59] Yet another considers it in terms of "how much punishment a natural system can take without total and permanent collapse."[60] All these definitions convey the idea of a particular threshold level of activity beyond which there will occur physical deterioration of the environment and/or irreversible damage to ecosystems as reflected by both the loss of species and their habitats.[61]

Any review of definitions that have been put forth for the concept of natural carrying capacities would quickly reveal that they almost uniformly imply an acceptance of limits to growth. As one source notes, "[e]nvironmental carrying capacity can be briefly defined as the limit at which human activity will lead to undesirable changes in the environment,"[62] or alternatively "that it refers to inherent limits in [natural] systems beyond which change cannot be absorbed without resulting in instability, degradation, or irreversible harm."[63] Another source defines it "as the measure of a region's ability to accommodate growth and development within limits defined by . . . natural resource capabilities."[64] It has, in fact, been noted that "[t]he concept rests on an assumption that there are certain limits that the environment itself imposes on development."[65] Conceding such limits has not, however, meant that there has been agreement on the nature of these limits. There are those, for example, who have pointed out the existence of different types of environmental carrying capacities, as in the distinction between "maximum" and "optimum" carrying capacities.[66] Under this distinction, "intrinsic constraints" on population density or development stemming from ecological limits are conceded, but it is additionally assumed that before "absolute limits" are reached "overloading" may cause unsafe, unhealthy, or unpleasant conditions. This assumption implies different possible carrying capacities, including a maximum capacity associated with a subsistence level of existence and an optimum capacity associated with a high quality of life and rights to a salubrious environment. Alternatively, it is possible to think of these distinctions in terms of different types of carrying capacities associated with the amount of environmental change considered acceptable.[67] One may, for example, set an environmental carrying capacity at the level of activity that can be accommodated before any significant alterations are experienced in a local environment. This type of capacity would place high value on maintaining the integrity of an existing environmental system, and would therefore imply a restrictive stance toward most forms of development. Another type of carrying capacity would be more accepting of change in natural systems, but would still limit environmental loading to levels that would not degrade certain aspects of the environment below predetermined standards. Setting such loading levels would be an exercise in human value judgment, basing carrying capacities on what people consider to be acceptable standards of environmental quality. A final type of carrying capacity would be based on the ability of the environment to accept development until that development became self-limiting. Under this type of carrying capacity massive changes would be tolerated in the environment, with the limit of acceptable degradation being that point at which a natural system collapses, whether temporarily or irreversibly. While ecological studies could help derive carrying capacities directed at maintaining the integrity of natural systems or at avoiding system collapse under overloading, the broad middle ground of capacities based on setting acceptable standards of environmental deterioration obviously complicates operationalizing a methodology for this form of environmental planning. As these examples illustrate, the idea of limits embodied in the concept of carrying capacities has meant different things to different people.

One response to the complexity associated with attempting to implement a carrying-capacity approach to environmental planning has been to determine the carrying capacity based on a limited range of environmental factors (for example, that based on available water supply) and then to set a limit based on the most restrictive of these factors.[68] However, this approach has not eliminated the controversy surrounding any potential application of this method, because even the proponents of this strategy argue "that carrying capacity is not fixed."[69] Those who take this position contend that "[t]he natural capacity of a resource to absorb growth is not fixed, but can be altered by human intervention."[70] This argument tends to be framed in the following terms:

> Most of the examples of apparently absolute physical environmental limits turn out to be based in part on certain assumptions. If the assumptions can be altered, then the physical limit itself can be pushed back. The critical assumptions have to do with technology, with economics, and with acceptable life styles.[71]

Under this line of reasoning, "there are a number of ways of increasing the natural environment's capacity to support growth."[72] One may either come up with new technological breakthroughs (a new pollution control technology), spend money on ameliorative measures (wetlands mitigation in the form of replacing lost wetlands), or change human behavior (a shift from private to public transportation), which would all "effectively reduce the impact of growth on critical resources . . . and thus expand a region's ability to accommodate growth."[73] As this illustrates, even the carrying-capacity approach to environmental planning, with its implied acceptance of limits, has not been able to make the necessary shift to conceding the existence of current limits to ongoing growth. Even under this approach, it is still possible to suggest an out from immediate ecological or natural resource constraints that may serve to impede further growth.

While the carrying-capacity approach to environmental planning may also evidence ongoing allegiance to the growth imperative, it nevertheless indicates a closer affinity to the concept of ecological sustainability than that exhibited by environmental planning based on impact assessments or suitability analyses. As characterized previously, the mitigation focus of impact assessments implies an ongoing acceptance of growth based on a faith in being able to address the problems associated with continued expansion. In this sense environmental planning based on mitigation efforts was said to represent the antithesis of ecological sustainability under current realities regarding the destruction of the natural world. Environmental planning based on suitability analyses may be thought of as being more attuned to the idea of ecological sustainability than that based on impact assessments. McHarg, for example, in presenting his methodology for determining the "intrinsic suitabilities" of different areas of the landscape for different uses made mention of "the necessity of sustaining nature as [the] source of life,"[74] and even referred to the need "to relate the density of prospective development, not only to the characteristics of land, but also to its carrying capacity."[75] Attempting to link development to the capability of land to absorb different intensities of use obviously reflects a respect for nature that seems to infer an ecologically sustainable outcome. However, as noted, the suitability approach, based on so-called land capability studies, may simply be viewed as a way of determining "the capacity of different areas to absorb development."[76] As such, the approach may be as antithetical to ecological sustainability as the impact assessment approach, but by its nature it may be assumed to afford greater prospects for an ecologically sustainable future than that associated with impact assessments. One would, after all, have to believe that basing land-use decisions on natural capabilities would be more likely to advance ecological sustainability than the manipulative engineering associated with the impact assessments approach. However, of the three approaches to environmental planning reviewed here, the one based on natural carrying capacities clearly evidences the most immediate association with the idea of ecological sustainability. By its very nature, the approach embodies an acknowledgment of limits to growth. Even if attempts to operationalize the approach demonstrate an unwillingness to accept the immediacy of limits, or reflect a belief in the ability to expand natural carrying capacities, it is more difficult to avoid the idea of limits under the natural carrying capacities approach to environmental planning than under impact assessments or suitability analyses. The approach also tends to expand the geographical realm of consideration to that of regions and beyond, which furthers the prospects for achieving ecological sustainability through environmental planning.

As presented here, the three approaches to environmental planning may be thought of as various stages in the evolution of such planning, with each stage representing a step toward the realization of ecological sustainability. Impact assessments contributed a significant advance by providing protection for the environment through mitigation measures intended to reduce the negative environmental effects associated with growth at different locations. The approach still left much to be desired, however, in that it represents an ongoing "imposition" of uses on the landscape. Suitability analyses address that problem by basing land-use decisions on the intrinsic or natural capabilities of different sites to accommodate growth. As is the case with impact assessment, however, the approach also tends to overlook the cumulative loading problem associated with overall growth in any particular planning environs. So while the suitability method of practicing environmental planning may appear to be superior to the impact assessment approach in advancing the goal of ecological sustainability, it may not be assumed to produce such an end. Only the natural carrying-capacities approach, with its implied acceptance of limits to growth, may be considered to afford a viable environmental planning route to the attainment of ecological sustainability.

The Nature of Environmental Planning Considerations in Statewide Growth Management Laws

A case has been made here that the different environmental planning approaches represented by impact assessments, suitability analyses, and carrying-capacity determinations represent different degrees of sensitivity to the critical matter of ecological sustainability. It was argued that prospects for sustainability advance as one moves from impact assessments through suitability analyses to carrying-capacity determinations. If that is the case, one may assess the move toward ecological sustainability in the United States by considering the degree to which environmental planning efforts have employed the three identified planning approaches. More specifically, with the focus of this work on growth management, it is possible to judge the extent to which growth management efforts have moved toward ecological sustainability by examining the degree to which the three environmental planning approaches appear in growth management programs. The findings of such a review are presented here in terms of the degree of emphasis placed on the three environmental planning approaches in the statewide growth management laws that have been passed to date.

As Table 5.1 shows, all of the existing statewide growth management laws contain environmental planning components that embody the mitigation focus of an impact-assessments approach to environmental planning. In some cases, these statewide laws transferred permitting authority to new bodies in order to achieve specific environmental-protection ends. With the 1961 passage of Act 187 in Hawaii, for example, the use of land in designated conservation districts became subject to the authority of a state department of natural resources, which was directed to base permits on such factors as the protection of watersheds and water sources. Vermont's Act 250, passed in 1970, created regional environmental commissions to issue permits for development projects of greater than local impact and required these commissions to protect such specific environmental resources as streams and wildlife habitats during the course of issuing permits. In the majority of cases, however, the statewide laws simply imposed new environmental protection requirements on local governments. Florida's 1985 statewide act, for example, required local land-use regulations to ensure the protection of environmentally-sensitive lands designated in local comprehensive plans. Washington's state law required all local governments to designate and protect such critical areas as wetlands and wildlife habitats. In the end, all the statewide growth management enactments reflect a continued faith in the possibility of protecting the environment under ongoing growth. The laws therefore uniformly assume that development-related problems can typically be mitigated. As such, this mitigation-based environmental planning approach makes no concessions to the idea of current or prospective limits to growth, and as a result contributes nothing to the needed transition to a state of ecological sustainability.

While all of the statewide laws evidence a continued faith in the impact and mitigation approach to environmental planning, 7 of the 10 statutes also contain provisions intended to advance environmental planning based on a suitability analysis approach. Oregon's enactment of Senate Bill 100 in 1973, for example, contained a stated goal for comprehensive physical planning of "ensur[ing] that the development of properties within the state [would be] commensurate with

Table 5.1
Environmental Components of Statewide Growth Management Laws

	Traditional Environmental Protection Elements	Land Suitability Analysis Elements	Carrying Capacity Study Elements	Traditional Growth Accommodation Provisions
Hawaii (1961)	+			x[a]
Vermont (1970 and 1988)	+	+	+	x
Florida (1972 and 1985)	+	+	+	x[a]
Oregon (1973)	+	+	+	x[a]
New Jersey (1985)	+			x[b]
Maine (1988)	+			x[a]
Rhode Island (1988)	+	+		x[a]
Georgia (1989)	+			x
Washington (1990 and 1991)	+	+		x[a]
Maryland (1992)	+	+		x[a]

x   Statewide laws contain provisions intended to promote ongoing growth.
x[a]   Legislative provisions actually mandate growth-accommodation measures on the part of local governments.
x[b]   Acknowledges limits for further growth within specific locations within the state, but maintains traditional accommodative stance for the remainder of the state.

Sources: The table is based on details gleaned from the statewide growth management laws in the 10 identified states that have passed such laws as of 1997.

the character and the physical limitations of the land."[77] Florida's 1985 legislation required coastal management elements of local plans to utilize "ecological planning principles and assumptions . . . in the determination of suitability and extent of permitted development,"[78] and under a mandated aquifer-recharge element of local plans required "soil surveys . . . [to] indicate the suitability of soils for septic tanks."[79] Rhode Island's statewide act of 1988 established a goal of "promot[ing] orderly growth and development that recognizes the natural characteristics of the land . . . [and] its suitability for use"[80] and required local comprehensive planning to "plan for future land use which relates development to land capability."[81] Vermont's 1988 law similarly identified a set of considerations under a required written report for plan amendments that included an assessment of "the suitability" of an area for proposed purposes based on "land capability" determinations.[82] To varying degrees, references to *suitability* determinations based on the natural *capability* of land appear in 7 of the 10 statewide growth management laws passed to date. It may therefore be argued that the majority of these statewide laws reflect at least some willingness to accept limits to growth at specific sites based on natural land characteristics. As a result of this circumscribed acceptance of limits, this form of environmental planning may be assumed to be superior to the impact-assessment approach in furthering the goal of ecological sustainability. However, as Table 5.1 also reveals, such requirements for engaging in environmental planning based on suitability analyses are contained in statewide laws that show no willingness to concede a need for communitywide limits to growth in any local governmental context. The suitability-analyses approach to environmental planning in these statewide enactments therefore only marginally advances the necessary shift to a form of planning that would actually advance the end of ecological sustainability.

Of the three environmental planning approaches treated here, only the natural carrying-capacities approach suggests a prospective route to realizing a state of ecological sustainability. It is the only approach that embodies an acceptance of areawide limits to growth across such broad planning jurisdictions as communities or regions. Any application of the carrying-capacity approach, with its implied acceptance of at least future, if not current, limits to growth, would therefore reveal prospects for moving toward a state of ecological sustainability. Unfortunately, as Table 5.1 indicates, only 3 of the 10 statewide growth management laws contain carrying-capacity provisions. Florida's 1972 legislation provided for a state comprehensive plan consisting of a set of state goals, and the land-use goal made specific reference to the requirement of directing development to areas with the "capacity to accommodate growth in an environmentally acceptable manner."[83] With the passage of Florida's 1985 statewide law requiring local comprehensive plans to be consistent with the state comprehensive plan,[84] one may assume local governments were actually required to deploy carrying capacity studies in order to fulfill the requirements of the noted state goal. Oregon's statewide growth management law introduced a number of carrying-capacity provisions. An air, water, and land resources quality goal imposed the requirement that all waste and process discharges from future development not "exceed the carrying capacity of such resources."[85] A natural resources goal required all local jurisdictions to inventory natural resources, and an accompanying guideline specified that development actions "should not exceed the carrying capacity of such resources."[86] For purposes of the law, carrying capacity was defined as that "level of use which can be accommodated and continued without irreversible impairment of natural resources productivity, the ecosystem and the quality of air, land, and water resources."[87] Vermont's 1988 statewide enactment established a system of regional planning commissions and required those commissions to conduct "capacity studies,"[88] which the act defined as "an inventory of available natural . . . resources, . . . which identifies the capacities and limits of those resources to absorb land development."[89]

Table 5.1 illustrates that while carrying-capacity provisions in three of the ten statewide growth management laws appear to indicate movement toward planning directed at ecological sustainability, the significance of the provisions is negated by the fact that two of the three noted states (Florida and Oregon) also mandate ongoing growth accommodation on the part of all local governments, while the third (Vermont) promotes continued growth.[90] So while the laws in these states appear to concede the existence of limits to growth, they continue to treat those limits as future constraints rather than current realities. It may therefore be argued that initial carrying-capacity provisions that have appeared in statewide growth management laws only represent tentative steps toward environmental planning directed at achieving ecological sustainability. To suggest the appropriateness of carrying-capacity determinations while promoting or mandating ongoing growth only serves to impede the needed transition to a state of ecological sustainability. With the case that was made for the existence of current limits to growth in the opening chapter of this book, and for the associated need to abandon the growth imperative on ecological grounds, carrying-capacity determinations are only relevant to the current era if they are employed to establish the needed degree of reduction in the present scale of the human enterprise in different regions. As long as the carrying-capacity approach to environmental planning is viewed merely as a technique for determining what is assumed to be unused capacity, it will contribute little to realizing the end of ecological sustainability. One may therefore conclude that environmental considerations in statewide growth management laws have done little to date to advance the primary end of ecological sustainability. None of the environmental planning approaches embodied in those laws has actually reflected an acceptance of current limits to growth. As they have appeared in the statewide laws to date, each of the three reviewed approaches in fact suggests ongoing prospects for additional growth, which promotes the oxymoronic idea of ecologically-sustainable growth.

If different approaches to environmental planning in statewide growth management laws have contributed little to introducing the idea of ecological sustainability into the growth management movement, the question remains as to whether the idea has found its way into the movement in other ways. The current era has, for example, demonstrated a keen interest in so-called "sustainable development," and such a focus may be assumed to provide a prospective avenue for consideration of sustainability in ecological terms. In the forthcoming section attention is given to providing a characterization of the idea of sustainable development. That treatment is followed by comment on the degree to which sustainable development considerations have appeared in the growth management movement and concluding remarks on whether those considerations have in any way advanced the idea of ecological sustainability within the movement.

SUSTAINABLE-DEVELOPMENT CONSIDERATIONS UNDER GROWTH MANAGEMENT

The idea of "sustainable development" was popularized during the 1980s by a series of publications,[91] but the work produced by the World Commission on Environment and Development in 1987 under the title *Our Common Future*[92] was arguably the most influential in advancing acceptance of the idea. This so-called Brundtland Report provided an often cited definition of sustainable development as "development that meets the needs of the present without compromising the ability of future generations to meet their own needs."[93] This view of future development attracted a sufficient number of supporters to have one observer in 1991 suggest that sustainable development was "poised to become the development paradigm of the 1990s."[94] There were others, however, who pointed out that the idea of sustainable development only evidenced widespread appeal because it "means different things to different people."[95] These critics noted that the term sustainable development was in danger of becoming a slippery cliché like "appropriate technology" or "environmental quality."[96] Since such terms are rarely defined explicitly, and are capable of being used in highly varied ways, advocates are apt to represent a broad spectrum of ideological positions. It has, for example, been possible for supporters of ongoing economic growth to endorse the idea of sustainable development. The Brundtland Report, to illustrate the point, advocated a policy of sustainable development, but also called for an expansion of the world economy by a factor of 5 to 10 in order to address global poverty. This position is troubling to those who see a basic incongruity between ongoing growth and sustainability. In order to understand why even advocates of the growth imperative are able to endorse the idea of sustainable development one must look both to the origins of the idea and to the different meanings that have been ascribed to the idea.

Origins of the Idea of Sustainability

The origins of the word "sustainability" appear to lie in the concept of "sustained yield" that appeared in Germany during the late 18th and early 19th centuries.[97] Germany at this time was dependent on its forests for wood to support its economy, and those forests were in a state of decline due to increased demands associated with an increasing population and an expanding economy. Fear of impending resource depletion and potential consequences in the form of poverty and social chaos prompted interest in a solution based on *management* of the nation's forests. It was a period of unwavering faith in science, and it was believed that science could ascertain the rate of resource extraction that would secure the long-term productivity of the forests. The line of reasoning during that era has been described in the following terms:

> Science, according to this ideal of sustained yield, could become the basis for a steady prosperity, a tool of economic growth, and could thereby lay the foundation for a lasting social order. Laws and regulations of harvest could be made scientific, and experts in the science of biological growth could become the architects of a more secure nation.[98]

In this regard, the concept of sustained yield may be viewed as a mechanism to ensure prosperity through ongoing economic growth. If forest managers merely assured a sustained yield of trees, which could be achieved through the practice of sustainable forestry, one could assume indefinite prospects for further growth under this perspective.

Americans like Gifford Pinchot imported the sustained-yield theory of environmental management into the United States in the last two decades of the 19th century. Advocates of this theory believed that the state, guided by professional foresters, had to "take an active role in managing the nation's natural resources in order to secure a sustainable future."[99] Embodied in this school of thought was the belief that nature was essentially a utilitarian commodity to be exploited in a managed way for the common good. People like Pinchot

> had absorbed completely the dominant world-view of their era, which taught that the primary goal of social life is economic progress—steadily increasing production over the long term— adding only the corollary that such production must be directed by the state and its experts to avoid destroying the organic social order.[100]

In this regard, the American advocates of a sustained-yield approach to environmental management also assumed, like their German counterparts, that a "wise use" of natural resources would make possible indefinite economic expansion. One may therefore conclude that the origins of the word sustainability in the concept of sustained yield imparted a decidedly pro-growth bias to any inferred meaning associated with early usage of the word. To make a case for a policy of sustainability in the use of a nation's resources did not therefore historically imply a rejection of the growth imperative.

As this consideration of the idea of sustained yield illustrates, the concept of sustainable development is certainly not a new issue, but rather one that has been around for at least two centuries. It may be viewed as a product of the European Enlightenment and, as such, linked to the noted faith of that period in science and an associated belief in an ability to manage nature. It is therefore possible to argue that the Brundtland Report and other sustainable-development documents of that ilk only differ from the earlier calls for a sustained-yield approach to the use of natural resources in the scale of the suggested management effort.[101] While the earliest sustained-yield strategists only proposed management of forest resources, the current advocates of sustainable development are pushing for management of the entire planet. For many of these present-day proponents of sustainable development the proper focus of the management effort is that of the whole global ecosystem, with the ultimate aim being pursuit of "the sustainable path to the summit of universal affluence."[102] To the extent that present calls for sustainable development are still grounded in the traditional reasoning associated with the concept of sustained yield, one may assume such appeals are still apt to reflect a continued faith in the ability to grow economically if resources are merely managed on a sustained-yield basis. This version of sustainability does not, therefore, imply an abandonment of further economic growth. For purposes of this work, the point of interest is whether different meanings ascribed to the idea of sustainability suggest other growth orientations than that associated with the notion of sustained yield.

Different Definitions of Sustainability

Any treatment of the different meanings attributed to the idea of sustainability might logically begin with consideration of the definition of the word *sustainability*. The lexical meaning of the term can be ascertained by reference to any dictionary, where one finds *sustainable* defined as "capable of being upheld; maintainable" and *to sustain* defined as "to keep in existence; to maintain or prolong."[103] Synonyms for *to sustain* are, in turn, listed as "to maintain, continue, prolong, keep intact; to preserve, conserve." The lexical meaning of sustainability appears therefore to provide little room for debate; to paraphrase the dictionary definition it means "the capacity of being maintained, or continued." If one focuses on the synonymous nature of the terms "to sustain" and "to continue," one may argue that when it comes to defining sustainability "the distinguishing characteristic is the ability to be continued."[104] In order for anything to be considered sustainable under this perspective, it would have to exhibit prospective continuity in time. Since continuous physical growth is not possible in a finite planetary system, one might expect definitions of sustainability that precluded ongoing growth, but as forthcoming definitions will illustrate that has not been the case. Many definitions of so-called sustainable behavior have in fact assumed continued prospects for further growth, particularly in economic terms.

With the distinguishing characteristic of sustainability being that of prospective continuity, there has been a natural emphasis on the temporal aspect of the concept. The focus on "continuity through time" is evident in the definition of sustainable development provided by the Brundtland Report, that is, development that meets the needs of the present without compromising the ability of future generations to meet their own needs. This concentration on supporting the current generation of humans while maintaining options for future generations has led some to argue that the "concept of intergenerational equity is the backbone of sustainability."[105] For many this has translated into a concern with leaving an equitable share of natural resources for future generations. This concern naturally returns considerations of sustainability to its origins in the notion of sustained yield and produces numerous examples of the use of "sustainability" as a modifier, as in the previous treatment of sustainable forestry. During the early years of the 20th century fisheries biologists joined foresters in advancing the idea of sustainable yields, and the notion of sustainable fisheries was introduced.[106] Over time sustained yields would come to be advocated as a management goal in the grazing of rangelands, water resource use, and agricultural production.

With the present interest in sustainability, it has become fashionable to speak of sustainable rangeland practices, sustainable water use, and sustainable agriculture. Most of these treatments of sustainable resource use imply a faith in being able to manage such resources for additional production beyond current levels of use. Sustainable yield has been defined as the "management of a resource for maximum continuing production, consistent with the maintenance of a constantly renewable stock."[107] Such a focus on "management" has all too often inferred a belief in the ability to intelligently exploit renewable resources in a manner that would support ongoing growth. As noted previously, the origins of the word sustainability in the concept of sustained yield imparted a decidedly pro-growth bias, and that bias has not been abandoned as the idea has spread to the newer concerns of sustainable rangeland practices, sustainable water use, and sustainable agriculture.

In the realm of sustainable resource use it has been typical to consider the concept of sustainability as "a viable alternative to uncontrolled exploitation" and to advance the idea of "sustainable exploitation."[108] The challenge has come to be seen as one of developing sustainable approaches to resource use that conserve each individual resource base without degrading it, rather than one of giving up on the growth imperative. Sustainable agriculture would, for example, be defined in terms of agricultural practices that maintained the productivity of the cropland resource base without degrading it. Under this perspective it has been possible to define sustainable resource use in terms of enlightened management practices and to advance the argument that a "wise use" of such resources will support further growth of the human enterprise. In spite of the mounting evidence that we have already surpassed the sustainable global limits of forestry, rangeland, water, and cropland resources,[109] definitions of sustainable resource use have done little to further the idea of current limits to growth. These definitions have instead promoted the idea that intelligent management practices afford an out from current and prospective constraints on additional growth.

Additional uses of "sustainability" as a modifier outside of the realm of sustainable resource use may be illustrated by reference to the recent interest in such concepts as "sustainable economies" and "sustainable societies." These usages of sustainability have produced different meanings associated with the term, but the alternative meanings have continued to convey a traditional pro-growth orientation. In the field of economics, the idea of sustainability has not brought about a shift in the discipline's historical pro-growth bias. For most economists "conventional approaches to development have been set in terms of economic growth."[110] The modern neoclassical approach to economic development tends to "view continued growth as an essential element of a sustainable economy."[111] When members of this school of thought consider the notion of sustainability, they are apt to "focus on the point where societies achieve a critical take-off into long-term, continuous growth, investment, and profit in a market economy."[112] The concept of "sustainable growth" is derived from this perspective, and seen to be "economic growth that can be supported by physical and social environments for the foreseeable future."[113]

While "mainstream economists have more or less ignored the relationship between the environment and development,"[114] proponents of the so-called "sustainable-growth mode" concede that economic growth only represents an appropriate development model if it does not come at the expense of natural resource conservation.[115] From this perspective, ongoing economic growth is possible if natural resources are properly managed on a sustained-yield basis. In this sense, this line of reasoning merely represents a correlative formulation of the sustainable resource-use logic employed to justify prospects for further growth. The idea of "sustainable economies" does not, therefore, imply an abandonment of the growth imperative.

The concept of "sustainable societies" has come to represent a number of different things to different people. Alternative formulations of such societies invariably address the temporal aspect of sustainability, arguing that a sustainable society would be "an enduring one,"[116] "one that to all intents and purposes can be sustained indefinitely while giving optimum satisfaction to its members,"[117] and one that would ultimately ensure the existence of the human race on the earth for as long as possible.[118] From the social perspective, continuity is assumed to depend on meeting the needs of human beings. A social definition of sustainability would therefore typically "include the continued satisfaction of basic human needs—food, water, shelter—as well as higher-level social and cultural necessities such as security, freedom, education, employment, and recreation."[119] As a result of the focus on human living standards, "socially defined sustainability might specify the survival and happiness of the maximum number of people"[120] as the central aim of any sustainable society.

In keeping with the earlier noted concern with intergenerational equity, any consideration of a sustainable society would also be likely to advance "the concept that current decisions should not damage prospects for maintaining or improving living standards in the future."[121] With a focus on the quality of life for humans, some formulations of social sustainability emphasize the empowerment of excluded groups and fair access to the benefits of human progress.[122] Formulations that focus on physical accessibility associate sustainability with access to basic public facilities and services, such as health care, schools, and transportation, as well as housing and employment opportunities. Yet other formulations of social sustainability associate sustainable societies with "sustainable institutions," defining sustainability in terms of the ability of institutions or ruling groups to generate enough public support to renew themselves and hold onto power.[123] Under this viewpoint "[s]ustainable societies are then simply those that are able to reproduce their political or social institutions."[124] Whether these formulations focus on living standards, the empowerment of excluded groups, accessibility issues, or sustainable institutions, prospects for attaining any of these ends have all tended to be seen in terms of ongoing economic growth. As was the noted case with the idea of "sustainable economies," the notion of "sustainable societies" has also remained wedded to the idea of the desirability of ongoing growth.

All of the noted definitions of sustainability exhibit a number of similarities. Irrespective of whether one is referring to sustainable resource use, sustainable economies, or sustainable societies, all of the definitions evidence a decidedly utilitarian and anthropocentric bias. In each case the central focus is one of meeting the material needs of the human species, and the fulfillment of those needs is assumed to depend on further growth. All of the noted definitions, therefore, convey a clear pro-growth bias. With this bias all of these alternative sustainability perspectives treat ecological issues as ancillary, instead of in an integrative way.[125] As such, these sustainability formulations contribute nothing to a meaningful consideration of ecological sustainability. Even if these meanings attributed to sustainability were to be included in growth management programs in the United States, and they have not been incorporated into the movement, they would not advance the idea of ecological sustainability. To the extent that growth management efforts have exhibited natural resource concerns, the interest has been one of preventing the conversion of agricultural and forest lands to other uses and not one of advancing the idea of a sustained use of resource lands. As noted, however, even if management programs were to include sustained-yield considerations, the traditional pro-growth bias of the sustained-yield concept would not further serious reflection on the notion of ecological sustainability. As for the ideas of sustainable economies and sustainable societies, neither of these terms has found its way into the growth management movement. In light of the pro-growth orientation of these definitions of sustainability, their omission from the movement may be for the best, for neither could be expected to advance the end of ecological sustainability.

As this treatment of different meanings ascribed to "sustainable development" and "sustainability" reveals, it is possible to endorse these concepts without rejecting the growth imperative or addressing ecological sustainability. It must be conceded, however, that the idea of sustainability has come to represent more than that conveyed by the alternative definitions that have been presented here. The notion of sustainability has increasingly been put forward in terms of operational measures of sustainable development. Some of those measures may be directly linked to the critical issue of ecological sustainability, and they thereby provide a prospective avenue for incorporating ecological-sustainability concerns into the growth management movement. A brief overview of the operational measures of sustainable development suggested to date will illustrate the nature of these measures. The overview will also permit conclusions on whether any of these operational measures of sustainable development appear among the objectives of growth management, and whether any of those measures have in turn specifically advanced the idea of ecological sustainability within the movement.

Operational Measures of Sustainable Development

If different definitions of "sustainable development" and "sustainability" have tended to ignore the need to reject further growth and the necessity of addressing the matter of ecological sustainability, that has not been the case when various sources have suggested operational measures of sustainable development and sustainability. Those who have attempted to formulate such measures have been inclined to argue for an end to population and economic growth as a necessary condition of sustainability.[126] In such considerations of the means necessary to bring a sustainable society to fruition, some have been willing to concede "that widespread provision of even basic survival needs will become increasingly unsustainable if population growth is not controlled."[127] Others addressing the matter of operationalizing sustainability have been willing to go beyond the matter of controlling population increases to suggesting "action to curb human population and consumption patterns."[128] Among those seeking to formulate measures of sustainability during the closing years of this century, there appears to be a growing awareness of the need to end growth in both human and economic terms if there is to be any hope for a sustainable future. In terms of operational measures of sustainability, further human and economic growth would therefore be considered to represent evidence of unsustainable behavior under current demographic, economic, and ecological realities. With evidence of the unsustainable character of even the present scale of the human enterprise, the actual measure of sustainability would be one of shrinkage in that enterprise to a level capable of being sustained indefinitely.

Efforts to devise operational measures of sustainable development and sustainability have also been inclined to acknowledge the essential role of the natural world in setting the parameters for sustainability. Take, for example, the operational principles of sustainability suggested by the steady-state economist Herman Daly:

> Rates of use for *renewable resources* that do not exceed their rates of regeneration. (Resources such as soils, aquifers, forests, and fish would be used at rates that represented an extraction of income rather than a destruction of the capital wealth they represent.)

Rates of use for *nonrenewable resources* that do not exceed the rate at which sustainable renewable substitutes are developed. (Resources such as fossil fuels would be used at rates no greater than the rate at which a renewable resource, used sustainably, could be substituted for it.)

Rates of *pollution* emission that do not exceed the assimilative capacity of the environment. (Pollutants such as sewage would only be put into the environment at a rate at which that pollutant would be recycled, absorbed, or rendered harmless by the environment.)[129]

These operational principles of sustainability concede that there are limits to possible rates of resource extraction and pollution emission set by the ecosystems that comprise the natural world. As a result, these formulations of operational principles or measures of sustainability tend to emphasize the importance of maximizing *efficiency* in the use of all resources.[130] Such efficiency would limit the scale of resource throughput and thereby limit pollution output. With respect to the role of nonrenewable resources in providing sources of energy, a measure of sustainability would be the degree of transition from an energy system based on consuming depletable fossil fuels to a sustainable system based on solar energy.[131] In this regard, "[a]n increasing reliance on incoming solar energy would seem to be a key ingredient in achieving sustainability."[132] This increasing reliance on solar energy would represent expanded prospects for the kind of nonrenewable resource use that Daly associates with sustainability, as well as increased prospects for sustainable emission rates for certain pollutants.

With respect to these measures of sustainability, there is little evidence of sustainable behavior, either at a global level or at lesser geographical scales. Considerable evidence exists to support the claim that renewable resources are being used at rates that exceed their regenerative capabilities in virtually every geographical context. Current rates of use for nonrenewable resources are not based on the rate at which sustainable renewable substitutes are being developed, and there is no discernible shift to a sustainable solar energy system. As for pollution, little progress has been made at any level on setting rates of emission at the assimilative capacity of specific environments. In short, these measures of sustainability suggest little progress toward a state of sustainable human behavior.

Other efforts to formulate operational measures of sustainable development and sustainability have gone beyond the *temporal* focus of most sustainability considerations to addressing the *spatial* dimension of a sustainable future. In addition to the typical focus on meeting the needs of the present generation without compromising the ability of future generations to meet their own needs, such extended definitions of sustainable development address meeting "the needs of a specific region without curtailing the ability of other regions to meet their own needs."[133] Adding this spatial dimension acknowledges that meeting the needs of a region with external resources may exert deleterious effects on other regions and that such parasitic behavior may in fact curtail the ability of other regions to meet their own needs. This interest in the spatial dimension of sustainability tends to be expressed in terms of bioregions or the concept of bioregionalism. Advocates of this idea are apt to make a case for sustainability based on the self-sufficiency or self-sustaining capability of any region, arguing that the cumulative impact of development ought not to exceed the rate of resource consumption and waste discharge that can be sustained indefinitely in a defined planning region without causing permanent degradation of the productivity of the ecosystems on which the regional population is dependent.[134] Current formulations of sustainable development evidence little willingness to accept the principle that regions ought to demonstrate self-sustaining behavior, that is, meeting the needs of those within a region without degrading the productivity of that region's ecosystems or the ecosystems of external regions. This measure of sustainability again suggests little progress toward a state of sustainable human behavior, because spatial development models have yet to incorporate the idea of self-sustaining bioregions into their operational frameworks.

When consideration of the spatial dimension of sustainability has been undertaken at the level of human settlements, it has yielded additional operational measures of sustainable development or sustainability. At the scale of urban settlements, the issue of sustainability has produced the view that most "urban areas have outgrown and overstressed their natural support systems."[135] This viewpoint, in turn, produces the conclusion that "the optimum size of human settlements is likely to be far smaller [than today's large megalopolises] in a sustainable society."[136] Both the ecology and economics of renewable energy sources, as well as other factors, suggest that a sustainable future would be composed of smaller cities than those currently supported by fossil fuels.[137] When this view of cities is linked to the concept of bioregions it produces a description of urban places far different from those existing today:

> Sustainability implies that the use of energy and materials in an urban area be in balance with what the region can supply continuously through natural processes such as photosynthesis, biological decomposition, and the biochemical processes that support life. The immediate implications of this principle are a vastly reduced energy budget for cities, and a smaller, more compact urban pattern interspersed with productive areas to collect energy, grow crops for food, fiber and energy, and recycle wastes.[138]

These measures of sustainability certainly do not govern the development of today's cities, and current urban settlement patterns evidence little in terms of making the transition to a state of sustainable human behavior.

When the spatial dimension of sustainability has been considered across a range of possible types of human settlements (cities, towns, villages, and suburbs), it has produced additional measures of sustainability. These measures address a range of land-use practices, including land-use patterns, alternative transportation modes, types of buildings, and energy-based design. In the broadest of terms, sustainable communities are assumed to be those that strive to reduce resource consumption (for example, water and energy) and the generation of wastes (for example, solid waste and air pollution). More specifically, such communities are assumed to reflect a set of land-use policies and programs, including: a focus on more compact and contiguous development patterns; an emphasis on reducing automobile dependency and promoting alternative forms of transportation; and attention to advancing mixed-use development and infill growth.[139] With respect to reducing energy consumption as a prerequisite of sustainability, sustainable communities are presumed to exhibit a range of energy-based practices: conservation and solar retrofit of existing buildings; passive solar design of all new buildings; solar water heating; on-site production of gas from biomass resources; on-site electrical cogeneration to reduce peak demand; convenient alternatives to automobile use; recycling of water and wastes to agriculture and tree crops, and so on.[140] While examples of some of these policies and programs associated with sustainable communities may be found in individual American and international communities, no widespread evidence of a shift to such practices heralds an actual transition to a future settlement pattern based on sustainable communities.

As the previous range of examples illustrates, the notion of sustainability has come to be expressed in terms of operational measures of sustainable development. Many of those measures are capable of being directly linked to the crucial issue of ecological sustainability. Those operational measures that have been put forth in terms of a needed shrinkage in the human enterprise have tended to be based on the belief that even the current scale of that enterprise imposes unsustainable pressures on the global ecosystem. The operational measures of sustainability based on possible rates of resource extraction and pollution emission are directly tied to the principle of ecological sustainability, because without healthy ecosystems there can be no prospects for a sustainable production of renewable resources, a sustainable source of renewable substitutes for nonrenewable resources, or environments capable of recycling, absorbing, or rendering harmless emitted pollutants. Similarly, the operational measure of sustainability framed in terms of self-sustaining bioregions is also dependent on a state of ecological sustainability, since these bioregions are premised on the condition of maintaining the productivity of regional ecosystems. Operational measures of sustainability associated with sustainable communities were also revealed to be grounded in a state of ecological sustainability. The focus of those measures on reducing the consumption of resources and the generation of wastes is again explicitly based on the need to maintain healthy ecosystems capable of providing a sustained yield of essential resources and of processing pollutants on a sustained basis. Advocates of the sustainable communities concept propose such specific measures of sustainability as compact and contiguous development patterns, mixed-use development, and infill growth principally because of prospects for reduced resource use and waste generation. If any of the above noted operational measures of sustainability were to be found among the objectives currently advanced by the growth management movement in the United States, one might be tempted to assume that the idea of ecological sustainability was beginning to surface within the movement.

The Sustainable-Development Gap in Growth Management

As the earlier treatment of environmental planning considerations under growth management revealed, the nature of environmental planning approaches evident in current growth management programs has done little to advance the idea of ecological sustainability. Since those environmental planning efforts have only marginally employed a carrying-capacity approach, most environmental planning under growth management has skirted the issue of ecological sustainability. Consideration of the origins of the idea of sustainability, and the different meanings that have been attributed to the idea, also disclosed the extent to which it has been possible to think about sustainability without addressing the matter of ecological sustainability. Different formulations of sustained yield, sustainable economies, and sustainable societies were shown to demonstrate a decidedly pro-growth orientation that would do little to further the concept of ecological sustainability within the growth management movement even if those formulations appeared among the movement's explicitly stated ends. As noted, however, such formulations have not been listed as goals within the movement. The ideas of sustained yield, sustainable economies, and sustainable societies have not, therefore, served as prospective avenues for introducing ecological-sustainability considerations into the growth management movement. If these ideas have not advanced the concept of ecological sustainability within the movement, the recent interest in operational measures of sustainability has afforded another possible route for bringing the concern of ecological sustainability into growth management.

If sustainability has become a catchword of the development community in the 1990s, it is hard to understand why the concept has not been incorporated into the growth management movement. Given the pro-growth bias of the growth management movement portrayed in this work, one might understand a reluctance to accept the concept of sustainability if it negated the prospects for further growth. However, as illustrated here, it has been possible to embrace the concept without abandoning the growth imperative. In spite of the pro-growth orientation of the different definitions of sustainability described above, the concept has not been embraced by the growth management movement. One might only guess that a perceived incongruity between sustainability and ongoing growth may explain why the movement has been reluctant to broach the concept of sustainability in spite of the fact that it can be defined in a pro-growth fashion. If the growth management movement has shown no willingness to embrace the idea of sustainability embodied in general pro-growth-biased definitions, it might be assumed that the movement would be even less inclined to adopt the operational measures that have been suggested for sustainability. Since many of the operational measures of sustainable development are capable of being directly linked to the critical issue of ecological sustainability and the related need to give up on further growth, one might logically expect no evidence of such measures among the movement's identified objectives. That has not, however, entirely been the case.

With the commitment to a pro-growth position on the part of the growth management movement, it is obvious that the movement would ignore the operational measure of sustainability that directly posits a requisite shrinkage in the human enterprise. Operational measures of sustainability based on possible rates of resource extraction and pollution emission are also absent from the list of goals associated with the growth management movement. While the movement has addressed the loss of resource lands and the mitigation of pollution effects caused by development, it has neglected the broader issues of basing resource use on the regenerative capacity of renewable resources (or the ability to find sustainable renewable substitutes for nonrenewable resources) and pollution emissions on the assimilative capacity of the environment. The movement has additionally failed to include the operational measure of sustainability framed in terms of self-sustaining bioregions among its goals. It has similarly ignored those operational measures of sustainability associated with the concept of sustainable communities that focus on reducing both the consumption of resources and the generation of wastes. The attention paid to a sustainable energy system based on solar energy in developing operational measures for sustainable communities has also been missing from lists of objectives typically associated with the growth management movement. Since the movement has not addressed these measures they have not served to further consideration of the question of sustainability in growth management. More specifically, to the extent that all these measures are capable of being linked to the crucial issue of ecological sustainability, their absence has allowed the management movement to completely disregard the question of ecological sustainability.

The growth management movement has, however, dealt with a few of the issues presented as operational measures of sustainability for sustainable communities. Many growth management programs have pursued the end of compact and contiguous development via regulations designed to contain growth within designated growth boundaries. This focus on infill growth intended to achieve communities characterized by compact and contiguous development has also represented an operational measure of sustainability within the sustainable-communities literature. However, the rationales used to justify such compact settlements have not been the same as those employed in the growth management movement. Advocates of the concept of sustainable communities argue the case for compact settlements mainly on grounds of prospective reductions in resource consumption and waste generation. With their focus on a sustainable energy system based on solar energy these advocates argue a case for a vastly reduced energy budget for cities, with the implication that settlements would be smaller and more compact than those of the present and as a result capable of recycling wastes without overwhelming local biological processes. Those who make a case for sustainable communities tend to accept the current reality of limits to growth and to acknowledge that development must ultimately be based on the concept of ecological sustainability.

The growth management movement has, in contrast, shown no willingness to give up on the growth imperative or to adopt ecological sustainability as the primary guiding principle for the management movement. When the movement has pursued the end of containing growth within designated urban growth boundaries, the aim has not usually been motivated by a desire to reduce resource consumption or waste generation. The primary rationale for containing sprawl and promoting compact settlements has rather been one of avoiding costly and inefficient facility and service provisions across the landscape. When containment policies have been associated with reduced prospects for the loss of agricultural and forestry resource lands, they have not been based on a concern with achieving sustainability in the use of such resources, but rather on avoiding declines in resource-based sectors of state economies. Similarly, when containment policies have been argued on the grounds of a need to protect such sensitive environmental lands as wetlands from sprawl development, the proposed aim has not been based on an acknowledgment of the role of such lands in the sustainable functioning of local ecosystems, but rather on an accepted need to balance development with environmental protection. In short, while the growth management movement has addressed some of the same issues as those reflected in operational measures associated with the attainment of sustainable communities, these concerns have not advanced the idea of ecological sustainability within the movement. In spite of mounting evidence that current behavior is not ecologically sustainable, and the fact that our species is as dependent on the sustainable functioning of ecosystems as any other species, the growth management movement has yet to address the matter of ecological sustainability. The following section provides an overview of some of the definitions that have been provided for ecological sustainability, suggests some operational measures for such sustainability, and makes a case for accepting ecological sustainability as the primary focus of future growth management activity.

ECOLOGICAL SUSTAINABILITY AS THE PRIMARY GROWTH MANAGEMENT FOCUS

This treatment of sustainability has noted that most formulations of the concept have evidenced a clear anthropocentric bias.[141] Irrespective of whether the focus has been on sustainable resource use, sustainable economies, sustainable societies, or other versions of sustainability, the central interest has consistently been one of human welfare. When sustainability has been considered in terms of the more general notion of sustainable development, this anthropocentric orientation has continued to occupy center stage. As one observer has put it, "[w]ithout doubt, the anthropocentric perspective dominates the paradigm of sustainable development."[142] That perspective is patently evident in the definition of sustainable development from the Brundtland Report, which considers development as sustainable if it meets the needs of the present generation of humans without compromising the ability of future generations to meet their own needs. For those who believe that anthropocentrism is the root of our current environmental problems,[143] this preoccupation with human welfare is seen as ill advised. With the growing perception that anthropocentrism is inherently "unecological,"[144] and thus threatening to all life on this planet, there has been a growing interest in ecological sustainability. Part of that interest has found expression in attempts to define sustainability in ecological terms.

Definitions of Ecological Sustainability

Although most definitions of sustainability have excluded explicit ecological components, there have been attempts to define the concept of ecological sustainability. The following examples serve to illustrate the nature of concerns embodied in such definitions:

> Ecological sustainability refers to . . . development activity that acknowledges biophysical limits and the need to maintain essential ecological processes and life-support systems upon which all life depends.[145]

> The ecological definition of sustainability focuses on natural biological processes and the continued productivity and functioning of ecosystems. Long-term ecological sustainability requires the protection of genetic resources and the conservation of biological diversity.[146]

> [Sustainability implies] management practices that will not degrade the exploited [ecological] systems or any adjacent systems . . . and . . . consumption standards that are within the bounds of ecological possibility and to which all can aspire.[147]

> A 'sustainable biosphere' can be envisioned in which the diversity of life on earth persists [and serves as the ecological basis of sustainability].[148]

These attempts to define ecological sustainability evidence a number of recurring themes. They all reveal a biological perspective that extends beyond a concern with the survival of our species to an expressed need to maintain the diversity represented by all life forms on the planet. Since ecosystems by definition are composed of biotic and abiotic components, and an ecological understanding recognizes the role played by living and nonliving portions of ecosystems, the definitions also assert a need to retain the basic functions of natural ecosystems. The definitions additionally convey an acceptance of limits to the demands that may be put on the biotic and abiotic components of ecosystems, and the associated warning that surpassing those limits threatens the life-support systems upon which all life depends.

It is possible to explain the interest in maintaining biodiversity and the integrity of ecosystems in selfish anthropocentric terms. From this perspective the loss of biodiversity is only lamented on the grounds that it may reduce prospects for utilizing other species to meet the needs of people. Similarly, from this point of view threats to the integrity of ecosystems would only be deplored to the extent that they represented an erosion in the quality of life for humans. There are those, however, who defend biodiversity and ecological integrity in a way that has nothing to do with whether they have instrumental value in satisfying a variety of human needs. That defense is based on ethical principles.[149] With respect to maintaining species diversity, proponents of this ethics-based position argue that species have an inherent right to existence, regardless of the utility or value they may hold for humans. Under this view other species should be conserved simply because they exist, that is, "[l]ong-standing existence in Nature is deemed to carry with it the unimpeachable right to continued existence."[150] For those who hold this biocentric position it naturally follows that at the very least humans have a moral obligation to refrain from actions that cause other species to become extinct. Other biocentrists extend that moral obligation further, as evidenced by the ethical standard espoused by Aldo Leopold in his pioneering work *A Sand County Almanac*: "A thing is right when it tends to preserve the integrity, stability, and beauty of the biotic community. It is wrong when it tends otherwise."[151]

Ecocentrists, in turn, may take this line of reasoning a step further and make a case for assigning intrinsic moral value to the abiotic components of ecosystems: mountains, landforms such as plains and valleys, rivers, and the like. The case for extending moral obligations to these components is based on an understanding of the role they play in the functioning of ecological systems. Since ecosystems could not maintain essential ecological processes without the roles played by both biotic and abiotic elements, ecocentrists are apt to make a case for extending ethical obligations to all components of ecological systems, and then to ecosystems in their entirety. This ethical obligation would not necessarily be based on the value that ecosystems hold for humans, or because they support other forms of life, but rather because of their uniqueness and complexity. That uniqueness and complexity is assumed to confer inherent value or worth, a good of its own, which is again deemed to carry with it the unimpeachable right to continued existence based on prior long-term existence in Nature. Such reasoning is then apt to produce an ethical standard that goes beyond addressing implications for the biotic community to implications for entire ecological systems. One formulation of such an ethical standard has been offered in the following terms: "Something is right when it tends to maintain the earth's life-support systems for us and all other species and wrong when it tends otherwise."[152] Since ecosystems represent life-support systems, the ethical standard infers a minimal moral obligation to refrain from actions that eliminate ecosystems. More broadly, the moral obligation may be assumed to extend to the level of a duty to maintain the ecological integrity of all ecosystems. From this perspective, "engaging in a mode of development that is anything less than ecologically sustainable would be not only contradictory but immoral."[153]

Operational Measures of Ecological Sustainability

The prior noted definitions of ecological sustainability suggest a few operational measures for directing the transition to a state of ecological sustainability. First, the definitions affirm that preserving the diversity of life is a necessary condition for ecological sustainability. From this perspective, *actions that serve to reduce biodiversity are by definition ecologically unsustainable.* On anthropocentric grounds, such reductions are to be condemned because they reduce prospects for utilizing other species to meet human needs. On moral grounds, the loss of other life forms is condemned because it is seen as a negation of their inherent worth and their resultant right to continued existence regardless of their utility to humans. As noted, this at the very least implies a moral obligation to refrain from actions that cause other species to become extinct. For deep ecologists, however, it infers a good deal more. They argue that "all things in the biosphere have an equal right to live and blossom and to reach their own individual forms of unfolding and self-realization within the larger self-realization."[154] This view connotes an obligation to minimally impact other living things as we meet our needs, and to thereby allow them the opportunity to attain their own forms of self-realization. Far short of assuming this modest position in the world, the operational measure of ecological sustainability is clear: *no further loss of biodiversity due to anthropogenic causes.* The loss of any species is recognized to represent a threat to ecological sustainability, and the transition to a sustainable state therefore requires an immediate cessation of such unsustainable behavior.

The noted definitions of ecological sustainability suggest a second operational measure for directing the transition to a state of ecological sustainability. They hold that maintaining the integrity of ecosystems is a necessary condition for ecological sustainability. In this respect, *actions that serve to reduce the number or integrity of ecosystems are by definition ecologically unsustainable.* On selfish anthropocentric grounds, these actions are to be censured because they require futile attempts to create functional substitutes for the life-support systems provided by ecosystems. On moral grounds, actions that reduce the number or integrity of ecosystems are to be condemned because they serve to negate the uniqueness and complexity that give ecosystems their inherent worth and their resultant right to continued existence based on prior long-term existence. As noted, this infers a minimal moral obligation to refrain from actions that eliminate ecosystems. More broadly, it extends the moral obligation to the duty of maintaining the ecological integrity of all ecosystems. Since ecosystems are composed of both biotic and abiotic components, this amounts to a requirement of limiting our own need fulfillment to a level that allows other species to meet their needs and abiotic portions of ecosystems to carry out their natural functions. This reasoning suggests another operational measure of ecological sustainability: *no further loss of ecosystems or impairment of their continued productivity and functioning due to anthropogenic causes.* The loss or impairment of ecosystems is understood to represent the antithesis of ecological sustainability, and the transition to a sustainable state is again understood to require the cessation of such unsustainable behavior.

A third operational measure for directing the transition to a state of ecological sustainability is suggested by the previously noted definitions of ecological sustainability. Those definitions infer an acceptance of limits to the demands that may be put on both the biotic and abiotic components of ecosystems, which if surpassed would erode the essential ecological processes and life-support systems on which all life depends. With regard to the biotic components of ecosystems, "[n]o one doubts that species are disappearing at an accelerating rate."[155] An assessment of this phenomenon in the mid-1990s by some 1,500 scientists worldwide concluded that the natural wealth referred to as biodiversity is disappearing at an "unprecedented" and alarming rate.[156] Since "[h]abitat destruction is the chief cause of the global extinction rate,"[157] the loss of species is obviously reflective of a loss of ecosystems that house those species. As the opening chapter of this book pointed out, our species has already appropriated some 40% of the planet's terrestrial food supply and at least an equal percentage of the planet's land surface. With continued growth in the scale of the human enterprise, "the accelerated extinction rate of species and destruction of habitats will continue."[158] As a consequence, *further growth in the scale of the human enterprise is also by definition ecologically unsustainable.* Even if the global population were to stabilize at its current level, the attempt of developing nations to imitate the living standards of developed countries would produce further losses in both ecosystems and species. This suggests a third operational measure of ecological sustainability: *an ongoing reduction in the scale of the human enterprise to a level capable of being supported indefinitely without eroding biodiversity or the integrity of ecosystems.* Anything short of such an ongoing reduction would be seen as incongruous with ecological sustainability, and the transition to a sustainable state would be assumed to depend on an ongoing process of scaling back our presence on the planet to an ecologically-sustainable level.

Accepting Ecological Sustainability as the Primary Growth Management Focus

By the 1990s ecologists were joining the chorus of voices cataloging threats to the natural world from anthropogenic causes.[159] Like members of other disciplines, ecologists expressed concerns over "the rapidly deteriorating state of the environment."[160] In a report from the Ecological Society of America they claimed that human activities were "currently leading to unprecedented changes in the Earth's atmospheric, terrestrial, freshwater, and marine environments."[161] Referring to such anthropogenic effects as deforestation, soil depletion, contamination of air and water resources, and depletion of biological diversity, the ecologists who authored the report maintained that our species had already "caused massive changes in the biosphere."[162] As a result of these changes, they argued that "Earth's life support systems are changing, and their ability to sustain human society is being degraded rapidly."[163] This led them to conclude that "[e]nvironmental problems resulting from human activities have begun to threaten the sustainability of Earth's life support systems."[164] For these ecologists, the underlying issue of the day is clearly one of ecological sustainability.[165]

The primacy of ecological sustainability was acknowledged in the opening section of this chapter with the statement that the human economy and civilization itself are utterly dependent on the life-support services provided by sound ecosystems. More specifically, the nature of that dependency may be thought of in the following terms:

> Human survival requires sufficient food, potable water, uncontaminated air, adequate shelter and clothing, energy, and minerals. . . . These needs are closely tied to the continued functioning of the supporting ecological systems which maintain nutrient, air, and water cycles, and to the maintenance of renewable biological resources such as forests and fisheries stocks. . . . [E]ach of the conditions for survival has its own complex set of support systems which must be sustained. Adequate food, [for example], requires an agricultural system which can function on a continuing basis without losses of land area, soil fertility, soil moisture, resistance to pests and disease, or nutritional quality. . . . *At all scales, food, water, air, shelter, and clothing can be very closely linked to the sustained functioning of natural ecosystems.*[166] [italics added]

The conclusion emphasized in the prior citation is so self-evident that it is remarkable that it even needs to be stated. Without ecosystems providing a host of such essential life-support services as maintaining a benign mix of atmospheric gases, regulating the hydrologic cycle, purifying air and water, generating and maintaining fertile soils, disposing of wastes, recycling of nutrients, providing pest control and pollination services, supplying forest products and food from the oceans, and creating and maintaining biodiversity our species could not exist. Without sound ecosystems, in turn, we cannot count on the continued provision of any of these essential services. Human well-being cannot, in short, be achieved at the expense of ecological integrity. As ecologists continue to present evidence that human activities have begun to threaten the sustainability of Earth's life-support systems, nothing seems more pressing than to acknowledge the primacy of ecological sustainability as a guiding principle for all human behavior, including that of growth management.

Much of the current preoccupation with the concept of sustainability ignores the reality "that sustainability is at bottom *an ecological concept*."[167] Without ecological sustainability no other forms of sustainability will be possible. As the underlying basis of all other forms of sustainability, "the biosphere conditions the possibilities for development."[168] This reality infers the obligation to preserve an ecological base for future development. It also imposes the condition that other formulations of sustainability (such as social sustainability and economic sustainability) must "draw upon the ecological perspective for guidance as they attempt to develop strategies necessary to meet the requirements of ecologically sustainable development."[169] To the extent that these other versions of sustainability are based on further growth in the scale of the human enterprise they must be acknowledged to be ecologically unsustainable, because such growth can now occur only at the expense of other species and the planet's ecosystems. These losses are by definition ecologically unsustainable. In the present era, even the current scale of the human enterprise is eliminating species and ecosystems, so current reality calls not only for a cessation of growth, but also for a reduction in the scale of that enterprise to a level that is ecologically sustainable.

Relinquishing the growth imperative will not come easily, for it occupies a prominent place in the world's dominant social paradigm. The "technological enthusiasts" will continue to make a case for technical efficiencies providing a route "to ease the human economy down below the planet's limits with grace and without sacrifice."[170] That route suggests that technology will enable us to squeeze more out of available resources, while simultaneously allowing us to reduce pollution emissions. Others will continue to espouse the virtues of the market mechanism, arguing that price adjustments will solve problems of resource availability and pollution remediation.[171] Yet others will contend the most important feature of achieving sustainable development consists of the art of compromise; specifically, reaching an "essential optimal compromise . . . between economic growth and [an] environmental protection level."[172] Proponents of this view emphasize the need to achieve a balance between development and conservation, arguing for the possibility of pursuing both ends.[173] All of these perspectives convey prospects for further growth. Given what ecologists are now telling us about the effects of ongoing growth on other species and ecosystems, and the realization that those effects are incongruous with ecological sustainability, it seems that we have no option but to accept the current reality of present limits to any further growth. Ecological realities call out for the abandonment of the growth imperative and the adoption of an alternative imperative: the imperative of ecological sustainability. In the same way that the global community must accept the primacy of this new imperative, the growth management movement in the United States must also accept ecological sustainability as its new primary focus if it is to remain relevant to the needs of the day.

FUTURE PROSPECTS FOR THE GROWTH MANAGEMENT MOVEMENT

The growth management movement in the United States has staked out a clear position on growth. It has shown no inclination whatsoever to accept the idea of a current need to abandon the growth imperative driving present behavior at all levels, and has instead endorsed the idea that it is possible to practice continued adherence to that imperative by controlling the deleterious effects of growth. Rather than accepting the view of growth as the central problem of the era, the movement has subscribed to the view that the country can have quantity with quality if future growth is properly planned and regulated. Current ecological realities are presenting serious challenges to this perspective, but the movement remains committed to the assumed wisdom of further growth.

The Unsustainable Nature of Current Growth Management Activity in the United States

As the prior treatment of the growth management movement in the United States illustrated, the overwhelming majority of management programs have allowed, facilitated, or actually mandated ongoing growth accommodation. Virtually every local growth management program evidences the clear intent of accommodating future growth, irrespective of whether programs are based on statewide growth management laws. For local programs adopted in states with these statewide laws, local governments are typically required to plan for ongoing growth accommodation by specific mandates written into the statewide enabling acts. In these contexts, local programs are actually barred from instituting management efforts intended to stop growth. The movement has, therefore, continued to support ongoing allegiance to the growth imperative.

Growth management was shown to represent different things to different participants in the movement. For some, the proper focus of the movement is one of maintaining the traditional promotion and stimulation of further growth. For others, the principal interest has become one of planning properly for what is considered to be inevitable growth. Then there are those who have stressed a need to influence, guide, channel, or redistribute growth in order to minimize any associated negative impacts. Yet others have directed attention to the increasing need to regulate, control, and even limit future growth in response to a host of growth-induced problems. These varying emphases have allowed participants in the movement to pursue a number of different management objectives: the conservation of resource lands and the protection of environmentally-sensitive areas; growth containment to avoid costly and destructive sprawl; the timely provision of public services and facilities; and rate controls to allow the timely assimilation of growth without destroying community character or a current way of life. All of these objectives allow ongoing growth. With respect to conserving resource lands and protecting sensitive environmental areas, the position taken by members of the movement tends to be one of arguing that both ends may be realized merely by channeling ongoing growth to appropriate locations. As for containing growth within urban growth boundaries, the participants in the movement advance the view that such boundaries need to be adjusted over time to allow for the future growth needs of an area. Management efforts directed at the timely provision of services and facilities needed by new growth have tended to consist of programs that assure the financing and construction of service centers and facilities so that their absence would not serve to impede ongoing growth. The use of rate controls in management programs has served to limit the amount of growth allowed in a specified period, but these programs have provided for subsequent allowances for growth in future time periods. In short, none of the typical objectives advanced by the movement has acted to stop future growth. In fact, the movement has evidenced no receptivity to the idea that management efforts might legitimately be directed at stopping growth.

Participants in the growth management movement have not been content with merely dismissing the idea that management programs might justifiably be intended to stop growth they have actually condemned that possible end. They have tended to censure any suggested pursuit of no-growth as a management objective by associating such a quest with socially unacceptable motives and undesirable social consequences. The no-growth option for growth management programs has been written off by members of the movement, repeatedly being characterized as inefficient, unjust, and irresponsible. Even management programs that have sought only to limit future growth, as an alternative to actually stopping it, have been labeled as the worst, unenlightened, unrealistic, immature, and improperly defined efforts. In contrast, ongoing attempts to accommodate growth have been characterized as the best, enlightened, realistic, mature, and properly defined programs. *The growth management movement represents a wholehearted endorsement of ongoing growth accommodation.*

In spite of mounting evidence of the damage continuing growth is inflicting on other species and natural ecosystems, participants in the movement have been unable to perceive an alternative to ongoing growth accommodation and have shown no willingness whatsoever to entertain management efforts directed at stopping growth. The movement instead continues to endorse the "balance" argument, which suggests that growth and environmental protection represent equally legitimate objectives, and that a balance can be achieved between these ends without compromising either. As the 1990s come to a close, and we prepare to embark on another millennium, a leading spokesperson for the movement still suggests the following definition for growth management:

> Growth management is defined as a balance between the equally legitimate need to protect natural systems and provide for the population growth and economic development necessary to assure a healthy economy. It assumes that a healthy environment and a strong economy are not in conflict with each other, but are in fact mutually supporting.[174]

With a general acceptance of this perspective, growth management programs in the 1990s have evidenced a shift from the environmental focus of the 1970s to a current preoccupation with growth-accommodating economic policies. This increasing reference to promoting growth and economic development in growth management programs represents a continued belief in the legitimacy of further growth in spite of accumulating documentation of current limits to growth. So as the century winds down, the majority of participants in the movement remain wedded to their belief in the merit of the growth imperative.

To continue to portray growth accommodation as "responsible" behavior in light of effects stemming from even the current scale of the human enterprise will increasingly put the movement at risk of losing its relevance. Ongoing growth will surely demonstrate the "irresponsible" nature of further growth accommodation as future growth-induced problems inevitably increase. Support for growth under those circumstances will certainly come to be seen as irresponsible support for an obsolete ideology. If members of the growth management movement are to play a meaningful societal role during the opening years of the next century, they must come to recognize that in impeding the needed transition to a state of nongrowth they are hindering the essential transition to a sustainable future. Current ecological realities call out for a new focus for the movement, one directed at downsizing and redesigning the human enterprise to a level and form that is ecologically sustainable.

The Role of the Planning Profession in Unsustainable Growth Management Efforts

As part of the prior treatment of the role of the planning profession in the growth management movement, members of the profession were shown to play important roles in the movement. By taking part in structuring the policy agenda that addresses growth in America's communities, planners have been in the position of being able to influence the development process that has historically supported ongoing growth. Planners have also been able to affect development policy through the key roles they play in creating the comprehensive plans and associated land-use regulations that set the parameters for future growth. Unfortunately, the profession's historical pro-growth orientation has blocked an alternative role for planners that would represent something other than ongoing growth facilitation. That pro-growth orientation has been clearly reflected in different types of planning activity over time. The profession's comprehensive plan-making approach has continued to employ an outdated demand-based methodology that merely calculates future demand for land and facilities based on past trends and then presents a design scheme for accommodating that demand. The second dominant view of planning as a rational decision-making process, with its belief in the superiority of having ends imposed by political and market processes rather than by a previous determination of the public interest, clearly links this type of planning to a pro-growth orientation. In reality, these and other types of planning all serve to illustrate the extent to which the profession has associated itself with a pro-growth stance. Regrettably, that stance has changed only marginally during the growth management era, during which time planners have been willing to accept a need for the management of growth, but have been unable to back away from continued endorsement of future growth.

Planners have been able to maintain their historical pro-growth stance during the growth management era by endorsing the concept of "balanced growth." As noted, that concept assumes equal legitimacy for the objectives of ongoing growth and environmental protection. This perspective presupposes that it is possible to accommodate ongoing growth in a responsible way if growth is properly planned and its negative effects adequately mitigated. From this point of view, it appears unnecessary to moderate the profession's historical anthropocentric focus on meeting the needs of our species (for example, planning directed at ensuring an employment base, housing opportunities, transportation options, recreation prospects, and so forth), because it is believed that those needs are capable of being met without compromising the environment. Unfortunately, such an anthropocentric focus on meeting the needs of humans appears fated to run headlong into the paradox of anthropocentrism, which "is that a world conceived of only with human ends in mind seems destined to become inhospitable to any human ends in the long run."[175] Given what ecologists are now revealing about anthropogenic impacts on other species and ecosystems associated with ongoing growth, continued support for the idea of further growth only serves to endorse the pursuit of an unsustainable end. Surprisingly, the planning profession's involvement with growth management has contributed nothing to an acceptance of the idea that ongoing growth is now clearly unsustainable. Rather than accepting that reality, planners continue to support the growth imperative.

Even during the latter 1990s the planning profession appears committed to supporting unsustainable growth management practices directed at ongoing growth accommodation. One of the most recent growth management texts authored by members of the profession claims to provide insights into "desirable ways of accommodating growth," and in the process of doing so refers to "sustainable growth."[176] In those rare instances when planners have addressed planning for sustainable communities during the 1990s, they have still been apt to suggest that "sustainable growth" represents a legitimate aspect of such sustainability.[177] As we approach the end of this century, the planning profession continues to support what is increasingly being revealed as the obsolete ideology of growth and the oxymoronic idea of sustainable growth. If the profession is to play a meaningful role in reshaping the present into a sustainable future, it must relinquish the growth imperative. If it is unable to do so, it will be destined to become as obsolete as those other actors in the movement that are blocking the crucial transition to a sustainable state of nongrowth. By its nature the planning profession could play a critical role in helping society redesign the present into an ecologically sustainable future, but if it is to play a part in realizing this end it must abandon its historical pro-growth posture because of its incongruity with ecological sustainability.

The Role of the Courts in Impeding the Needed Transition to a Sustainable Society

The essence of the growth management movement has been its regulatory nature. In response to growth-related problems, state and local governments began to experiment with an expanded realm of police-power regulations in order to impose a new level of control on growth during the course of the management process. Although the majority of growth management programs have continued to maintain an accommodative stance toward growth, they have nevertheless introduced additional police-power regulations designed to control the amount, rate, location, and quality of development. These land-use regulations associated with the growth management movement have collectively served to reduce the scope of private property rights associated with property ownership in this country. The increase in regulatory activity that placed new limits on the use of private property, and thereby brought about this reduction in property rights, generated inevitable conflict, and that conflict often ended up in the courts. This put the courts in the business of defining the permissible limits of governmental regulation. More specifically, it has put them in the position of judging the legality of land-use regulations created to implement growth management ends. The courts therefore play a pivotal role in shaping growth management programs, because they ultimately decide whether new management regulations are lawful.

American courts have used a broad array of constitutional, statutory, and case-law standards to decide how far police-power regulations of land may go before they are found to be beyond the permissible limits of the law. As the review of these standards revealed, most police-power regulations that have commonly been employed during the course of attempting to manage growth are capable of surviving legal challenges. In fact, when litigated, the courts have confirmed the general legality of most growth management controls attempted to date by upholding the majority of challenged management efforts. However, that willingness to validate an expanded set of restrictions on private property may be attributable to the fact that the overwhelming majority of those programs have continued to provide for ongoing growth. While the courts have historically allowed even severe limitations on use and associated diminutions in value when justified by a legitimate public purpose, they have not condoned a denial of all use and value. To the extent that growth management programs moved toward implementing programs actually intended to stop further growth, these programs would impose even more serious restrictions on use and value than those associated with earlier growth management efforts. With the traditional attention that courts in this country have given to defending the right to make use of private property, they could be expected to scrutinize any extension of use limitations associated with growth management efforts directed at stopping growth.

The reluctance on the part of the courts to accept the land-use limitations associated with stopping growth could also be attributable to the traditional progrowth bias of the courts. Court opinions reveal a reluctance on the part of the judiciary to sanction efforts to impede continued growth. These opinions refer to "natural" and "normal" growth, and display a general belief that ongoing growth furthers the general welfare in spite of its associated problems. In the handful of states where courts have established a regional-welfare standard for judging the legality of land-use controls, these courts have actually imposed a requirement that local governments must accommodate growth in furtherance of the general welfare. However, even that requirement is violable, and the standard is capable of being waived in certain circumstances, as when environmental concerns make further growth impractical. Even though the courts have a real interest in protecting private property rights, and a bias in favor of ongoing growth as a route for protecting those rights and associated general welfare interests, they have not considered these factors in isolation. The courts have also recognized a need to balance the public interests served by police-power regulations against the degree of intrusion into private property rights. If the growth management movement decides to pursue the end of stopping growth, the legal challenge will become one of convincing the judiciary that current ecological realities justify a new level of restrictions on private property usage.

American courts have a long history of protecting private property rights from excessive land-use regulations, and that tradition can certainly be expected to present challenges to any attempts to stop growth by limiting use options for private property. The courts also mirror society's general pro-growth bias, and that bias can similarly be expected to hinder programs intended to shut down growth. The support for private property rights and pro-growth perspectives displayed by courts might be expected to impede the critical transition to a sustainable future based on nongrowth. However, land already in use carries with it no inherent right to use it more intensely, even though property owners might want to increase its value through more intense use. Vacant land, which may not be regulated to the point of denying all use and value, may in many instances be legally limited to uses (for example, agricultural and recreational) that do not allow ongoing growth (for example, residential, commercial, and industrial). To take this position on use rights will not come easily, but the transition to an ecologically-sustainable future appears to demand a new view of how intensely private land may be used. Communities will face the challenge of having to convince the courts that they are pursuing a legitimate public purpose in their quest for a sustainable future based on nongrowth, and that in pursuing that end they are still allowing economically viable uses for private property. While this may represent a substantial challenge, it need not be viewed as insurmountable. In the same manner that society must come to recognize the need to stop growth as a necessary condition of ecological sustainability, the courts must be made to understand that legal support of further growth will only serve to impede the essential transition to a sustainable future.

The Primacy of Ecological Sustainability as a New Growth Management Focus

Growth management programs in the United States have sought to advance a broad range of environmental ends, for example, preventing further environmental deterioration of air and water quality, minimizing a range of negative environmental impacts, protecting environmentally-sensitive lands, and conserving resource lands. In attempting to further these ends, management programs have utilized three different environmental planning approaches, but none of these approaches has required an abandonment of the growth imperative. The predominant approach based on impact assessments and associated mitigation measures assumes that growth can continue if its impacts are mitigated. The approach based on suitability analyses similarly assumes continued prospects for growth, if land is merely put to suitable uses as indicated by an assessment of its natural capabilities. Even the environmental planning approach based on the concept of natural carrying capacities suggests continued growth options, under the assumption that natural capacities are not fixed and can be overcome by new technologies or expenditures on ameliorative measures. To the extent that all of these approaches sanction ongoing growth, they contribute little to the needed transition to a state of ecological sustainability. We are at a point where further growth can occur only at the expense of other species and natural ecosystems, which by definition constitutes ecologically unsustainable behavior. If growth management programs are to assist in the necessary societal transition to a state of ecological sustainability, they will have to be directed at forms of environmental planning that permit no further erosion in biodiversity or the integrity of ecosystems. Current forms of environmental planning utilized in growth management programs do not serve to further such an end.

In the same way that environmental planning considerations under growth management have not advanced the end of ecological sustainability, the concept of sustainable development has not found its way into the growth management movement in a way that would promote the needed transition to a state of ecological sustainability. The growth management movement has largely ignored the issue of sustainable development. When the movement's stated objectives have corresponded with those identified in the sustainable communities literature, the management movement has used a different set of rationales to justify those objectives. Rather than making the case for compact development patterns on the basis of prospective reductions in resource consumption and waste generation in the manner of the sustainable communities literature, the movement has justified this end on the grounds of avoiding costly and inefficient facility and service provisions. While proponents of the concept of sustainable communities have tended to accept the current reality of limits to growth, and to acknowledge that development must ultimately be based on the concept of ecological sustainability, the participants in the growth management movement have yet to acknowledge either of these obvious realities. By continuing to support the growth imperative the movement is effectively blocking the urgently needed shift to ecologically-sustainable behavior.

The growth management movement in America must be recognized for what it really is: an institutionalized form of support for the growth imperative. In the majority of states with statewide growth management laws those statutes mandate ongoing growth accommodation by local governments. In states without such laws the overwhelming majority of local management programs provide for continued accommodation of growth. In reality, most growth management programs are directed at a "managing to grow" option, rather than toward actual efforts to control or limit future growth. The movement can therefore be critically assessed as representing little more than development facilitation. At a time when ongoing growth is revealing itself to be lethal to other species and natural ecosystems, the growth management movement continues to defend the idea that a "balance" can still be realized between future growth and environmental protection. Participants in the movement appear unable to recognize that ongoing compromise between these ends is no longer possible. When the country's virgin old-growth forests have been reduced to something like 5 to 10% of their original stands, then ongoing compromise between further cutting and preservation must be recognized to represent compromising such forests out of existence. With diminishing levels of resource availability across all renewable resources, such forms of "balance" between competing objectives must be correctly labeled as unsustainable behavior. Ecological realities cry out for the abandonment of such unsustainable behavior, and that shift requires a prior rejection of the growth imperative.

A point in history has been reached where the ongoing elimination of species and ecosystems must be condemned as insane behavior. From an ecological perspective, which in the long run is the only one that matters, such behavior is simply incapable of being sustained. The current war on the community of life and the habitats that support it must end if our species hopes to experience an indeterminate future. In order to keep that option open, ecological sustainability must become the primary focus of both the growth management movement and society at large. With an acceptance of that focus the incongruity of further growth with ecological sustainability will become increasingly more difficult to reconcile. As the primacy of ecological sustainability is accepted, the necessity of rejecting the growth imperative will become increasingly self-evident. It must be conceded that our species can persist without growth, but not without sustainable ecosystems. If people can accept this obvious truism, the requisite transition from the artificial growth imperative to an indispensable ecological imperative can finally occur. Under that transition the growth management movement can finally shift its focus from its current irrelevant growth accommodation position to a new focus on overseeing the required downsizing and re-designing of the human enterprise to a level and form that is ecologically sustainable. The current growth management movement is committed to an obsolete growth imperative. Whether the movement will appropriately serve society's future needs will depend on its willingness to replace the growth imperative currently driving the movement with the imperative of ecological sustainability.

Notes

1 THE GROWTH MANAGEMENT CONTEXT

1. Paul R. Ehrlich and Anne H. Ehrlich, 1991, *Healing the Planet: Strategies for Resolving the Environmental Crisis*, New York: Addison-Wesley, 249.

2. This relationship between a relentless pursuit of growth and the destruction of the natural world is clearly illustrated in the following works: Carolyn Merchant, 1980, *The Death of Nature: Women, Ecology and the Scientific Revolution*, San Francisco: Harper & Row; Paul R. Ehrlich and Anne H. Ehrlich, 1981, *Extinction: The Causes and Consequences of the Disappearance of Species*, New York: Random House; Bill McKibben, 1989, *The End of Nature*, New York: Anchor Books-Doubleday.

3. See John Delafons, 1962, *Land-Use Controls in the United States*, Cambridge, Massachusetts: The MIT Press, 114.

4. Donella H. Meadows, Dennis L. Meadows, and Jorgen Randers, 1992, *Beyond the Limits: Confronting Global Collapse, Envisioning a Sustainable Future*, Post Mills, Vermont: Chelsea Green Publishing Company, 161.

5. Ibid., 3.

6. Ehrlich and Ehrlich, *Healing the Planet*, 216.

7. Paul R. Ehrlich and Anne H. Ehrlich, 1990, *The Population Explosion*, New York: Simon and Schuster, 162.

8. Mancur Olson, Hans H. Lansberg, and Joseph L. Fisher, 1973, Epilogue, *Daedalus: The No-Growth Society* 102,4: 231.

9. Christopher Manes, 1990, *Green Rage: Radical Environmentalism and the Unmaking of Civilization*, Boston: Little, Brown and Company, 241.

10. See Zachary A. Smith, 1995, *The Environmental Policy Paradox*, Englewood Cliffs, New Jersey: Prentice-Hall, 7-22; and Ehrlich and Ehrlich, *Healing the Planet*, 251-3.

11. B. F. Skinner, 1971, *Beyond Freedom and Dignity*, New York: Bantam Books, 168.

12. Lester R. Brown, 1974, *In the Human Interest: A Strategy to Stabilize World Population*, New York: WW Norton, 185.

13. Paul R. Ehrlich, Anne H. Ehrlich, and John P. Holdren, 1977, *Ecoscience: Population, Resources, Environment*, San Francisco: WH Freeman, 777.

14. Alfred Sauvy, 1976, *Zero Growth*, New York: Praeger, 3.

15. Ehrlich, Ehrlich, and Holdren, *Ecoscience*, note that the greeting reflects the fact that women in India are judged primarily by their fertility, with barrenness being considered a disgrace, 777.

16. See Paul R. Ehrlich and Anne H. Ehrlich, 1970, *Population, Resources, and Environment: Issues in Human Ecology*, San Francisco: WH Freeman, for reference to "the common idea that not only is growth of the GNP highly desirable, but that population increase, at least in DCs, *promotes* such growth," 281.

17. E. J. Mishan, 1969, *Technology and Growth: The Price We Pay*, New York: Praeger, for example, notes that "one of the factors insistently stressed as being conducive to rapid economic expansion is an increase of population," 79.

18. Reference to population increases in terms of their contribution to increased production potential may be found in Richard Zechhauser, 1973, The Risks of Growth, *Daedalus: The No-Growth Society* 102,4: 107, while reference to such increases in terms of their contribution to increased consumption potential appears in Warren A. Johnson, 1971, The Guaranteed Income as an Environmental Measure, in *Economic Growth vs. the Environment*, edited by Warren A. Johnson and John Hardesty, Belmont, California: Wadsworth, 109.

19. See S. Fred Singer, The Price System as a Control of Growth, *Society* (January/February), 48, Kingsley Davis, 1973, Zero Population Growth: The Goal and the Means, *Daedalus: The No-Growth Society* 102,4: 18, and John P. Holdren, 1973, Population and the American Predicament: The Case Against Complacency, *Daedalus: The No-Growth Society* 102,4: 40, for mention of such an "economies of scale" rationale behind positive perceptions of population growth.

20. See Norman B. Ryder, Two Cheers for ZPG, *Daedalus: The No-Growth Society* 102,4: 57, for reference to such an argument.

21. Ibid., 57.

22. A similar point is noted in Singer, The Price System as a Control of Growth, 48.

23. See Davis, Zero Population Growth: The Goal and the Means, 18.

24. Ibid., 21.

25. Ryder, Two Cheers for ZPG, 59-0.

26. Ehrlich and Ehrlich, *Population, Resources, and Environment*, 279.

27. Walter A. Weisskopf, 1973, Economic Growth versus Existential Balance, in *Toward a Steady-State Economy*, edited by Herman E. Daly, San Francisco: WH Freeman, 241.

28. See Wilfred Beckerman, 1972, Two Cheers for Economic Growth, *Lloyds Bank Review* (October), 52.

29. An example of reference to the desirability of increased affluence in terms of what it represents for increases in the range of human choices appears in Arthur W. Lewis, Is Economic Development Desirable?, 1970, in *Economic Development: Challenge and Promise*, edited by Stephen Spiegelglas and Charles J. Welsh, Englewood Cliffs, New Jersey: Prentice-Hall, 17, while an example of a noted expansion of choice in terms of collective action through government appears in Mancur Olson, 1973, Introduction, *Daedalus: The No-Growth Society* 102,4: 5.

30. See David T. Bazelon, 1968, The New Factor in American Society, in *Environment and Change: The Next Fifty Years*, edited by William R. Ewald, Bloomington: Indiana University Press, 269.

31. See Herman E. Daly, 1971, Toward a New Economics—Questioning Growth, in *Economic Growth vs. the Environment*, edited by Johnson and Hardesty, 82, for mention of the postulate of nonsatiety, and in the same edited work see John Hardesty

The Political Economy of Environmental Destruction, 93, for reference to economists' general faith in such a postulate.

32. Barbara Ward and René Dubos, 1972, *Only One Earth*, New York: WW Norton, 120.

33. See Garrett J. Hardin, 1972, *Exploring New Ethics for Survival: The Voyage of the Spaceship Beagle*, New York: Viking Press, 20, for such an observation.

34. A point commented on by Kimon Vlaskakis, Peter S. Sindell, J. Graham Smith, and Iris Fitzpatrick-Martin, 1979, *The Conserver Society: A Workable Alternative for the Future*, New York: Harper & Row, 15.

35. See the interview with Margaret Mead, 1974, in *On Growth*, edited by William L. Oltmans, New York: Capricorn Books, 21, for such an identified link between material and spiritual well-being.

36. An example of perceived ties between technology and maximization of material productivity may be found in Alan S. Kravitz, 1970, Mandarinism: Planning as the Handmaiden to Conservative Politics, in *Planning and Politics*, edited by Thad Beyel and George Lathrop, New York: Odyssey Press, 266-7.

37. From the interview with Edward Goldsmith in Oltmans, *On Growth*, 174.

38. See E. F. Schumacher, 1973, *Small is Beautiful: Economics as if People Mattered*, New York: Harper & Row, 23, for reference to historically assumed ties between economic growth and the preservation of world peace.

39. John Kenneth Galbraith, 1958, *The Affluent Society*, New York: Mentor Books, 157.

40. Lewis, Is Economic Development Desirable?, 18.

41. Ibid., 19.

42. Ibid., 20.

43. Herman E. Daly, 1973, makes a similar point in The Steady-State Economy: Toward a Political Economy of Biophysical Equilibrium and Moral Growth, in *Toward a Steady-State Economy*, edited by Herman E. Daly, San Francisco: W. H. Freeman and Company, 151.

44. For references to such an attribute of economic growth see Daly, ibid, 167; Harvey Brooks, 1973, The Technology of Zero Growth, *Daedalus: The No-Growth Society* 102,4: 149; and Anthony J. Wiener, 1978, Growth as Ideology, *Society* (January/February), 50.

45. See the interviews with Carl Kaysen, 69, and Leonard M. Ross/Peter Passell, 95, in Oltmans, *On Growth*, for expressions of such an assumed relationship between economic growth and reduced prospects for poverty, and Richard P. Applebaum, 1976, City Size and Urban Life: A Preliminary Inquiry into Some Consequences of Growth in American Cities, *Urban Affairs Quarterly* (December), 140, for mention of economic growth being linked to prospects for eliminating poverty.

46. See Daniel Bell, 1978, Mediating Growth Tensions, *Society* (January/February), 35.

47. Treatment of such arguments may be found in Marc J. Roberts, 1973, On Reforming Economic Growth, *Daedalus: The No-Growth Society* 102,4: 120, and in John P. Holdren, Population and the American Predicament: The Case Against Complacency, *Daedalus: The No-Growth Society* 102,4: 32.

48. See Wiener, Growth as Ideology, 50, for an example of the argument tying needed social expenditures to future economic growth, and Weisskopf, Economic Growth versus Existential Balance, 242, for reference to continued economic growth being rationalized on the grounds of defense needs.

49. For a classic statement of the argument that pollution is more likely to be reduced in a growing economy see Beckerman, Two Cheers for Economic Growth, 97.

50. For expression of the view that population growth has been equated with progress see chapter one of The Report of the Commission on Population Growth and the American Future, 1972, *Population and the American Future*, New York: Signet,

while illustration of the assumed link between economic growth and progress may be found in the introduction to Johnson and Hardesty, *Economic Growth vs. the Environment*, 1-5.

51. See the interview with Sir Julian S. Huxley in Oltmans, *On Growth*, 161. In the literature of economic development, such an association is felt to result from overpopulation of rural lands, thereby necessitating rural-urban migration, and because the industrial revolution in agriculture has reduced the need for population growth in the countryside.

52. See Herman Kahn and Anthony J. Wiener, 1967, *The Year 2000*, New York: McMillan.

53. Lewis Mumford, 1961, *The City in History*, New York: Harcourt, Brace, & World, 425.

54. For a typical expression of such a traditional view, see United Nations, 1970, *International Social Development Review*, No. 1, New York: United Nations, 72, and United Nations, 1970, *International Social Development Review*, No. 2, New York: United Nations, 16.

55. See Paul Sjoberg, 1966, International Development Strategies, *International Development Review* (September), 246.

56. United Nations, *International Social Development Review*, No. 1, 72.

57. Ibid., 71, 85; United Nations, *International Social Development Review*, No. 2, 15, 17; Tarlok Singh, 1962, Problems of Integrating Rural, Industrial, and Urban Development, in *India's Urban Future*, edited by Roy Turner, Los Angeles, California: University of California Press, 327; Gerald Breese, 1966, *Urbanization in Newly Developing Countries*, Englewood Cliffs, New Jersey: Prentice-Hall, 143.

58. United Nations, 1971, *Planning for Urban and Regional Development in Asia and the Far East*, New York: United Nations, 22.

59. United Nations, *International Social Development Review*, No. 1, 79.

60. G. M. Desmond, 1973, The Impact of National Development Policies on Urbanization: South and South-East Asia, *Urbanization Policy Planning Essays*, Urban Planning/Development Series, No. 11, Seattle, Washington: University of Washington (November), 17.

61. A bias evident in Albert O. Hirschman, 1958, *The Strategy of Economic Development*, New Haven, Connecticut: Yale University Press, 53, and Lloyd Rodwin, 1970, *Nations and Cities: A Comparison of Strategies for Urban Growth*, Boston, Massachusetts: Houghton-Mifflin 26.

62. Sjoberg, International Development Strategies, 257-8.

63. See Niles M. Hansen, 1971, *Intermediate-Size Cities as Growth Centers*, New York: Praeger Publishers, 68; Hirschman, *The Strategy of Economic Development*, 183-4, 187; and Rodwin, *Nations and Cities*, 25, for expressions of such an acceptance.

64. Such spread effects include the growth-inducing impact of purchases and investments on the part of these growth centers in their outlying areas and their ability to increase marginal labor productivity and per capita consumption levels in outlying areas by their absorption of unemployment from those areas.

65. See John Friedmann, 1968, The Strategy of Deliberate Urbanization, *Journal of the American Institute of Planners* 34,6: 364-3, for elaboration of this view.

66. United Nations, *International Social Development Review*, No. 2, 14.

67. See Friedmann, The Strategy of Deliberate Urbanization, 364-3.

68. For illustration of the large city bias in development literature see Surinder K. Mehta, Some Demographic and Economic Correlates of Primate Cities, in *The City in Newly Developing Countries*, edited by Gerald Breese, Englewood Cliffs, New Jersey: Prentice-Hall, 299. For additional elaboration of the positive attributes of large urban places see John Hoselitz, 1953, Economic Development Policies, *Journal of Economics* (June), 195; Sjoberg, International Development Strategies, 258; United

Nations, *International Social Development Review*, No. 1, 72-3, 78; and Desmond, The Impact of National Development Policies on Urbanization: South and South-East Asia, 35.

69. United Nations, *International Social Development Review*, No. 1, 82.

70. See Sjoberg, International Development Strategies, 259, for such a claim.

71. Industrialization is believed to offer such impetus based on arguments of productivity (see Robert L. Heilbroner, 1963, *The Great Ascent: The Struggle for Economic Development In Our Time*, New York: Harper & Row, 39, 70, 81), assumed superiority of linkage effects (see Albert O. Hirshman, 1958, *The Strategy of Economic Development*, New Haven, Connecticut: Yale University Press, 109-10), and the promise of relatively direct, quick, and predictable payoffs in additional output (see John P. Lewis, 1964, *Quiet Crisis in India*, Garden City, New Jersey: Doubleday, 89).

72. See Oswald Spengler, 1967, The Path to Economic Development, *International Development Review* (September), 60.

73. For examples of publications from that period that were offering counter arguments to many of the traditional supportive rationales for ongoing growth see the compiled articles in the fall issue of the 1973 *Daedalus* journal titled The No-Growth Society, and the articles in the 1978 January/February issue of *Society*. A detailed presentation of supportive rationales and their counter arguments appears in an unpublished doctoral dissertation, Gabor M. Zovanyi, 1981, *Toward a No-Growth Urban Planning Philosophy*, Department of Urban Planning, Seattle, Washington: University of Washington, 85-229.

74. See The Report of the Commission on Population Growth and the American Future, *Population and the American Future*, 48.

75. See Donella H. Meadows, Dennis L. Meadows, Jorgen Randers, and William W. Behrens, III, 1972, *The Limits to Growth*, New York: Signet, 183.

76. Robrt L. Heilbroner, 1974, *An Inquiry into the Human Prospect*, New York: WW Norton, 17.

77. For examples of works from that period attributing environmental problems to growth see Ehrlich and Ehrlich, *Population, Resources, and Environment*, 117-151, and Report of the Study of Critical Environmental Problems, 1970, *Man's Impact on the Global Environment*, Cambridge, Massachusetts: MIT Press.

78. Heilbroner, *An Inquiry into the Human Prospect*, 47.

79. Meadows, *The Limits to Growth*.

80. For reference to human ingenuity negating limits to growth see Lewis, Is Economic Development Desirable?, 20-1, and Harold J. Barnett and Chandler Morse, 1971, Scarcity and Growth: The Economics of Natural Resource Availability, in Johnson and Hardesty, *Economic Growth vs. the Environment*, 162. For examples of faith in the market-price system to permit an expansion of limits and a corresponding furtherance of growth see S. Fred Singer, 1978, The Price System as a Control of Growth, 44, and Daniel Bell, 1978, Mediating Growth Tensions, 36, in *Society*. Faith in the role technology might play in making continued growth possible is illustrated by Kenneth D. Wilson, 1978, Forecasting Futures, 25, in the same issue of *Society*, and a classic statement of such reasoning is provided by William Ophuls, 1974, The Scarcity Society, *Harper's Magazine* (April), 48.

81. See the interviews with Edward Teller and Herman Kahn in Oltmans, *On Growth*, 325, 414.

82. See, for example, Edward Goldsmith, Robert Allen, Michael Allaby, John Davoll, and Sam Lawrence, 1974, *Blueprint for Survival*, New York: Signet.

83. From the dust jacket to Oltman's, *On Growth*. An interview with Aurelio Peccei in the same work refers to "a debate of truly transnational and transideological character, which has spread like wildfire," 475.

84. Examples of such illustrations of population doubling times appear in Ehrlich and Ehrlich, *Population, Resources, and Environment*, 6-7, and Bernard Berelson, 1974, *World Population: Status Report 1974*, Reports on Population/Family Planning, No. 15, New York: The Population Council.

85. See Ansley J. Coale, 1974, The History of the Human Population, *Scientific American* 231,3: 46.

86. See The Report of the Commission on Population Growth and the American Future, *Population and the American Future*, 9, and Goldsmith, *Blueprint for Survival*, 3.

87. The classic rejection of population growth during this period appears in Paul R. Ehrlich, 1968, *The Population Bomb*, New York: Ballantine. For a rejection of the merit of continued population growth in the American context see The Report of the Commission on Population Growth and the American Future, *Population and the American Future*.

88. Ibid., 1.

89. Ibid., 13, 200.

90. Ibid., 19-1.

91. Meadows, *The Limits to Growth*, 45-1.

92. Ibid., 45.

93. Such a 1000-fold increase associated with 10 doublings is illustrated by the simple example of the following number sequence: 1, 2, 4, 8, 16, 32, 64, 128, 256, 512, 1024.

94. Reference to such car to people ratios appears in Marcia D. Lowe, 1994, Reinventing Transport, in Lester R. Brown, Alan Durning, Christopher Flavin, Hilary French, Nicholas Lenssen, Marcia Lowe, Ann Misch, Sandra Postel, Michael Renner, Linda Starke, Peter Weber, and John Young, 1994, *State of the World*, Worldwatch Institute, New York: WW Norton, 82. The production and registration figures for motor vehicles in general, and passenger cars in particular, are from Motor Vehicle Manufacturers Association of the United States, Inc., *Facts & Figures*, Detroit, Michigan, with most of the data coming from 1982 and 1992 editions containing comparative figures.

95. See Michael Renner, 1988, *Rethinking the Role of the Automobile*, Worldwatch Paper 84, Washington, D.C.: World Watch Institute, Figure 2, 20.

96. The Report of the Commission on Population Growth and the American Future, *Population and the American Future*, 45-3.

97. See E. J. Mishan, 1967, *The Costs of Economic Growth*, New York: Praeger; Schumacher, *Small is Beautiful*; and Daly, *Toward a Steady-State Economy*.

98. Herman E. Daly, 1973, Introduction: Biophysical Constraints on Economic Growth, in *Toward a Steady-State Economy*, 33.

99. Herman E. Daly, 1973, The Steady-State Economy: Toward a Political Economy of Biophysical Equilibrium and Moral Growth, *Toward a Steady-State Economy*, 149.

100. For a figure illustrating these changes in patterns of urbanization within this century see G. Tyler Miller, Jr., 1991, *Environmental Science: Sustaining the Earth*, Belmont, California: Wadsworth, 125.

101. For acknowledgment of such a fact see Berelson, *World Population*, 13.

102. Council on Environmental Quality and the Department of State, 1982, *The Global 2000 Report to the President: Entering the Twenty-First Century*, Great Britain: Penguin Books, 407.

103. The figures are taken from tables appearing in Barclay G. Jones and William F. Shepard, 1987, Cities of the Future: Implications for the Rise and Relative Decline of the Cities of the West, *Journal of Planning Education and Research* 6,3: 162-6.

104. See, for example, the reference to such urban increases as "one of the more sobering implications of current population trends" in Berelson, *World Population*, 15.

105. Thomas R. Detwyler, and Melvin G. Marcus, 1972, *Urbanization and Environment*, Belmont, California: Duxbury, vii; for another expression of the view that the city represents our species' greatest impact on nature see G. Tyler Miller, Jr., 1975, *Living in the Environment: Concepts, Problems, and Alternatives*, Belmont, California: Wadsworth, 179.

106. See, for example, Garrett Hardin, 1974, Lifeboat Ethics: The Case Against Helping the Poor, *Psychology Today* 8,4: 124. Similar sentiments appeared in Paul R. Ehrlich and John P. Holdren, 1971, Impact of Population Growth, *Science* 171(March): 1212-17, and Lester Brown, 1974, *In the Human Interest: A Strategy to Stabilize World Population*, New York: WW Norton, 13.

107. Daly, The Steady-State Economy: Toward a Political Economy of Biophysical Equilibrium and Moral Growth, 152.

108. The original formulation appeared in Ehrlich and Holdren, Impact of Population Growth.

109. See Miller, *Environmental Science: Sustaining the Earth*, 3.

110. N. Keyfitz, 1989, The Growing Human Population, *Scientific American*, 261,7: 119-26.

111. Lester R. Brown and Hal Kane, 1994, *Full House: Reassessing the Earth's Population Carrying Capacity*, New York: WW Norton, 49.

112. *New York Times*, Oct. 20, 1985. Excerpts from the statement appear in Ehrlich and Ehrlich, 1990, *The Population Explosion*, 191-2.

113. World Commission on Environment and Development, 1987, *Our Common Future*, Oxford: Oxford University Press, 95.

114. Ehrlich and Ehrlich, *The Population Explosion*, 23.

115. Such figures appear in Brown and Kane, *Full House*, 59.

116. See Ehrlich and Ehrlich, *Healing the Planet*, 41; Ehrlich is quoted in Miller, *Environmental Science*, 5, as claiming that a baby born in the United States will damage the planet 20 to 100 times more in a lifetime than a baby born into a poor family in a less developed country, and that a rich person in the United States would do 1,000 times more damage.

117. Ehrlich and Ehrlich, *Healing the Planet*, xi.

118. Brown and Kane, *Full House*, 59.

119. Meadows, *Beyond the Limits*, 37.

120. Ibid., Figure 1-2, 5.

121. Ibid., 2.

122. The figures are from Motor Vehicle Manufacturers Association of the United States, Inc., *Facts & Figures*, Detroit, Michigan, with most of the data coming from 1982 and 1992 editions containing comparative figures.

123. Renner, *Rethinking the Role of the Automobile*, 20.

124. A Report by the World Resources Institute, *World Resources 1994-95*, Oxford: Oxford University Press, 31.

125. Ibid.

126. Ibid.

127. Council on Environmental Quality and the Department of State, *The Global 2000 Report to the President*, 407.

128. The Population Institute, 1987, *Global Population: Gaining People, Losing Ground*, Institute Pamphlet, Washington, D.C.

129. Department of International Economic and Social Affairs, 1989, *Prospects of World Urbanization, 1988*, New York: United Nations, Table A-9, 76.

130. The noted figures are again taken from tables appearing in Jones and Shepard, Cities of the Future, 162-6.

131. See, for example, Lester R. Brown and Jodi L. Jacobson, 1987, *The Future of Urbanization: Facing the Ecological and Economic Constraints*, Worldwatch Paper 77, Washington, D.C.: Worldwatch Institute, 6.

132. See, for example, Warren M. Hern, 1990, Why Are There So Many of Us? Description and Diagnosis of a Planetary Ecopathological Process, *Population and Environment: A Journal of Interdisciplinary Studies* 12,1: 9-39.

133. Ehrlich and Ehrlich, *Healing the Planet*, 245.

134. Meadows, *The Limits to Growth*, placed the limits to growth within a century of the publication of that work, while Goldsmith, *Blueprint for Survival*, placed the limits within the lifetimes of the children alive at the time of that publication.

135. Lester R. Brown, 1981, *Building a Sustainable Society*, New York: WW Norton, 6.

136. Ehrlich and Ehrlich, *The Population Explosion*, 38-9.

137. Ehrlich and Ehrlich, *Healing the Planet*, 6-7.

138. Ibid., 35.

139. Ehrlich and Ehrlich, *The Population Explosion*, 23.

140. Ehrlich and Ehrlich, *Healing the Planet*, 249.

141. Meadows, *Beyond the Limits*, 7-8, 44-103.

142. Ibid., xv.

143. Ibid., 206.

144. Ibid., 210.

145. A population figure of 8 billion is surprisingly close to the U.N. medium population projection of the early 1990s, showing world population reaching 8.9 billion by 2030 and leveling off at 11.5 billion around 2150. See Sandra Postel, 1994, Carrying Capacity: Earth's Bottom Line, in Brown, *State of the World 1994*, 7, for reference to such projections and a source citation to a private communication as the origin of the figures.

146. Ibid., 3.

147. Ibid., 11.

148. Brown and Kane, *Full House*, 211.

149. Ibid., 22-3.

150. Ibid., 65, 95.

151. Ibid., 22.

152. Ibid., 203.

153. Ehrlich and Ehrlich, *Healing the Planet*, 4.

154. Ibid., 131.

155. The Ehrlich's treatment of the planet's life-support systems may be found throughout their book *The Population Explosion*, and in a focused form in a chapter within their more recent book *Healing the Planet*, Chapter One, Our Life-Support Systems, 15-37.

156. Ehrlich and Ehrlich,*The Population Explosion*, 57.

157. Ibid., 134.

158. Peter M. Vitousek, Paul R. Ehrlich, Anne H. Ehrlich, and Pamela A. Matson, 1986, Human Appropriation of the Products of Photosynthesis, *BioScience* 36,6: 368-73.

159. See Ehrlich and Ehrlich, *Healing the Planet*, 150-1, for the figures and source citations regarding the percentages of the Earth's surface used by humanity.

160. Figures cited by Ehrlich and Ehrlich, 151.

161. Ibid., 34.

162. Ibid., 91; Ehrlich and Ehrlich, *The Population Explosion*, 31.

163. Ehrlich and Ehrlich, *Healing the Planet*, 91.

164. Ehrlich and Ehrlich, *Extinction*, 6.

165. See Edward O. Wilson, 1989, Threats to Biodiversity, *Scientific American*, 261,3: 108-6, and Ehrlich and Ehrlich, *Healing the Planet*, 33.

166. Meadows, *Beyond the Limits*, 64.

167. See Table 6-2 in Ariel E. Lugo, 1988, Estimating Reductions in the Diversity of Tropical Forest Species in *Biodiversity*, edited by Edward O. Wilson and Francis M. Peter, Washington D.C.: National Academy Press, 64, and Ehrlich and Ehrlich, *Healing the Planet*, 163-4.

168. Ibid., 34.

169. The term is attributed to Jasper Carlton, a member of Earth First!, by Manes *Green Rage*, 26.

170. Ibid., 243.

171. Reference to such a claim in a 1987 document titled Technologies to Maintain Biological Diversity, published by the Office of Technology Assessment, appears in Suzanne Winckler, 1992, Stopgap Measures, *The Atlantic* 269,1: 78.

172. Brown and Kane, *Full House*, 80.

173. Paul Koberstein, 1994, Dammed Salmon, *Willamette Week* 20,10: 14.

174. F. Talbot, 1990, Earth, Humankind, and Our Responsibility, Plenary Address to the American Association of Museums (mimeograph), noted in Ehrlich and Ehrlich, *Healing the Planet*, 32.

175. Les Line, 1993, Silence of the Songbirds, *National Geographic* 183,6: 68-91.

176. A similar estimate by Peter Hoch, of the Missouri Botanical Garden, is noted in Charles C. Mann and Mark L. Plummer, 1992, The Butterfly Problem, *The Atlantic* 269,1: 50.

177. Ehrlich and Ehrlich, *Healing the Planet*, 37.

178. Paul R. Ehrlich and Harold A. Mooney, 1983, Extinction, Substitution, and Ecosystem Services, *BioScience* 33,4: 248-4.

2 THE EVOLUTION OF THE GROWTH MANAGEMENT MOVEMENT IN THE UNITED STATES

1. Randall W. Scott, 1975, Management and Control of Growth: An Introduction and Summary, in *Management and Control of Growth: Issues, Techniques, Problems, and Trends*, Vol. I, edited by Randall W. Scott, David J. Brower, and Dallas D. Miner, Washington, D.C.: The Urban Land Institute, 2.

2. Willian K. Reilly, editor, 1973, *The Use of Land: A Citizens' Policy Guide to Urban Growth*, A Task Force Report sponsored by the Rockefeller Brothers, New York: Thomas Y. Crowell Company.

3. Council on Environmental Quality, 1974, Memorandum for CEQ Correspondents, (mimeographed, July 31).

4. Elizabeth G. Patterson, 1975, Municipal Self-Determination: Must Local Control of Growth Yield to Travel Rights?, *Arizona Law Review* 17,1: 145-6.

5. Ibid., 145.

6. For a sample reference to the existence of a growth management movement by the 1970s see David R. Godschalk, David J. Brower, Larry D. McBennett, and Barbara A. Vestal, 1977, *Constitutional Issues of Growth Management*, Chicago: The ASPO Press, 7.

7. A statement of what would become the growth management movement's attitude toward growth is aptly illustrated by the title of the Report of the National Goals Research Staff, 1970, *Toward Balanced Growth: Quantity with Quality*, Superintendent of Documents, Washington, D.C. : U.S.G.P.O.

8. For reference to the growth management movement as a phenomenon of the late 1960s and subsequent decades see Dennis E. Gale and Suzanne Hart, 1992, Public Support for Local Comprehensive Planning Under Statewide Growth Management: Insights From Maine, *Journal of Planning Education and Research* 11,3: 192.

9. See Eric D. Kelly, 1993, *Managing Community Growth: Policies, Techniques, and Impacts*, Westport, Connecticut: Praeger, 7.

10. Benjamin Chinitz, 1990, Growth Management: Good for the Town, Bad for the Nation?, *American Planning Association Journal* 56,1: 5-6.

11. Eugenie L. Birch, 1993, Stop the World . . . and Look What Planners Can Do!, *American Planning Association Journal* 59,4: 414.

12. See Kelly, 1993, *Managing Community Growth*, 16-9, for an overview of the development of subdivision regulations.

13. Excerpted from a book review by Anthony J. Catanese, 1977, Land Use and the States, *American Institute of Planners Journal* 43,1: 96.

14. J. Barry Cullingworth, 1993, *The Political Culture of Planning*, New York: Routledge, 245.

15. Scott, Management and Control of Growth, 23.

16. For a listing of such typical growth management objectives see Katherine E. Stone and Robert H. Freilich, 1991, Writing a Defensible Growth Ordinance, in *Balanced Growth: A Planning Guide for Local Government*, edited by John M. De-Grove and Patricia M. Metzger, Washington, D.C.: International City Management Association, 106.

17. See Douglas R. Porter, editor, 1986, Forward, in *Growth Management: Keeping on Target?*, Washington, D.C.: Urban Land Institute, 1, for reference to the term and concept being popularized during the 1970s.

18. Donald E. Priest, 1975, Epilogue: Managed Growth and the Future of City Building, in *Management and Control of Growth*, Vol III, edited by Scott, Brower, and Miner, 537.

19. See Paul L. Niebanck, 1984, Dilemmas in Growth Management, *Journal of the American Planning Association* 50,4: 403.

20. John M. Levy, 1994, *Contemporary Urban Planning*, Englewood Cliffs, New Jersey: Prentice Hall, 224-5.

21. See ibid., 224, and Lawrence B. Burrows, 1978, *Growth Management: Issues, Techniques, and Policy Implications*, New Brunswick, New Jersey: The Center for Urban Policy Research, Rutgers University, 13.

22. See Robert W. Burchell and James W. Hughes, 1974, Issues in Planned Unit Development, in *New Dimensions in Urban Planning: Growth Controls*, edited by James W. Hughes, New Brunswick, New Jersey: The Center for Urban Policy Research, Rutgers University, 211; Levy, *Contemporary Urban Planning*, 225-6; and John M. DeGrove and Deborah A. Miness, 1992, *The New Frontier for Land Policy: Planning and Growth Management in the States*, Cambridge, Massachusetts: Lincoln Institute of Land Policy, 52.

23. The claim that "environmental concerns sparked much of the early development of growth management systems" appears in Douglas R. Porter, 1989, Significant Research Needs in the Policy and Practice of Growth Management, in *Under-*

standing Growth Management: Critical Issues and a Research Agenda, edited by David J. Brower, David R. Godschalk, and Douglas R. Porter, Washington, D.C.: The Urban Land Institute, 192.

24. Gale and Hart, Public Support for Local Comprehensive Planning, 192.

25. Levy, *Contemporary Urban Planning*, 226.

26. See ibid., 225, and Burchell and Hughes, Issues in Planned Unit Development, 211.

27. See Robert C. Einsweiler, Michael E. Gleeson, Ian Traquair Ball, Alan Morris, and Diane Sprague, 1975, Comparative Descriptions of Selected Municipal Growth Guidance Systems, in *Management and Control of Growth: Issues, Techniques, Problems, and Trends*, Vol. II, edited by Scott, Brower, and Miner, 290.

28. Robert C. Larson, 1975, Growth as a Metropolitan Issue, in *Management and Control of Growth*, Vol. III, edited by Scott, Brower, and Miner, 485.

29. John M. DeGrove, 1993, The Emergence of State Planning and Growth Management Systems: An Overview, in *State and Regional Comprehensive Planning: Implementing New Methods for Growth Management*, edited by Peter A. Buchsbaum and Larry J. Smith, Chicago: American Bar Association, 8.

30. DeGrove and Miness, *The New Frontier for Land Policy*, 1.

31. See Einsweiler, Comparative Descriptions of Selected Municipal Growth Guidance Systems, 294.

32. This distinction is treated in Kelly, *Managing Community Growth*, 19-1.

33. Ibid., 22-5.

34. For a description of urban growth boundaries as one component of a limited set of features associated with typical growth management programs see Kelly, ibid., 23-4.

35. Ibid., 23.

36. John D. Landis, 1992, Do Growth Controls Work? A New Assessment, *American Planning Association Journal* 58,4: 490-1.

37. Levy, *Contemporary Urban Planning*, 225.

38. Elizabeth Deakin, 1989, Growth Controls and Growth Management: A Survey and Review of Empirical Research, in *Understanding Growth Management*, edited by Brower, Godschalk, and Porter, 3.

39. Willian J. Toner, 1974, Introduction to Nongrowth Economics, in Earl Finkler and David L. Peterson, *Nongrowth Planning Strategies: The Developing Power of Towns, Cities, and Regions*, New York: Praeger, xviii.

40. Earl Finkler, 1972, *Nongrowth as a Planning Alternative: A Preliminary Examination of an Emerging Issue*, Planning Advisory Service Report No. 283, Chicago: American Society of Planning Officials, 6.

41. Reference to the report's conclusions regarding the inevitability of future growth in this country appears in Finkler, ibid., 29. The noted federal report was put out by the Advisory Commission on Intergovernmental Relations in 1968 under the title *Urban and Rural America: Policies for Future Growth*, Washington, D.C.: U.S. Government Printing Office.

42. Reilly, *The Use of Land*, 18.

43. William K. Reilly, 1975, Six Myths—About Land Use in the United States, in *Management and Control of Growth*, Vol. I, edited by Scott, Brower, and Miner, 101.

44. Steve Carter, Kendall Bert, and Peter Nobert, 1975, Local Government Techniques for Managing Growth, in *Management and Control of Growth*, Vol. II, edited by Scott, Brower, and Miner, 332.

45. Larson, Growth as a Metropolitan Issue, 485.

46. A decision to implement a social policy of limiting births to a single child per family in this country during the 1970s would, for example, have brought on an immediate cessation of population growth.

47. Niebanck, Dilemmas in Growth Management, 405.

48. Paul L. Niebanck, 1989, Growth Controls and the Production of Inequality, in *Understanding Growth Management*, edited by Brower, Godschalk, and Porter, 106.

49. Fred Bosselman, 1973, Can the Town of Ramapo Pass a Law to Bind the Rights of the Whole World?, *Florida State University Law Review* 1,3: 249.

50. See Elizabeth L. Hollander, Leslie S. Pollock, Jeffry D. Reckinger, and Frank Beal, 1988, General Development Plans, in *The Practice of Local Government Planning*, Second Edition, edited by Frank S. So and Judith Getzels, Washington, D.C.: International City Management Association, 69.

51. Robert C. Ellickson, 1977, Suburban Growth Controls: An Economic and Legal Analysis, *Yale Law Journal* 86,3: 385-511.

52. Bernard J. Frieden, 1979, *The Environmental Protection Hustle*, Cambridge, Massachusetts: MIT Press.

53. Source citations for works attributing such negative effects to growth controls appear in Thomas I. Miller, 1986, Must Growth Restrictions Eliminate Moderate-Priced Housing?, *American Planning Association Journal* 52,3: 319, and in Deakin, Growth Controls and Growth Management: A Survey and Review of Empirical Research, 6.

54. See William A. Fischel, 1991, Good for the Town, Bad for the Nation? A Comment, *American Planning Association Journal* 57,3: 341.

55. Miller, Must Growth Restrictions Eliminate Moderate-Priced Housing?, 319.

56. See, for example, Miller, ibid., and Deakin, Growth Controls and Growth Management: A Survey and Review of Empirical Research, 18.

57. Finkler, *Nongrowth as a Planning Alternative*, 4.

58. Ibid., 4.

59. Scott, Management and Control of Growth, 4.

60. Godschalk, Brower, McBennett, and Vestal, *Constitutional Issues of Growth Management*, 8.

61. Levy, *Contemporary Urban Planning*, 224.

62. DeGrove and Miness, *The New Frontier for Land Policy*, 1, 161.

63. Forster Ndubisi and Mary Dyer, 1992, The Role of Regional Entities in Formulating and Implementing Statewide Growth Policies, *State and Local Governmental Review* (Fall), 117.

64. See Cullingworth, *The Political Culture of Planning*, 9-14.

65. William Fulton, 1991, The Second Revolution in Land-Use Planning, in *Balanced Growth*, edited by DeGrove and Metzger, 118.

66. Cullingworth, *The Political Culture of Planning*, 10; for another statement of the fact that land-use control "take[s] place largely at the local government level" in the United States see Kelly, *Managing Community Growth*, 8.

67. Fred P. Bosselman, 1975, Town of Ramapo: Binding the World?, in *Management and Control of Growth*, Vol. II, edited by Scott, Brower, and Miner, 103.

68. Stone and Freilich, Writing a Defensible Growth Ordinance, 104.

69. Such nonregulatory techniques may include such components as public acquisitions of land, public improvements to influence growth, development rights transfer programs, and tax and fee systems. See Einsweiler, Comparative Descriptions of Selected Municipal Growth Guidance Systems, 290-9, and Michael E. Gleeson, Ian Traquair Ball, Stephen P. Chinn, Robert C. Einsweiler, Robert H. Freilich, and Patrick Meagher, 1975, *Urban Growth Management Systems*, Planning Advisory Service, Report Numbers 309 and 310, Chicago, Illinois: American Society of Planning Officials for a description of such nonregulatory techniques.

70. Priest, Epilogue: Managed Growth and the Future of City Building, 538.

71. David Dubbink, 1984, I'll Have My Town Medium-Rural, Please, *American Planning Association Journal* 50,4: 406.

72. See Gale and Hart, Public Support for Local Comprehensive Planning Under Statewide Growth Management, 192.

73. Deakin, Growth Controls and Growth Management, 4.

74. See Kelly, *Managing Community Growth*, 28, for reference to this early attempt to control the rate of growth within a community.

75. Ibid., 27-9; Finkler and Peterson, *Nongrowth Planning Strategies*, 22, describe the Clarkstown management ordinance as a "development scheduling ordinance."

76. See David Callies, 1980, The Quiet Revolution Revisited, *American Planning Association Journal* 46,2: 138, for reference to court rulings upholding the Ramapo and Petaluma rate control ordinances and the subsequent proliferation of similar growth management ordinances.

77. Thomas C. O'Keefe, 1975, Time Controls on Land Use: Prophylactic Law for Planners, in *Management and Control of Growth,* Vol. II, edited by Scott, Brower, and Miner, 66.

78. See Israel Stollman, 1975, Ramapo: An Editorial & the Ordinance as Amended, in *Management and Control of Growth*, Vol. II, edited by Scott, Brower, and Miner, 10, for excerpts from the ordinance referring to the intent of providing facilities and services to *all* land in the town so as to make all properties capable of being developed in accordance with proper planning.

79. Finkler and Peterson, *Nongrowth Planning Strategies*, 20.

80. *Golden* v. *Planning Board of the Town of Ramapo*, 285 N.E.2d at 302 (1972).

81. 409 U.S. 1003 (1972).

82. O'Keefe, Time Controls on Land Use, 67.

83. See Seymour I. Schwartz, David E. Hansen, and Richard Green, 1986, The Effect of Growth Control on the Production of Moderate-Priced Housing, in *Growth Management: Keeping on Target?*, edited by Porter, 16, for reference to the degree to which the rate control system slowed down the issuance of building permits.

84. *Construction Industry Ass'n of Sonoma County* v. *City of Petaluma*, 375 F. Supp. 574 (1974).

85. *Construction Industry Ass'n of Sonoma County* v. *City of Petaluma*, 522 F.2d 897 (1975).

86. Finkler and Peterson, *Nongrowth Planning Strategies*, 21.

87. Ibid., 21.

88. See Paul D. Danish, 1986, Boulder's Self-Examination, in *Growth Management: Keeping on Target?*, edited by Porter, 27, for a description of an attempt via the initiative to force the elected officials of Boulder to set a cap on the city's future growth.

89. See Finkler and Peterson, *Nongrowth Planning Strategies*, 22.

90. See Danish, Boulder's Self-Examination, 27.

91. See ECO Northwest, Inc., 1986, Growth Management Study of Boca Raton, in *Growth Management: Keeping on Target?*, edited by Porter, 57-8.

92. *City of Boca Raton* v. *Boca Villas Corporation*, 371 So.2d 154 (Fla.Ct.App.1979).

93. See Levy, *Contemporary Urban Planning*, 236.

94. See "Sanibel Island: A Paradise Lost and Saved," in Richard F. Babcock and Charles L. Siemon, 1985, *The Zoning Game Revisited*, Boston, Massachusetts: Oelgeschlager, Gunn & Hain, 94-118, and David L. Callies, Robert H. Freilich, and Thomas E. Roberts, 1994, *Cases and Material on Land Use*, Second Edition, St. Paul, Minnesota: West Publishing, 608. It is of interest to note that the cap on dwelling units reduced the allowable number from some 35,000 units to the noted 6,000.

95. Ivonne Audirac, Anne H. Shermyen, and Marc T. Smith, 1990, Ideal Urban Form and Visions of the Good Life: Florida's Growth Management Dilemma, *American Planning Association Journal* 56,4: 473.

96. Norman L. Christeller, 1986, Wrestling with Growth in *Growth Management: Keeping on Target?*, edited by Porter, 82-3.

97. Michael J. Stepner, 1986, San Diego's System: Is It Working?, in *Growth Management: Keeping on Target?*, Porter, 65.

98. Madelyn Glickfeld and Ned Levine, 1991, *Growth Controls: Regional Problems—Local Responses*, Cambridge, Massachusetts: Lincoln Institute of Land Policy. A table summarizing the distribution of growth control versus growth management measures adopted by cities and counties in California drawn from the work by Glickfeld and Levine appears in Landis, Do Growth Controls Work? A New Assessment, 491.

99. William Alonso, 1975, Urban Zero Population Growth, in *Management and Control of Growth*, Vol. I, edited by Scott, Brower, and Miner, 408.

100. Francis H. Parker, 1975, Regional Imperatives & Managed Growth, in *Management and Control of Growth*, Vol. III, edited by Scott, Brower, and Miner, 284.

101. Cullingworth, *The Political Culture of Planning*, 132.

102. Landis, Do Growth Controls Work? A New Assessment, 502.

103. Priest, Epilogue: Managed Growth and the Future of City Building, 542.

104. Christeller, Wrestling with Growth, 84.

105. In 1973 the U.S. House of Representatives considered land-use policy legislation in the form of the Land Use Policy and Planning Assistance Act (S. 268), which had previously passed the Senate. That legislation was seen by its Senate sponsors "as the framework for developing a national growth policy," but its defeat by the house left the United States without such a policy. See Norman Beckman, 1974, National Urban Growth Policy: 1973 Congressional and Executive Action, *Journal of the American Institute of Planners* 40,4: 235-6.

106. See The Pinelands: A Radical Experiment Works, in Babcock and Siemon, *The Zoning Game Revisited*, 135-57, for an example of such a regional growth management effort being directed at the redistribution of ongoing growth to supposedly suitable sites.

107. The noted citation comes from two Canadians, Michael I. Jeffery and Michael B. Vaughan, 1993, Toward Environmentally Sound Planning and Development in Ontario, in *State and Regional Comprehensive Planning*, edited by Buchsbaum and Smith, 200.

108. For one source of such a claim see the book review by David Johnson, 1977, Land: State Alternatives for Planning and Management, *Journal of the American Institute of Planners* 43,1: 96-7.

109. Accounts of the Hawaiian experience may be found in Fred Bosselman and David Callies, 1971, *The Quiet Revolution in Land Use Control*, Washington, D.C.: Government Printing Office, and in John M. DeGrove, 1984, *Land, Growth, and Politics*, Chicago, Illinois: American Planning Association Press.

110. John M. DeGrove, 1989, Growth Management and Governance, in *Understanding Growth Management*, edited by Brower, Godschalk, and Porter, 23.

111. John M. DeGrove and Nancy E. Stroud, 1987, State Land Planning and Regulation: Innovative Roles in the 1980s and Beyond, *Land Use Law* 39,3: 3.

112. For a discussion of the relationship between states and local governments concerning the matter of the power to regulate land see excerpts from a Council of State Governments report titled The Dominant Issues in State Growth Management, in *Management & Control of Growth*, Vol. IV, edited by Frank Schnidman, Jane A. Silverman, and Rufus C. Young, 1978, Washington, D.C.: The Urban Land Institute, 255.

113. Bosselman and Callies, *The Quiet Revolution in Land Use Control*, 1.

114. Ibid., 1.

115. A description of these statewide growth management laws appears in DeGrove and Miness, *The New Frontier for Land Policy*.

116. DeGrove, Growth Management and Governance, 31.

117. Deborah A. Howe, 1991, Review of Growth Management Strategies Used in Other States, Report prepared for the Oregon Department of Land Conservation and Development, Salem, Oregon, 1.

118. Fulton, The Second Revolution in Land-Use Planning, 116.

119. DeGrove and Stroud, State Land Planning and Regulation, 8.

120. Fulton, The Second Revolution in Land-Use Planning, 117.

121. Descriptions of the Washington and Maryland laws appear in DeGrove and Miness, *The New Frontier for Land Policy*, 117-35, 169-70.

122. See Patricia E. Salkin, 1993, Statewide Comprehensive Planning: The Next Wave, in *State and Regional Comprehensive Planning,* edited by Buchsbaum and Smith, 238; DeGrove, Growth Management and Governance, 32; and Sylvia Lewis, 1992, Goodbye, Ramapo. Hello, Yakima and Isle of Palms, *Planning* 58,7: 9-16.

123. Peter A. Buchsbaum and Larry J. Smith, 1993, Introduction, in *State and Regional Comprehensive Planning*, edited by Buchsbaum and Smith, xi.

124. DeGrove and Miness, *The New Frontier for Land Policy*, 170.

125. Bosselman and Callies, *The Quiet Revolution in Land Use Control*, 3.

126. DeGrove, Growth Management and Governance, 23.

127. DeGrove and Miness, *The New Frontier for Land Policy*, 2.

128. Ibid., 2-4.

129. Scott A. Bollens, 1992, State Growth Management: Intergovernmental Framework and Policy Objectives, *American Planning Association Journal* 58,4: 455.

130. David R. Godschalk, 1975, State Growth Management: A Carrying Capacity Approach, in *Management and Control of Growth*, Vol. III, edited by Scott, Brower, and Miner, 328.

131. H. Milton Patton and Janet W. Patton, 1975, Harbingers of State Growth Policies, in *Management and Control of Growth*, Vol. III, edited by Scott, Brower, and Miner, 318.

132. For the results of that survey showing that moratoria represented the most frequently used growth control mechanism by the latter 1970s see Burrows, *Growth Management*, 5-9.

133. DeGrove, The Emergence of State Planning and Growth Management Systems: An Overview, 11.

134. DeGrove and Miness, *The New Frontier for Land Policy*, 100.

135. See DeGrove, The Emergence of State Planning and Growth Management Systems, 11, note 22.

136. Larry J. Smith, 1993, Planning for Growth, Washington Style, in *State and Regional Comprehensive Planning*, edited by Buchsbaum and Smith, 138.

137. DeGrove and Miness, *The New Frontier for Land Policy*, 29.

138. Finkler and Peterson, *Nongrowth Planning Strategies*, 83.

139. The noted citation is from Gerrit J. Knaap, 1987, Self-Interest and Voter Support for Oregon's Land Use Controls, *American Planning Association Journal* 53,1: 92, who summarizes such a conclusion on the part of Richard A. Walker and Michael K. Heiman, 1981, Quiet Revolution for Whom?, *Annals of the Association of American Geographers* 71: 68-83.

140. See Bollens, State Growth Management, 459-62, for summary descriptions of how Vermont, Florida, Oregon, and New Jersey have attempted to "incorporate growth-accommodating initiatives into their growth management strategies," 459.

141. Thomas G. Pelham, 1993, The Florida Experience: Creating a State, Regional, and Local Comprehensive Planning Process, in *State and Regional Comprehensive Planning*, edited by Buchsbaum and Smith, 100, 102.

142. See Thomas R. Melloni and Robert I. Goetz, 1993, Planning in Vermont, in *State and Regional Comprehensive Planning*, edited by Buchsbaum and Smith, 169.

143. A point noted in DeGrove and Miness, *The New Frontier for Land Policy*, 120.

144. H. Jeffrey Leonard, 1983, *Managing Oregon's Growth: The Politics of Development Planning*, Washington, D.C.: The Conservation Foundation, 4.

145. See such a reference to the Hawaiian statute in Bosselman and Callies, *The Quiet Revolution in Land Use Control*, 36, note 14.

146. Act 250, Chapter 151, Subchapter 3, Section 6042, 150.

147. Florida's 1985 Local Government Comprehensive Planning and Land Development Act, Chapter 163, Section 3177(6)(a), 949.

148. Oregon's Statewide Planning Goals, Land Conservation and Development Commission, Goal 14: Urbanization, 12.

149. State Planning Act of 1985, 52:18A-200(d), 15.

150. Comprehensive Planning and Land Use Regulation Act of 1988, Sections 4960(C)4C(1)(a) and 4960(C)4C(2), 15-6.

151. Rhode Island Comprehensive Planning and Land Use Act of 1988, Section 45-22.2-3(B)5, 3.

152. Georgia Planning Act of 1989, Section 2.1, 50-8-3(a)(5), 4.

153. Engrossed Substitute House Bill No. 2929 of 1990, Section 13(3), 14.

154. Maryland's Economic Growth, Resource Protection, and Planning Act of 1992, Section 1, Article 66B, 3.05(a)(1)(vi)(3), 5.

155. DeGrove and Miness, *The New Frontier for Land Policy*, 1.

156. Bollens, State Growth Management, 454.

157. Dennis E. Gale, 1992, Eight State-Sponsored Growth Management Programs: A Comparative Analysis, *American Planning Association Journal* 58,4: 425.

158. See Porter, *Growth Management*, for descriptions of some of these local programs that were developed without statewide management laws to direct them.

159. Bollens, State Growth Management, 458.

160. See DeGrove, Growth Management and Governance, 32, and DeGrove and Stroud, State Land Planning and Regulation, 4.

161. Burrows, *Growth Management*, 4.

162. Porter, Afterword, Growth Management: Keeping on Target, *Growth Management: Keeping on Target?*, 218.

163. DeGrove, Introduction, in *Balanced Growth*, edited by DeGrove and Metzger, xiii.

164. Stone and Freilich, Writing a Defensible Growth Ordinance, 104.

165. DeGrove and Miness, *The New Frontier for Land Policy*, 1.

166. Levy, *Contemporary Urban Planning*, 239.

167. Cullingworth, *The Political Culture of Planning*, 241.

168. See Bollens, State Growth Management, 454.

169. DeGrove, Introduction, in *Balanced Growth*, edited by DeGrove and Metzger, xiii.

170. DeGrove, Introduction, DeGrove and Miness, *The New Frontier for Land Policy*, 5.

171. Robert W. Burchell, 1993, Issues, Actors, and Analyses in Statewide Comprehensive Planning, in *State and Regional Comprehensive Planning*, edited by Buchsbaum and Smith, 34.

3 THE ROLE OF THE PLANNING PROFESSION IN GROWTH MANAGEMENT

1. Earl Finkler, 1972, *Nongrowth as a Planning Alternative: A Preliminary Examination of an Emerging Issue*, Planning Advisory Service Report No. 283, Chicago: American Society of Planning Officials, 7.

2. A statement attributed to the economist Kenneth E. Boulding and quoted by Lewis Grant, 1988, Too Many Old People or Too Many Americans? Thoughts About the Pension Panic, *NPG Forum* (July).

3. Arthur W. Lewis, 1971, Ecology and Politics, *New York Times*, March 6, 31.

4. G. Clay, 1973, No Growth: Hot Property or a Hot Potato?, *Landscape Architecture* 63,4: 332.

5. Laurence C. Gerkins, 1988, Historical Development of American City Planning, in *The Practice of Local Government Planning*, edited by Frank S. So and Judith Getzels, Washington, D.C.: International City Management Association, 20.

6. Ibid., 21.

7. Herbert J. Gans, 1968, City Planning in America: A Sociological Analysis, in *People and Plans: Essays on Urban Problems and Solutions*, edited by Herbert J. Gans, New York: Basic Books, 57.

8. See the listing of fifty "firsts" in modern American city planning in Gerkins, Historical Development of American City Planning, 24-5.

9. Gans, City Planning in America, 58.

10. See ibid., 57-9; John Hancock, 1967, Planners in the Changing American City, 1900-1940, *Journal of the American Institute of Planners* 33,5: 292; and Alan S. Kravitz, 1970, Mandarinism: Planning as the Handmaiden to Conservative Politics, in *Planning and Politics*, edited by Thad L. Beyel and Goerge T. Lathrop, New York: Odyssey Press, 243-4.

11. See Doris B. Holleb, 1969, *Social and Economic Information for Urban Planning*, Vol. 1, Chicago: University of Chicago Press, 15.

12. Gans, City Planning in America, 58.

13. See Mel Scott, 1969, *American City Planning Since 1890*, Berkeley: University of California Press, 75.

14. See Scott, ibid., 43-65, for observations on the "City Beautiful" movement and the role of architects in setting up such a movement and as forebears of the planning profession.

15. Ibid., 163.

16. Ibid., 43, 45-6.

17. Gans, City Planning in America, 59.

18. See Kravitz, Mandarinism, 247.

19. Scott, *American City Planning*, 123.

20. Kravitz, Mandarinism, 248.

21. Kravitz, ibid., 249-50, links such a reform movement to "a rich and powerful coalition of the old elite and the new upper class" who sought to develop "an alliance with the propertied portion of the middle class" with whom they shared common interests, particularly with regard to protecting and promoting property values.

22. Ibid., 249.

23. Holleb, *Social and Economic Information for Urban Planning*, 15.

24. See Scott, *American City Planning*, 83-270, for an extensive treatment of the nature of planning during the "age of business."

25. Ibid., 230.

26. See Gans, City Planning in America, 59.

27. Kravitz, Mandarinism, 249.

28. Scott, *American City Planning*, 252.

29. Ibid., 252.

30. Kravitz, Mandarinism, 247.

31. Ibid., 247.

32. See Scott, *American City Planning*, 192-8, for a description of the nation's love affair with zoning during the early 1920s.

33. Gans, City Planning in America, 59, comments on upper- and middle-class voters lending their support to zoning proposals because of their role in promoting and protecting property values during the period that zoning first came on the scene in the United States.

34. Scott, *American City Planning*, 193.

35. Ibid., 199.

36. Ibid., 182.

37. Ibid., 161.

38. A quotation cited by Scott, ibid., 224.

39. Quoted by Scott, ibid., 224, as part of his discussion of the nineteenth annual conference on city planning.

40. See Thomas D. Galloway and Riad G. Mahayni, 1977, Planning Theory in Retrospect: The Process of Paradigm Change, *Journal of the American Institute of Planners* 43,1: 67, for a characterization of the development of competing schools of thought regarding different types of planning, and a suggested evolution of two dominant models and a set of partial planning models over time.

41. Gans, City Planning in America, 61.

42. Scott, *American City Planning*, 117.

43. Ibid., 615.

44. See Scott, *American City Planning*, 614-8, for the source of the citation and a discussion of the attempt to amend such language in 1965 at the profession's annual conference by deleting the entire phrase referring to land uses; an attempt that failed at that national conference but that succeeded when it was tried again at the national meeting of 1967.

45. Henry Fagin, 1967, The Evolving Philosophy of Urban Planning, in *Urban Research and Policy Planning*, edited by Leo F. Schnore and Henry Fagin, Beverly Hills, California: Sage, 311.

46. Galloway and Mahayni, Planning Theory in Retrospect, 62.

47. Ibid., 69.

48. Ibid., 66.

49. Gans, City Planning in America, 61-5, comments on many of the perceived shortcomings of the comprehensive plan as part of his sociological analysis of planning in the United States. Also see Martin Meyerson, 1956, Building the Middle-Range Bridge for Comprehensive Planning, *Journal of the American Institute of Planners* 22,3: 58-64 and Constance Perin, 1967, A Noiseless Secession From the Comprehensive Plan, *Journal of the American Institute of Planners* 33,5: 336-46 for additional formulations of changes that would have to occur in noted features of traditional comprehensive plans in order for them to maintain their relevance.

50. Thomas D. Galloway, 1972, *The Role of Urban Planning in Public Policymaking: A Synthesis and Critique of Contemporary Procedural Planning Thought*, Ph.D. Dissertation, Seattle, Washington: University of Washington.

51. Galloway and Mahayni, Planning Theory in Retrospect, 67.

52. T.J. Kent, 1964, *The Urban General Plan*, San Francisco, California: The Chandler Press, 132.

53. Alan Black, 1968, The Comprehensive Plan, in *Principles and Practice of Urban Planning*, edited by William I. Goodman and Eric C. Freund, Washington, D.C.: International City Manager's Association, 349.

54. John T. Howard, 1961, City Planning as a Social Movement, a Governmental Function, and a Technical Profession, in *Planning and the Urban Community*, edited by Harvey S. Perloff, Pittsburgh, Pennsylvania: University of Pittsburgh Press, 163-4.

55. Bernard J. Frieden, 1967, The Changing Prospects for Social Planning, *Journal of the American Institute of Planners* 33,5: 312.

56. Kravitz, Mandarinism, 252-3.

57. Jerome L. Kaufman, 1974, Contemporary Planning Practice: State of the Art, in *Planning in America: Learning From Turbulence*, edited by David R. Godschalk, Washington, D.C.: American Institute of Planners, 117.

58. Melville C. Branch, 1978, Critical Unresolved Problems of Urban Planning Analysis, *Journal of the American Institute of Planners* 44,1: 56.

59. A claim made by Galloway and Mahayni, Planning Theory in Retrospect, 69, and supported by reference to a number of planning works.

60. See the The Plan as Law: The Consistency Doctrine, in *Cases and Materials on Land Use*, Second Edition, by David L. Callies, Robert H. Freilich, and Thomas E. Roberts, 1994, St. Paul, Minnesota: West Publishing Company, 372-89.

61. A quote from a legal article by Sullivan, 1992, titled The Plan as Law, cited in Callies, Freilich, and Roberts, *Cases and Materials on Land Use*, ibid., 372.

62. See John W. Dyckman, 1961, Planning and Decision Theory, *Journal of the American Institute of Planners*, November, 343, for comment on the fact that the utopian function has been well-entrenched in the profession; also see Thomas A.

Reiner, 1963, *The Place of the Ideal Community in Urban Planning*, Philadelphia, Pennsylvania: University of Pennsylvania Press.

63. Gans, City Planning in America, 61.

64. See Kaufman, Contemporary Planning Practice, 117.

65. Gans, City Planning in America, 62.

66. Donald L. Foley, 1964, An Approach to Metropolitan Spatial Structure, in *Explorations into Urban Structure*, by Melvin M. Webber, John W. Dyckman, Donald L. Foley, Albert Z. Guttenberg, William L. C. Wheaton, and Catherine Bauer Wurster, Philadelphia, Pennsylvania: University of Pennsylvania Press, 59.

67. John Friedman, 1971, The Future of Comprehensive Urban Planning, *Public Administration Review* 31,3: 325.

68. Melvin M. Webber, 1965, The Roles of Intelligence Systems in Urban-Systems Planning, *Journal of the American Institute of Planners* 31,6: 293.

69. Lowdon Wingo, 1973, The Quality of Life: Toward a Microeconomic Definition, *Urban Studies* 10,1: 4.

70. Melville C. Branch, 1972, Continuous Master City Planning, in *Decision-Making in Urban Planning: An Introduction to New Methodologies*, Ira M. Robinson, editor, Beverly Hills, California: Sage Publications, 409.

71. See Edgar Rose, 1974, in *The Spirit and Purpose of Planning*, edited by Michael J. Bruton, London, England: Hutchinson & Company, Ltd., 43.

72. Scott, *American City Planning*, 237.

73. As cited by Scott, ibid., 141.

74. Alan A. Altshuler, 1965, *The City Planning Process: A Political Analysis*, Ithaca, New York: Cornell University Press, 87.

75. See Hans Blumenfeld, 1968, The Modern Metropolis, in *Cities*, a Scientific American book, New York: Alfred A. Knopf, Incorporated, 54.

76. Scott, *American City Planning*, 451.

77. Fagin, The Evolving Philosophy of Urban Planning, 319.

78. David R. Godschalk, 1973, Reforming New Community Planning, *Journal of the American Institute of Planners* 39,5: 307.

79. Richard S. Bolan, Mapping the Planning Theory Terrain, in *Planning in America*, edited by Godschalk, 23.

80. Donald A. Barr, 1972, The Professional Urban Planner, *Journal of the American Institute of Planners* 38,3: 156.

81. F. Stuart Chapin, Jr., 1965, *Urban Land Use Planning*, Urbana, Illinois: University of Illinois Press.

82. Ibid., 159.

83. Ibid., 199.

84. Ibid., 211.

85. Ibid., 254.

86. Ibid., 255.

87. Ibid., 300.

88. Ibid., 380.

89. F. Stuart Chapin, Jr. and Edward J. Kaiser, 1979, *Urban Land Use Planning*, Urbana, Illinois: University of Illinois Press, 22.

90. A claim made regarding the F. Stuart Chapin, Jr. and Edward J. Kaiser edition in the preface to the newest edition by Edward J. Kaiser, David R. Godschalk, and F. Stuart Chapin, Jr., 1995, *Urban Land Use Planning*, Urbana, Illinois: University of Illinois Press, xiv.

91. See David R. Godschalk, 1975, State Growth Management: A Carrying Capacity Policy, in *Management and Control of Growth: Issues, Techniques, Problems, and Trends*, Vol. III, edited by Randall W. Scott, David J. Brower, and Dallas D. Miner, Washington, D.C.: The Urban Land Institute, 329.

92. James A. Clapp, 1975, *Growth Management: Practices and Issues*, A report prepared for the California State Assembly Committee on Local Government, Sacramento, California, February, 20.

93. Earl Finkler and David L. Peterson, 1974, *Nongrowth Planning Strategies: The Developing Power of Towns, Cities, and Regions*, New York: Praeger Publishers, Inc., 89-90.

94. For discussions of such a possible planning approach see: Godschalk, State Growth Management, 329, for comments on a "supply-based" style of planning; Clapp, *Growth Management*, 21, for comments on "supply-activated" planning; and Finkler and Peterson, *Nongrowth Planning Strategies*, 90, for their observations on a "carrying capacity" approach.

95. Gans, City Planning in America, 60.

96. Finkler and Peterson, *Nongrowth Planning Strategies*, 89.

97. John Delafons, 1962, *Land-Use Controls in the United States*, Cambridge, Massachusetts: MIT Press, 29-30.

98. Clapp, *Growth Management*, 5.

99. Kaiser, Godschalk, and Chapin, *Urban Land Use Planning*.

100. Ibid., 196.

101. Ibid., 115.

102. Ibid., 196.

103. Ibid., 279.

104. Ibid., 304.

105. Ibid., 172.

106. See Martin Meyerson and Edward C. Banfield, 1955, *Politics, Planning, and the Public Interest*, New York: The Free Press.

107. Gans, City Planning in America, 71.

108. Galloway and Mahayni, Planning Theory in Retrospect, 67.

109. Robinson, *Decision-Making in Urban Planning*, 22, 26.

110. A more detailed portrayal of the steps associated with the rational planning process may be found in Robinson, ibid., 28. Other portrayals appear in Meyerson and Banfield, *Politics, Planning, and the Public Interest*, 312-22, and in Britton Harris, 1967, The Limits of Science and Humanism in Planning, *Journal of the American Institute of Planners* 33,5: 324-25.

111. Gans, City Planning in America, 69.

112. Kravitz, Mandarinism, 253.

113. Gans, City Planning in America, 71.

114. Norman Beckman, 1964, The Planner as Bureaucrat, *Journal of the American Institute of Planners* 30,4: 327.

115. Foley, An Approach to Metropolitan Spatial Structure, 69.

116. Ibid., 59.

117. See Galloway and Mahayni, Planning Theory in Retrospect, 67, for their discussion of "partial planning models."

118. Meyerson, Building the Middle-Range Bridge.

119. Ibid., 60-1.

120. Ibid., 60.

121. Ibid., 60-1.

122. Scott, *American City Planning,* 570.

123. See Harvey S. Perloff, New Directions in Social Planning 31,4: 297-04; John W. Dyckman, 1966, Social Planning, Social Planners, and Planned Societies 32,2: 66-76; Robert Perlman, 1966, Social Welfare Planning and Physical Planning 33,2: 237-41; and Martin Rein, 1969, Social Planning: The Search for Legitimacy 35,2: 233-44, all of which appeared in the *Journal of the American Institute of Planners,* for examples of such works on social planning.

124. Perloff, New Directions in Social Planning, 299, suggests a list of the planning concerns that might constitute what he calls "the logical core of a social planning effort."

125. Melvin M. Webber, 1963, Comprehensive Planning and Social Responsibility: Toward an AIP Consensus on the Profession's Roles and Purposes, *Journal of the American Institute of Planners* 29,4: 235.

126. Perloff, New Directions in Social Planning, 299.

127. Paul Davidoff, 1965, Advocacy and Pluralism in Planning, *Journal of the American Institute of Planners* 31,4: 331-8.

128. Paul Davidoff, Linda Davidoff, and Neil N. Gold, 1970, Suburban Action: Advocate Planning for an Open Society, *Journal of the American Institute of Planners* 36,1: 12.

129. For a typical argument illustrating such a defense of mobility and economic growth see Mimi Winslow, 1973, Growth Control and the Poor, *Equilibrium* (January): 16.

130. See Anthony Downs, 1973, *Opening Up the Suburbs: An Urban Strategy for America,* New Haven, Connecticut: Yale University Press, 22.

131. See Paul Davidoff, Linda Davidoff, and Neil N. Gold, 1971, The Suburbs Have to Open Their Gates, *New York Times Magazine,* November 7, 40-1, for such a noted opposition to controls that would stop growth in the suburbs and an expression of the authors' growth bias in the following words: "In a nation that has highly valued growth, it is strange to find growth disdained as a matter of policy."

132. Arthur L. Silvers and Allan K. Sloan, 1965, A Model Framework for Comprehensive Planning in New York City, *Journal of the American Institute of Planners* 31,3: 246.

133. William L. C. Wheaton, 1967, Metro-Allocation Planning, *Journal of the American Institute of Planners* 33,2: 103-7.

134. Silvers and Sloan, A Model Framework, 247.

135. Wheaton, Metro-Allocation Planning, 106.

136. Galloway, *The Role of Urban Planning in Public Policymaking*, 221.

137. Ibid., 230; for a description of the suggested changes under a radical planning formulation see Kravitz, Mandarinism, 266-7.

138. Stephen Grabow and Allan Heskin, 1973, Foundations for a Radical Concept of Planning, *Journal of the American Institute of Planners* 39,2: 106.

139. Ibid., 106.

140. Kravitz, Mandarinism, 266.

141. Grabow and Heskin, Foundations for a Radical Concept of Planning, 110.

142. See Finkler, *Nongrowth as a Planning Alternative*; Finkler and Peterson, *Nongrowth Planning Strategies*; and Earl Finkler, William J. Toner, and Frank J. Popper, 1976, *Urban Nongrowth: City Planning for People*, New York: Praeger Publishers.

143. Finkler, Toner, and Popper, *Urban Nongrowth*, 1.

144. Finkler, *Nongrowth as a Planning Alternative*, 2.

145. William J. Toner, 1974, Introduction to Nongrowth Economics, in *Nongrowth Planning Strategies*, by Finkler and Peterson, xxii.

146. Ibid., xxii.

147. Henry Fagin, 1970, Advancing the 'State of the Art,' in *Urban Planning in Transition*, edited by Ernest Erber, New York: Grossman Publishers, 132.

148. Constantinos A. Doxiadis, 1968, *Ekistics: An Introduction to the Science of Human Settlements*, New York: Oxford University Press, 215-7, 430.

149. Marion Clawson and Peter Hall, 1973, *Planning and Urban Growth: An Anglo-American Comparison*, Baltimore, Maryland: The Johns Hopkins University Press, 273-4.

150. From *AIP Planning Policies*, adopted by the American Institute of Planners during October 1977, 8.

151. Paul L. Niebanck, 1984, Dilemmas in Growth Management, *Journal of the American Planning Association* 50,4: 403-4.

152. Excerpted wording from Douglas R. Porter's book *Growth Management: Keeping on Target* cited in a journal book review of that work by Christy Supp, 1988, *Journal of the American Planning Association* 54,3: 390.

153. Ivonne Audirac, Anne H. Shermyen, and Marc T. Smith, 1990, Ideal Urban Form and Visions of the Good Life: Florida's Growth Management Dilemma, *Journal of the American Planning Association* 56,4: 473.

154. From a book review by Michael Chandler, 1991, of Irving Schiffman's *Alternative Techniques for Managing Growth*, *Journal of the American Planning Association* 57,2: 246-7.

155. David R. Godschalk, 1992, In Defense of Growth Management, *Journal of the American Planning Association* 58,4: 424.

156. John M. DeGrove, 1989, Growth Management and Governance, in *Understanding Growth Management: Critical Issues and a Research Agenda*, edited by David J. Brower, David R. Godschalk, and Douglas R. Porter, Washington, D.C.: Urban Land Institute, 32.

157. Godschalk, In Defense of Growth Management, 423.

158. For a claim of such a focus on the concept of balance in current growth management efforts see John M. DeGrove, 1993, The Emergence of State Planning and Growth Management Systems: An Overview, in *State & Regional Comprehensive Planning: Implementing New Methods for Growth Management*, edited by Peter A. Buchsbaum and Larry J. Smith, Chicago: American Bar Association, 9.

159. John M. DeGrove and Deborah A. Miness, 1992, *The New Frontier for Land Policy: Planning and Growth Mangement in the States*, Cambridge, Massachusetts: Lincoln Institute of Land Policy, 9.

160. See John M. DeGrove and Patricia M. Metzger, editors, 1991, *Balanced Growth: A Planning Guide for Local Government*, Washington, D.C.: International City Management Association.

161. Dennis E. Gale and Suzanne Hart, 1992, Public Support for Local Comprehensive Planning Under Statewide Growth Management: Insights From Maine, *Journal of Planning Education and Research* 11,3: 192.

162. Kaiser, Godschalk, and Chapin, 1995, *Urban Land Use Planning*, 172.

163. Nico Calavita and Roger Caves, 1994, Planners' Attitudes Toward Growth, *Journal of the American Planning Association* 60,4: 483.

164. See Calavita and Caves, ibid., 484, for reference to works addressing the power of planners to set and influence policy agendas in local communities.

165. See DeGrove and Miness, *The New Frontier for Land Policy*, 161, for reference to such a "managing to grow" side of current growth management programs.

166. Richard P. Appelbaum, 1976, City Size and Urban Life: A Preliminary Inquiry Into Some Consequences of Growth in American Cities, *Urban Affairs Quarterly* 12,2: 140.

167. Calavita and Caves, Planners' Attitudes Toward Growth, 496.

168. An observation attributed to Edgar Rust during the course of a review of his book *No Growth: Impacts on Metropolitan Areas* by Robert C. Einsweiler, 1976, *Journal of the American Institute of Planners* 42,4: 449.

169. See John W. Dyckman, 1969, The Practical Uses of Planning Theory, *Journal of the American Institute of Planners* 35,5: 299, for mention of the skepticism in planning literature regarding the existence of an identifiable single public interest.

170. See E. F. Schumacher, 1973, *Small is Beautiful: Economics as if People Mattered*, New York: Harper & Row, 100, for observations on the role of relativism in recent Western thought.

171. Paul Davidoff and Thomas A. Reiner, 1962, A Choice Theory of Planning, *Journal of the American Institute of Planners* 28,2: 110, make the point that since there are no such things as "correct" decisions it is improper for planners to impose their ideas on others. Also see Davidoff, Advocacy and Pluralism in Planning, 335, for mention of the view that there are no right solutions, and Harvey Cox, 1965, *The Secular City: Secularization and Urbanization in Theological Perspective*, Toronto, Ontario: The Macmillan Company, 27, for the opinion that people have no right to inflict their values on others because of their relativism.

172. John Friedmann, 1973, *Retracking America: A Theory of Transactive Planning*, New York: Anchor Press/Doubleday, 204.

173. See, for example, Robert C. Weaver, 1960, *The Urban Complex*, New York: Anchor Books, 57, who makes the claim that planners are unable to control growth; Edgar Rose, 1974, Philosophy and Purpose of Planning, in *The Spirit and Purpose of Planning*, edited by Bruton, 43, for the view that the power that planners have to affect change is limited; and Altschuler, 1965, *The City Planning Process*, 354, for the opinion that planners control so little of their environment that an acceptance of its main features is a necessity for success in planning endeavors.

174. Branch, Critical Unresolved Problems, 50.

175. See Lawrence Haworth, 1963, *The Good City*, Bloomington, Indiana: Indiana University Press, 53, who states "With the growth of the city human beings meet increased opportunities" and James A. Clapp, 1971, *New Towns and Urban Policy: Planning Metropolitan Growth*, New York: Dunellen Publishing Company, 238, who notes "What is generally clear is that the modern metropolis offers unprecedented locational choice and opportunity for large segments of the population."

176. Webber, The Roles of Intelligence Systems in Urban-Systems Planning, 296.

4 THE ROLE OF THE COURTS IN SHAPING GROWTH MANAGEMENT EFFORTS

1. Earl Finkler, 1972, *Nongrowth as a Planning Alternative: A Preliminary Examination of an Emerging Issue*, Planning Advisory Service Report No. 283, Chicago: American Society of Planning Officials, 2.

2. C. Thomas Williamson, III, 1980, Constitutional and Judicial Limitations on the Community's Power to Downzone, *Urban Lawyer* 12,1: 166.

3. John M. Levy, 1994, *Contemporary Urban Planning*, Englewood Cliffs, New Jersey: Prentice Hall, 65.

4. Jacob H. Beuscher, Robert R. Wright, and Morton Gitelman, 1976, *Cases & Materials on Land Use*, 2nd Edition, St. Paul, Minnesota: West Publishing Company, 339.

5. G. Richard Hill, 1993, Forward to the Revised Printing: *Lucas* and Regulatory Taking Doctrine in the 1990s, in *Regulatory Taking: The Limits of Land Use Controls*, edited by G. Richard Hill, Chicago: American Bar Association, xv.

6. Beuscher, Wright, and Gitelman, *Cases & Materials on Land Use*, 339.

7. See, Early Legislative Controls on the Use of Land: Some Statutes Spanning the Centuries, in ibid., 1-16, for examples of such early controls.

8. Fred Bosselman, David Callies, and John Banta, 1971, *The Taking Issue: An Analysis of the Constitutional Limits of Land Use Control*, Washington, D.C.: U.S. Government Printing Office, 75.

9. Ibid., 80.

10. Ibid., 318-9.

11. For reference to the 12th century origins of the common law doctrine of nuisance and the subsequent seven centuries of case law developing a body of nuisance law see Ira M. Heyman, 1968, The Great 'Property Rights' Fallacy, *Cry California* III,3: 29.

12. *Commonwealth v. Tewksbury*, 11 Metcalf (Mass.)(1846), 57.

13. See Heyman, The Great 'Property Rights' Fallacy, 31, for reference to the historical progression of initially using land-use regulations to address nuisances, then to prohibit nuisance-like activities, and finally to positively enhance the general welfare.

14. *Village of Euclid, Ohio v. Ambler Realty Co.*, 272 U.S. 365, 386-7.

15. Robert H. Freilich, 1983, Solving the 'Taking' Equation: Making the Whole Equal the Sum of Its Parts, *Urban Lawyer* 15,2: 453.

16. A quote attributed to Lippman appears in Heyman, The Great 'Property Rights' Fallacy, 29.

17. A discussion of legal challenges to land-use regulations based on noncompliance with statutory requirements appears in Carl J. Seneker, II, 1974, *Land Use Regulations for Urban Growth Control: Selected Legal Principles*, Environmental Quality Series No. 20, University of California, Davis, California: Institute of Governmental Affairs, 3.

18. See David L. Callies, Robert H. Freilich, and Thomas E. Roberts, 1994, *Cases and Materials on Land Use*, 2nd Edition, St. Paul, Minnesota: West Publishing Company, 153, for reference to Dillon's Rule in the context of a treatment of the legality of subdivision regulations.

19. Mention of a willingness on the part of some courts to give a liberal reading to state enabling acts appears in Callies, Freilich, and Roberts, ibid., 153.

20. Such observations on the landmark case of *Golden v. Planning Board of Town of Ramapo*, 285 N.E.2d 291, appear in Robert R. Wright and Susan W. Wright, 1985, *Land Use in a Nutshell*, 2nd Edition, St. Paul, Minnesota: West Publishing Company, 99-101.

21. In Washington state, for example, Article XI, Section 11 of the state constitution states that "Any county, city, town or township may make and enforce within its limits all such local, police, sanitary and other regulations as are not in conflict with general laws."

22. *Chicago B. & Q. R. Co. v. City of Chicago*, 17 S.Ct. 581 (1897).

23. *Lawton v. Steele*, 152 U.S. 133 (1894).

24. Ibid., 152 U.S. 133, 137.

25. *French Investing Co., Inc. v. City of New York*, 350 N.E.2d 381 (1976): 385-6.

26. For a detailed treatment of such judicial standards used to assess the legality of land-use regulations under substantive due process challenges see David R. Godschalk, David J. Brower, Larry D. McBennett, and Barbara A. Vestal, 1977, *Constitutional Issues of Growth Management*, Chicago: The ASPO Press, 43-8.

27. For comments on such an assumed presumption of constitutionality regarding stated public purposes of land-use regulations see Brian W. Blaesser and Alan C. Weinstein, editors, 1989, *Land Use and the Constitution: Principles for Planning Practice*, Chicago: Planners Press, 51.

28. Godschalk, Brower, McBennett, and Vestal, *Constitutional Issues of Growth Management*, 47.

29. Ibid., 48.

30. See the 11th Circuit Court ruling in *Eide v. Sarasota County*, 908 F.2d 716 (1990): 720-2, and Callies, Freilich, and Roberts, *Cases and Materials on Land Use*, 311-2.

31. Freilich, Solving the 'Taking' Equation, 461.

32. *First English Evangelical Lutheran Church of Glendale v. County of Los Angeles*, 107 S.Ct. 2378 (1987): 2388-9.

33. For a detailed treatment of the two possible tests used to evaluate land-use regulations under the equal protection clause see Godschalk, Brower, McBennett, and Vestal, *Constitutional Issues of Growth Management*, 83-8.

34. See Blaesser and Weinstein, editors, *Land Use and the Constitution*, 60, for mention of the affect of a regulation determining the test used to judge its legality, and for the observation that the rational basis test applies in most land-use cases.

35. Godschalk, Brower, McBennett, and Vestal, *Constitutional Issues of Growth Management*, 83.

36. Blaesser and Weinstein, editors, *Land Use and the Constitution*, 61.

37. Bosselman, Callies, and Banta, *The Taking Issue*, 104.

38. Ibid., 238.

39. Ibid., 239.

40. Ibid., 325.

41. For a treatment of the distinction between the power of eminent domain and the police power see Freilich, Solving the 'Taking' Equation, 461.

42. See Bosselman, Callies, and Banta, *The Taking Issue*, 51, for such noted distinctions between the power of eminent domain and the police power.

43. *Mugler v. Kansas*, 123 U.S. 623 (1887).

44. Ibid., 668-9.

45. Michael M. Berger, 1993, Property Owners Have Rights; Lower Courts Need to Protect Them, in *After* Lucas*: Land Use Regulation and the Taking of Property Without Compensation*, edited by David L. Callies, Chicago: American Bar Association, 36.

46. Nathaniel S. Lawrence, 1988, Regulatory Takings: Beyond the Balancing Test, *Urban Lawyer* 20,2: 394-5.

47. Ibid., 393.

48. Callies, Freilich, and Roberts, *Cases and Materials on Land Use*, 248.

49. Robert H. Freilich and E. Stuhler, 1981, *The Land Use Awakening: Zoning Law in the Seventies*, 42, provide the noted wording for such a viewpoint, although it does not represent their position.

50. *Pennsylvania Coal v. Mahon*, 43 S.Ct. 158 (1922).

51. Callies, Freilich, and Roberts, *Cases and Materials on Land Use*, 245.

52. *Pennsylvania Coal v. Mahon*, 43 S.Ct. 158 (1922): 160.

53. See excerpts from *Williamson County Regional Planning Commission v. Hamilton Bank of Johnson City*, 105 S.Ct. 3108 (1985) in Callies and Freilich, *Cases and Materials on Land Use*, 463-4, that indicate that Holmes' earlier opinions for the Court made clear his opinion that excessive regulations were not to be considered as triggering compensation awards.

54. John Mixon, 1988, Compensation Claims Against Local Governments for Excessive Land-Use Regulations: A Proposal for More Efficient State Level Adjudication, *Urban Lawyer* 20,3: 679.

55. See Callies, Freilich, and Roberts, *Cases and Materials on Land Use*, 224.

56. See Robert H. Freilich and Elizabeth A. Garvin, 1993, Takings after *Lucas*: Growth Management, Planning, and Regulatory Implementation Will Work Better, in *After* Lucas, edited by Callies, 56-9. Freilich and Garvin note that "title takings" may significantly interfere with the incidents of ownership and deprive owners of a legally actionable right (for example, the right to use easements) or they may involve acquisition of title to property through development exactions (for example, land dedications).

57. Ibid., 59-1.

58. Callies and Freilich, *Cases and Materials on Land Use*, 416.

59. Freilich and Garvin, Takings after *Lucas*, 59.

60. Callies, Freilich, and Roberts, *Cases and Materials on Land Use*, 224.

61. Freilich, Solving the 'Taking' Equation, 466.

62. See Elaine Moss, editor, 1977, *Land Use Controls in the United States: A Handbook on the Legal Rights of Citizens*, National Resources Defense Council, New York: The Dial Press/James Wade, 7-11, for a summary treatment of such standards.

63. Callies makes note of the Supreme Court's rejection of the harm-based standard for exempting regulations from taking claims in Introduction: Taking the Taking Issue into the Twenty-first Century, in *After* Lucas, edited by Callies, 4.

64. For comment on the fact that Pennsylvania Coal established the so-called "balancing test" for making regulatory taking determinations see Bosselman, Callies, and Banta, *The Taking Issue*, 238.

65. *San Diego Gas & Electric Co. v. City of San Diego*, 450 U.S. 621 (1981).

66. *First English Evangelical Lutheran Church of Glendale v. County of Los Angeles*, 107 S.Ct. 2378 (1987).

67. Lawrence, Regulatory Takings, 432.

68. *Loretto v. Teleprompter Manhattan Corporation*, 458 U.S. 419 (1982): 432.

69. *Nollan v. California Coastal Commission*, 107 S.Ct. 3141 (1987).

70. Ibid., 3145.

71. *Lucas v. So. Carolina Coastal Council*, 120 L.Ed.2d 798 (1992).

72. Ibid., 813.

73. Ibid., 812.

74. *Agins v. City of Tiburon*, 100 S.Ct. 2138 (1980). See Berger, Property Owners Have Rights, 31, for reference to this categorical rule having been first expressed in *Agins*.

75. *Agins*, ibid., 2142.

76. *First English*, (1987): 2388.

77. *Nollan*, (1987): 3147.

78. Ibid., 3147.

79. *Dolan v. City of Tigard*, 62 LW 4576 (1994): 4580.

80. *Lucas*, (1992): 821.

81. *Keystone Bituminous Coal Association v. DeBenedictis*, 107 S.Ct. 1232 (1987): 1245, n. 22.

82. *Lucas*, (1992): 821.

83. *Agins*, (1980): 2141.

84. *Penn Central Transportation Co. v. City of New York*, 98 S.Ct. 2646 (1978).

85. Ibid., 2659.

86. The Supreme Court cited *Euclid v. Ambler Realty Co.*, 278 U.S. 365 (1926) (75% diminution in value) and *Hadacheck v. Sebastian*, 239 U.S. 394 (1915) (87.5% diminution in value) as examples of regulations that had been upheld in spite of substantial diminution in value effects, ibid., 2663.

87. Ibid., 2663.

88. Michael M. Berger, 1988, Happy Birthday, Constitution: The Supreme Court Establishes New Ground Rules for Land-Use Planning, *Urban Lawyer* 20,3: 767.

89. See Berger, ibid., 758, for the claim that courts have sought to resolve the economic impact issue by focusing on the extent of diminution in value.

90. Callies and Freilich, *Cases and Materials on Land Use*, 438.

91. See Freilich and Garvin, Takings after *Lucas*, 60, who make such a claim based on cited cases from Maryland, California, Pennsylvania, Virginia, and Oregon.

92. For comment on such a whole parcel rule see Fred P. Bosselman, 1993, Protecting Resources Under the Scalia Regime, *Land Use Forum* (Winter): 65. As the *Penn Central* Court noted: "'Taking' jurisprudence does not divide a single parcel into discrete segments and attempt to determine whether rights in a particular segment have been entirely abrogated. In deciding whether a particular governmental action has effected a taking, this Court focuses rather both on the character of the action and on the nature and extent of the interference with rights in the parcel as a whole," 98 S.Ct. 2646 (1978): 2662.

93. *MacDonald, Sommer & Frates v. County of Yolo*, 477 U.S. 340 (1986): 348.

94. While "as applied" challenges are evaluated on the basis of the multi-factor balancing test, "facial" challenges "face an uphill battle" according to the Court and need only satisfy the requirements of being reasonably related to a legitimate government objective and of leaving property owners with economically viable use.

95. *Williamson County Regional Planning Commission v. Hamilton Bank*, 473 U.S. 172 (1985).

96. *Agins*, (1980): 2143, n. 9.

97. *First English*, (1987): 2389.

98. The *Lucas* opinion itself refers to the denial of all economically beneficial use as representing "extraordinary circumstances" and occurring in "relatively rare situations," 120 L.Ed.2d 798 (1992): 814.

99. Hill, Forward to the Revised Printing: *Lucas*, xxvii.

100. One description of a court declared "regional welfare standard" in the states of Pennsylvania, New Jersey, Michigan, and New York appears in Godschalk, Brower, McBennett, and Vestal, *Constitutional Issues of Growth Management*, 66-70. Courts in the states of California and Washington have also established such regional welfare standards in the rulings handed down in *Associated Homebuilders v. City of Liv-*

ermore, 557 P.2d 473 (Cal.1976) and *S.A.V.E. v. City of Bothell*, 576 P.2d 401 (Wash.1978).

101. See Godschalk, Brower, McBennett, and Vestal, *Constitutional Issues of Growth Management*, 67-8, 74.

102. See *Vickers v. Township Committee of Gloucester Township*, 181 A.2d 129 (1962) and *So. Burlington Cty N.A.A.C.P. v. Mt. Laurel Tp.*, 456 A.2d 390 (1983) (*Mt. Laurel* II).

103. *Duckworth v. Bonney Lake*, 586 P.2d 860 (1978).

104. See Freilich and Garvin, Takings after *Lucas*, 79-80, n. 78, for the citation and for reference to case law rulings substantiating such a claim.

105. The *Agins* opinion held that mere fluctuations in value during the process of governmental decision making, absent extraordinary delay, are incidents of ownership that may not be considered a taking, and the *First English* ruling held that normal delays in obtaining development approval are similarly not to be considered a taking.

106. Freilich and Garvin, Takings after *Lucas*, 64.

107. Ibid., 63.

108. Ibid., 63.

109. Ibid., 63.

110. Ibid., 63.

111. See Godschalk, Brower, McBennett, and Vestal, *Constitutional Issues of Growth Management*, 100-1, for comment on the U.S. District Court ruling in *Construction Indus. Ass'n v. City of Petaluma*, 375 F. Supp. 574 (N.D. Cal. 1974).

112. See ibid., 101, for comment noting the reluctance of courts to apply the rigorous compelling state interest test whenever a land-use regulation in some way obstructs the ability of citizens to migrate and resettle.

113. Williamson, Constitutional and Judicial Limitations on the Community's Power to Downzone, 161.

114. See ibid., 157-5, for comment on such alternative bases for contesting the legality of downzonings.

115. See ibid., 181, for case law citations upholding a broad range of downzoning actions.

116. David L. Callies, 1988, Property Rights: Are There Any Left?, *Urban Lawyer* 20,3: 643.

117. Berger, Happy Birthday, Constitution, 749.

118. Callies, Property Rights, 638.

119. See *County of Ada v. Henry*, 668 P.2d 994 (Idaho 1983) and *Wilson v. County of McHenry*, 416 N.E.2d 426 (1981).

120. *Just v. Marinette County*, 201 N.W.2d 761 (1972).

121. Ibid., 769.

122. Ibid., 769.

123. See, for example, Callies, Introduction; Taking the Taking Issue into the Twenty-first Century, 9, and Fred P. Bosselman, 1993, Scalia on Land, in *After* Lucas, edited by David L. Callies, 86.

124. Kenneth B. Bley, 1993, Litigation Strategies for Landowners, *Land Use Forum* (Winter): 56.

125. *Lucas*, (1992): 815.

126. Ibid., 813-4, n. 7.

127. *National Land & Investment Co. v. Easttown Township Board of Adjustment*, 215 A.2d 597 (1966).

128. Ibid., 610, 612.

129. *Appeal of Girsh*, 263 A.2d 395 (1970).

130. Ibid., 398-9, n. 4.

131. *Kit-Mar Builder's Inc. v. Township of Concord*, 268 A.2d 765 (1970).

132. Ibid., 768-9.

133. *Oakwood at Madison, Inc. v. Township of Madison*, 283 A.2d 353 (1971).

134. Ibid., 358.

135. *Southern Burlington County NAACP v. Township of Mount Laurel*, 336 A.2d 713 (1975).

136. Ibid., 731-3.

137. *Berenson v. Town of New Castle*, 415 N.Y.S.2d 669 (1979).

138. Ibid., 679.

139. *Golden v. Planning Board of Town of Ramapo*, 285 N.E.2d 291(1972), *appeal dismissed*, 409 U.S. 1003.

140. Ibid., 302.

141. *Construction Industry Association of Sonoma County v. Petaluma*, 375 F. Supp. 574, revd., 522 F.2d 897 (1975), cert. den. 96 S.Ct. 1148 (1976).

142. Ibid. 375 F. Supp. 574 (1975): 583.

143. *Beck v. Town of Raymond*, 394 A.2d 847 (1978).

144. Ibid., 851-2.

145. *Convey v. Town of Stratham*, 414 A.2d 539 (1980).

146. Ibid., 540.

147. *Stoney-Brook Development Corp. v. Town of Fremont*, 474 A.2d 561 (1984).

148. Ibid., 563-4.

149. *Rancourt v. Town of Barnstead*, 523 A.2d 55 (1986).

150. Ibid., 58-9.

151. *Associated Home Builders Etc., Inc. v. City of Livermore*, 18 C.3d 582 (1976).

152. Ibid., 608-9.

153. *Arnel Development Company v. City of Costa Mesa*, 178 Cal.Rptr. 723 (1981).

154. Ibid., 727.

155. Ibid., 727-8.

156. *City of Del Mar v. City of San Diego*, 133 Cal.App.3d 401 (1982).

157. Ibid., 403-4, 411-5.

158. Ibid., 412.

159. *Albano v. Mayor and Township Committee of the Township of Washington*, 476 A.2d 852 (1984).

160. Ibid., 857.

161. *Sturges v. Town of Chilmark*, 402 N.E.2d 1346 (1980).

162. Ibid., 1352.

163. *Giuliano v. Town of Edgartown*, 531 F.Supp. 1076 (1982).

164. Ibid., 1083.

165. *La Salle National Bank & Trust Co. v. Cook County*, 402 N.E.2d 687 (1980).

166. Ibid., 699.

167. *Tisei v. Town of Ogunquit*, 491 A.2d 564 (1985).

168. *Begin v. Town of Sabattus*, 409 A.2d 1269 (1979).

169. Ibid., 1269.

170. *Tisei* (1985): 569.

171. This author's review of 30 randomly selected cases from the 1980s revealed, for example, that 20 of the challenged management programs were upheld by the courts, Gabor M. Zovanyi, 1989, The Growth Orientation of the Courts During the 1980s, a paper presented at the 31st Annual Conference of the Association of Collegiate Schools of Planning, Portland, Oregon.

172. See *Euclid v. Ambler Realty Co.*, 278 U.S. 365 (1926) and *Hadacheck v. Sebastian*, 239 U.S. 394 (1915) for two cases where the U.S. Supreme Court upheld land-use regulations in spite of the fact that they imposed use limitations resulting in four-fold and eight-fold diminutions respectively in the value of privately held land.

173. Callies, Property Rights: Are There Any Left?, 620.

174. Godschalk, Brower, McBennett, and Vestal, *Constitutional Issues of Growth Management*, 93.

175. Ibid., 101.

176. Ibid., 94.

177. Reference to the *Shapiro v. Thompson* case that announced the possible legality of reasonable restrictions appears in Godschalk, Brower, McBennett, Vestal, ibid., 94.

178. Ibid., 101.

179. Ibid., 101.

180. *Associated Home Builders Etc., Inc. v. City of Livermore*, 18 C.3d 582, 557 P.2d 473 (1976).

181. See the previously cited language from the 1980 *Sturges* opinion issued by the supreme court of Massachusetts, note 161, conceding a role for the "regional demand for primary housing" in deciding the legality of a contested land-use regulation.

182. See *Albano* (1984).

183. Pub. Resources Code, 21001.

184. *City of Boca Raton v. Boca Villas Corporation*, 371 So.2d 154 (1979).

185. Ibid., 154-5.

186. *City of Hollywood v. Hollywood, Inc.*, 432 So.2d 1332 (1983).

187. Ibid., 1335-6.

5 ECOLOGICAL SUSTAINABILITY AS THE NEW GROWTH MANAGEMENT FOCUS

1. Herman E. Daly, 1991, *Steady State Economics: Second Edition with New Essays*, Washington, D.C.: Island Press, 249.

2. See Paul R. Ehrlich and Anne H. Ehrlich, 1991, *Healing the Planet*, New York: Addison-Wesley Publishing Company, 6; Lester Brown and Hal Kane, 1994, *Full House: Reassessing the Earth's Population Carrying Capacity*, New York: WW Norton & Company, 201; Sandra Postel, 1994, Carrying Capacity: Earth's Bottom Line, in *State of the World 1994*, by Lester R. Brown, Alan Durning, Christopher Flavin, Hilary French, Nicholas Lenssen, Marcia Lowe, Ann Misch, Sandra Postel, Michael Renner, Linda Starke, Peter Weber, and John Young, New York: WW Norton & Company, 3-4, 13.

3. Donella H. Meadows, Dennis L. Meadows, and Jorgen Randers, 1992, *Beyond the Limits: Confronting Global Collapse, Envisioning a Sustainable Future*, Post Mills, Vermont: Chelsea Green Publishing Company, xv-xvi.

4. Brown and Kane, *Full House*, 49, 203.

5. Christopher Manes, 1990, *Green Rage: Radical Environmentalism and the Unmaking of Civilization*, Boston, Massachusetts: Little, Brown and Company, 43.

6. Ibid., preface.

7. Meadows, Meadows, and Randers, *Beyond the Limits*, xv.

8. See Ehrlich and Ehrlich, *Healing the Planet*, 15-30.

9. Paul R. Ehrlich and Anne H. Ehrlich, 1990, *The Population Explosion*, New York: Simon and Schuster, 110, 134.

10. Wording from *The Federal Programme of the German Green Party*, quoted in Manes, *Green Rage*, 134.

11. Ehrlich and Ehrlich, *Healing the Planet*, xiii, 279.

12. Ehrlich and Ehrlich, *The Population Explosion*, 110.

13. Brown and Kane, *Full House*, 213.

14. Ehrlich and Ehrlich, *The Population Explosion*, 35.

15. Brown and Kane, *Full House*, 12, 60.

16. Ehrlich and Ehrlich, *Healing the Planet*, 42.

17. Manes, *Green Rage*, 32.

18. Ehrlich and Ehrlich, *Healing the Planet*, 285.

19. See, for example, the 1990 added preface to Carolyn Merchant, 1980, *The Death of Nature: Women, Ecology and the Scientific Revolution*, San Francisco: Harper & Row, Publishers, xv-xviii.

20. See Ehrlich and Ehrlich, *The Population Explosion*, 181, for reference to converting the planet's economic system from one of "growthism" to one of sustainability.

21. Douglas R. Porter, 1989, Significant Research Needs in the Policy and Practice of Growth Management, in *Understanding Growth Management: Critical Issues and a Research Agenda*, edited by David J. Bower, David R. Godschalk, and Douglas R. Porter, Washington, D.C.: The Urban Land Institute, 192.

22. John M. DeGrove and Deborah A. Miness, 1992, *The New Frontier for Land Policy: Planning and Growth Management in the States*, Cambridge, Massachusetts: Lincoln Institute of Land Policy, 2.

23. See DeGrove and Miness, ibid., 2-4, for comment on the expanded set of concerns addressed by the second generation of statewide growth management enactments.

24. For reference to such a "managing to grow" component in the second generation of statewide growth management laws see DeGrove and Miness, ibid., 161.

25. George P. Marsh, 1864, *Man and Nature: or, Physical Geography as Modified by Human Action*, New York: Scribners. Published in 1970 as *The Earth as Modified by Human Action*, New York: Arno Press.

26. John W. Powell's report to the U.S. Congress was reprinted in 1983, Cambridge, Massachusetts: Harvard Common Press.

27. See William Toner, 1988, Environmental Land Use Planning, in *The Practice of Local Governmental Planning*, 2nd Edition, edited by Frank S. So and Judith Getzels, Washington, D.C.: The International City Management Association.

28. For a portrayal of a schism as reflected by the different opinions held by Gifford Pinchot and John Muir see Roderick Nash, 1967, *Wilderness and the American Mind*, 3rd Edition (copyright 1982), New Haven, Connecticut: Yale University Press, 129-40.

29. See L. H. Bailey, 1915, *The County Life Movement in the United States*, New York: Macmillan.

30. Thomas Adams, 1917, *Rural Planning and Development: A Study of Rural Conditions and Problems in Canada*, Ottawa, Ontario: Commission on Conservation.

31. Frank A. Waugh, 1914, *Rural Improvement*, New York: Orange Judd Company, and Frank A. Waugh, 1924, *Country Planning: An Outline of Principles and Methods*, New York: Harcourt, Brace and Company.

32. For a summary overview of environmental planning initiatives during Roosevelt's presidency see Toner, Environmental Land Use Planning, 120-1.

33. Edward H. Graham, 1944, *Natural Principles of Land Use*, London, England: Oxford University Press.

34. Ibid., 97.

35. Toner, Environmental Land Use Planning, 121.

36. David Hoeh, 1979, Environmental Planning, in *Introduction to Urban Planning*, edited by Anthony J. Catanese and James C. Snyder, New York: McGraw-Hill, Book Company, 212.

37. See, for example, Robert W. Burchell and David Listokin, 1975, *The New Environmental Impact Handbook*, Rutgers University, New Brunswick, New Jersey: Center for Urban Policy Research.

38. R. K. Jain, L. V. Urban, G. S. Stacey, and H. E. Balbach, 1993, *Environmental Assessment*, New York: McGraw-Hill, Incorporated, 59.

39. Ibid., 78.

40. Ibid., 59.

41. Frederick Steiner, 1991, *The Living Landscape: An Ecological Approach to Landscape Planning*, New York: McGraw-Hill, Incorporated, 14.

42. F. Stuart Chapin, Jr. and Edward J. Kaiser, 1979, *Urban Land Use Planning*, Urbana, Illinois: University of Illinois Press, 291.

43. Toner, Environmental Land Use Planning, 126.

44. Ian McHarg, 1969, *Design With Nature*, Garden City, New York: Doubleday/Natural History Press.

45. For a brief overview of that method and McHarg's reference to it as an "ecological method" see, ibid., 33-5.

46. Ibid., 56.

47. Ibid., 34.

48. Ibid., 57.

49. For reference to the role of suitability analyses in helping to ensure the continued health of "natural processes" see, ibid., 57, and for McHarg's faith in being able to accommodate further growth if it were simply "suitably" sited on the landscape see 80-6.

50. Ibid., 81.

51. Ibid., 158.

52. Ibid., 82.

53. Ibid., 86.

54. Ibid., 80.

55. Pacific Northwest River Basins Commission, 1973, *Ecology and the Economy: A Concept for Balancing Long-Range Goals*, Vancouver, Washington, 13.

56. David R. Godschalk, Francis H. Parker, and Thomas R. Knoche, 1974, *Carrying Capacity: A Basis for Coastal Planning?*, University of North Carolina, Chapel Hill, North Carolina: Center for Urban and Regional Studies, 137.

57. Devon M. Schnieder, David R. Godschalk, and Norman Axler, *The Carrying Capacity Concept as a Planning Tool*, Planning Advisory Service Report 338, Chicago: American Society of Planning Officials, 1.

58. Godschalk, Parker, and Knoche, *Carrying Capacity*, 131-2.

59. Mark von Wodtke, 1970, The Carrying Capacity of the Los Angeles Basin, *Cry California* 5,4: 24.

60. Bill Toner, 1977, Carrying Capacity Will Work – If It Doesn't Work Too Well, *Environmental Comment* (December), Washington, D.C.: Urban Land Institute, 12.

61. For reference to carrying capacities in such terms see *Carrying Capacity: A Status Report on Marine and Coastal Parks and Reserves*, Third International Seminar on Coastal and Marine Parks and Protected Areas, 1991, edited by John R. Clark, Washington, D.C.: The National Parks Service, United States Department of the Interior, 1-6.

62. Godschalk, Parker, and Knoche, 1974, *Carrying Capacity*, 134.

63. Ibid., 132.

64. George H. Nieswand and Peter J. Pizor, 1977, How to Apply Carrying Capacity Analysis, *Environmental Comment* (December), Washington, D.C.: Urban Land Institute, 8.

65. Godschalk, Parker, and Knoche, *Carrying Capacity*, 134.

66. For treatments of such a distinction between maximum and optimum carrying capacities see Kem Lowry, 1974, *Reflections on the Concept of Carrying Capacity*, Working Paper WP74-002, Honolulu, Hawaii: Hawaii Environmental Simulation Laboratory, University of Hawaii, 7-8, and Rice Odell, 1975, Carrying Capacity Analysis: Useful But Limited, in *Management and Control of Growth*, Volume III, edited by Randall W. Scott, David J. Brower, and Dallas D. Miner, Washington, D.C.: The Urban Land Institute, 23.

67. See Godschalk, Parker, and Knoche, *Carrying Capacity*, 135-7.

68. See, for example, Nieswand and Pizor, How to Apply Carrying Capacity Analysis, 8-10.

69. Ibid., 8.

70. Schnieder, Godschalk, and Axler, *The Carrying Capacity Concept as a Planning Tool*, 1.

71. Godschalk, Parker, and Knoche, *Carrying Capacity*, 135.

72. Schnieder, Godschalk, and Axler, *The Carrying Capacity Concept as a Planning Tool*, 1.

73. Ibid., 1.

74. McHarg, *Design With Nature*, 19.

75. Ibid., 156.

76. Schnieder, Godschalk, and Axler, *The Carrying Capacity Concept as a Planning Tool*, 4.

77. Senate Bill 100, Chapter 80, Section 48, (1), [(9)], (j), 12.

78. Local Governmental Comprehensive Planning and Land Development Regulation Act, 1985, Section 163.3177(6)(g)(5), 950.

79. Ibid., Section 163.3177(6)(c), 949.

80. Rhode Island Comprehensive Planning and Land Use Act, 1988, Section 45-22.2-3(C)(1), 3.

81. Ibid., Section 45-22.2-5(A)(1), 7.

82. Vermont Municipal and Regional Planning and Development Act, 1988, Section 4384(c)(4&5), 27.

83. State Comprehensive Plan, TITLE XIII, PLANNING AND DEVELOPMENT, CHAPTER 187, Section 187.201(16)(a), 1091.

84. Local Government Comprehensive Planning and Land Development Act, 1985, Section 163.3177(9)(c), 951.

85. Oregon Statewide Planning Goals, 1990, Land Conservation and Development Commission, Goal 6, Air, Water and Land Resources Quality, 7.

86. Ibid., Goal 5, Open Spaces, Scenic and Historic Areas, and Natural Resources, 7.

87. Ibid., Definitions, 23.

88. Vermont Planning and Development Act, 1988, Subchapter 3, Regional Planning Commissions, Section 4345a(5)(C), 15.

89. Ibid., Subchapter 1, General Provisions, Definitions, Section 4303(20), 5.

90. See Chapter Two for specific reference to the wording contained in the Florida, Oregon, and Vermont statewide growth management laws mandating or promoting ongoing growth accommodation on the part of local governments in those states, 59-0.

91. See, for example, the International Union for the Conservation of Nature, 1980, *World Conservation Strategy*, New York: United Nations; Lester R. Brown, 1981, *Building a Sustainable Society*, New York: W.W. Norton & Company; *Gaia: An Atlas of Planet Management*, 1984, edited by Norman Meyers; W. Clark and R. Munn, 1986, *Sustainable Development of the Biosphere*, Cambridge, England: Cambridge University Press; Michael Redclift, 1987, *Sustainable Development: Exploring the Contradictions*, New York: Routledge.

92. World Commission on Environment and Development, 1987, *Our Common Future*, New York: Oxford University Press.

93. Ibid., 43.

94. S. M. Lélé, 1991, Sustainable Development: A Critical Review, *World Development* 19,6: 607.

95. Michael Redclift, 1991, The Multiple Dimensions of Sustainable Development, *Geography* 76,3: 36.

96. See Lélé, Sustainable Development, and Becky J. Brown, Mark E. Hanson, Diana M. Liverman, and Robert W. Merideth, Jr., 1987, Global Sustainability: Toward Definition, *Environmental Management* 11,6: 713.

97. For a treatment of the origins of the word sustainability see Donald Worster, 1993, *The Wealth of Nature: Environmental History and the Ecological Imagination*, New York: Oxford University Press.

98. Ibid., 144-5.

99. Ibid., 145.

100. Ibid., 145.

101. Ibid., 146.

102. Ibid., 146.

103. For a treatment of the definition of the term sustainability see Brown, Global Sustainability, 713-9.

104. See Richard Shearman, 1990, The Meaning and Ethics of Sustainability, *Environmental Management* 14,1: 2.

105. Judy L. Meyer and Gene S. Helfman, 1993, The Ecological Basis of Sustainability, *Ecological Applications* 3,4: 569.

106. For reference to such an early use of the concept of sustained yield by fisheries biologists see *History of Sustained Yield Forestry*, 1984, edited by Harold

K. Steen, Santa Cruz, California: The Society for the International Union of Forestry Researchers.

107. See Joy Tivy and Greg O'Hare, 1982, *Human Impact on the Ecosystem*, Edinburgh, Scotland: Oliver and Boyd.

108. See Meyer and Helfman, The Ecological Basis of Sustainability, 569-70.

109. Summaries of such evidence appear in Brown, *State of the World 1994*, and Brown and Kane, *Full House*.

110. Shearman, The Meaning and Ethics of Sustainability, 6.

111. Brown, Global Sustainability, 716.

112. Worster, *The Wealth of Nature*, 147.

113. The cited definition and an associated treatment of so-called "sustainable growth" may be found in *The Sustainable Society: Implications for Limited Growth*, 1977, edited by D. Pirages, New York: Praeger.

114. Shearman, The Meaning and Ethics of Sustainability, 3-4.

115. For treatment of such a "sustainable growth mode" and its relationship to the conservation of natural resources see R. Carrie Turner, 1988, Sustainability, Resource Conservation and Pollution Control, in *Sustainable Environmental Management: Principles and Practice,* edited by R. Carrie Turner, Boulder, Colorado: Westview Press.

116. See Brown, *Building a Sustainable Society*.

117. See Edward Goldsmith, Robert Allen, Michael Allaby, John Davoll, and Sam Lawrence, 1972, *Blueprint for Survival*, Boston, Massachusetts: Houghton Mifflin.

118. See Herman E. Daly, 1973, *Towards a Steady State Economy*, San Francisco: WH Freeman.

119. Brown, Global Sustainability, 716.

120. Ibid.

121. See Charles S. Pearson, 1985, *Down to Business: Multinational Corporations the Environment, and Development*, Washington, D.C.: World Resources Institute.

122. See Michael Carley and Ian Christie, 1993, *Managing Sustainable Development*, Minneapolis, Minnesota: University of Minnesota Press, and John Young, 1990, *Sustaining the Earth*, Cambridge, Massachusetts: Harvard University Press.

123. See Derick W. Brinkerhoff and Arthur A. Goldsmith, 1990, *Institutional Sustainability in Agriculture and Rural Development: A Global Perspective*, New York: Praeger.

124. Worster, *The Wealth of Nature*, 147.

125. See Arne Naess, 1986, The Deep Ecology Movement: Some Philosophical Aspects, *Philosophical Inquiry* 8,2: 10-31.

126. For a statement of the need to stop population growth as a prerequisite for any attainment of sustainability see Lester R. Brown and Pamela Shaw, 1982, *Six Steps to a Sustainable Society*, Worldwatch Paper 48, Washington, D.C.: Worldwatch Institute, 13-21; for a statement of the need to give up on economic growth as a necessary prerequisite of sustainability see Herman E. Daly, 1991, Sustainable Development: From Concept and Theory Toward Operational Principles, in *Steady-State Economics*, by Herman E. Daly, Washington, D.C.: Island Press, 241-260.

127. Brown, Global Sustainability, 717.

128. Meyer and Helfman, The Ecological Basis of Sustainability, 570.

129. Daly, Sustainable Development, 256.

130. See, for example, Meadows, Meadows, and Randers, *Beyond the Limits*, 214, and Daly, Sustainable Development, 256.

131. See Jeanne Anderer, Alan Mc Donald, and Nebojsa Nakicenovic, 1981, *Energy in a Finite World: Paths to a Sustainable Future*, Cambridge, Massachusetts: Ballinger Publishing Company.

132. Meyer and Helfman, The Ecological Basis of Sustainability, 570.

133. Wen-Yuan Niu, Jonathan J. Lu, and Abdullah A. Khan, 1993, Spatial Systems Approach to Sustainable Development: A Conceptual Framework, *Environmental Management* 17,2: 181.

134. See William Rees, 1988, A Role for Environmental Assessment in Achieving Sustainable Development, *Environmental Impact Assessment* 8,3: 273-91.

135. Lester R. Brown and Jodi L. Jacobson, 1987, *The Future of Urbanization: Facing the Ecological and Economic Constraints*, Worldwatch Paper 77, Washington, D.C.: Worldwatch Institute, 44.

136. Brown, *Building a Sustainable Society*, 271.

137. See Brown and Jacobson, *The Future of Urbanization*, 35-49, and Brown, *Building a Sustainable Society*, 268-1.

138. Sim Van der Ryn and Peter Calthorpe, 1986, *A New Design Synthesis for Cities, Suburbs, and Towns: Sustainable Communities*, San Francisco: Sierra Club Books, ix.

139. For the rationales used to link such policies and programs to the attainment of sustainable communities see Van der Ryn and Calthorpe, ibid.

140. See, for example, Van der Ryn and Calthorpe, ibid., 64-5.

141. Treatment of such an anthropocentric perspective relative to the sustainability issue may be found in Shearman, The Meaning and Ethics of Sustainability, 4-6.

142. Ibid., 5.

143. See, for example, David W. Ehrenfeld, 1976, The Conservation of Non-Resources, *American Scientist* 64,6: 648-56, and George Sessions, 1987, The Deep Ecology Movement: A Review, *Environmental Review* 11,2: 105-25.

144. For the claim that there is a common perception that anthropocentrism is inherently "unecological" see Shearman, The Meaning and Ethics of Sustainability, 5.

145. Philip R. Berke and Jack Kartez, 1994, Sustainable Development as a Guide to Community Land Use Policy: A Conceptual Framework, College Station, Texas: Texas A&M University, 2. This paper was presented at the Annual Conference of the Association of Collegiate Schools of Planning, Tempe, Arizona, November 3-6, 1994.

146. Brown, Global Sustainability, 716.

147. Jane Lubchenco, Annette M. Olson, Linda B. Brubaker, Stephen R. Carpenter, Marjorie M. Holland, Stephen P. Hubbell, Simon A. Levin, James A. MacMahon, Pamela A. Matson, Jerry M. Melillo, Harold A. Mooney, Charles H. Peterson, H. Ronald Pulliam, Leslie A. Real, Philip J. Regal, and Paul G. Risser, 1991, The Sustainable Biosphere Initiative: An Ecological Research Agenda, *Ecology* 72,2: 394.

148. Meyer and Helfman, The Ecological Basis of Sustainability, 569.

149. For an overview of such ethical principles for defending biodiversity and ecological integrity see Timothy Beatley, 1994, Ethical Duties to the Environment, in *Ethical Land Use: Principles of Policy and Planning*, by Timothy Beatley, Baltimore, Maryland: The Johns Hopkins University Press, 102-33.

150. David Ehrenfeld, 1981, *The Arrogance of Humanism*, New York: Oxford University Press, 207.

151. Aldo Leopold, 1949, *A Sand County Almanac, and Sketches Here and There*, Oxford: Oxford University Press, 224-5.

152. G. Tyler Miller, Jr., 1991, *Environmental Science: Sustaining the Earth*, 3rd Edition, Belmont, California: Wadsworth Publishing Company, 28.

153. Shearman, The Meaning and Ethics of Sustainability, 7.

154. Bill Devall and George Sessions, 1985, *Deep Ecology: Living As If Nature Mattered*, Salt Lake City, Utah: Gibbs M. Smith, 67.

155. Meadows, Meadows, and Randers, *Beyond the Limits*, 65.

156. United Nations Environmental Program, 1995, *Global Biodiversity Assessment*, New York: United Nations.

157. Lubchenco, The Sustainable Biosphere Initiative, 388.

158. Ibid.

159. See A Report from the Ecological Society of America, Lubchenco, The Sustainable Biosphere Initiative.

160. Ibid., 371.

161. Ibid., 386.

162. Ibid., 387.

163. Ibid., 377.

164. Ibid.

165. Ibid., where the ecologists authoring the report refer to the sustainability of ecological systems as "one of the greatest challenges facing human society," 379.

166. Brown, Global Sustainability, 717.

167. Worster, *The Wealth of Nature*, 148.

168. Osvaldo Sunkel, 1980, The Interactions Between Styles of Development and the Environment in Latin America, *CEPAL Review* (December): 18.

169. Shearman, The Meaning and Ethics of Sustainability, 3.

170. Meadows, Meadows, and Randers, *Beyond the Limits*, 162.

171. For such a continued faith in the market see ibid., 162-3.

172. Niu, Lu, and Khan, Spatial Systems Approach to Sustainable Development, 184.

173. For an overview of the nature and extent of support for the idea of a possible balance between development and conservation see Shearman, The Meaning and Ethics of Sustainability, 4.

174. The noted citation is from a paper presented by John M. DeGrove, 1996, State Growth Management Systems That Integrate and Coordinate Land Use Planning: An Overview, at The Michigan State University Land Use Forum, and summarized by John Warbach in *Planning and Zoning News* 14,3: 8-9.

175. Manes, *Green Rage*, 141.

176. Arthur C. Nelson, James B. Duncan, Clancy J. Mullen, and Kirk R. Bishop, 1995, *Growth Management Principles and Practices*, Washington, D.C.: Planners Press, xi.

177. See, for example, Frederic O. Sargent, Paul Lusk, José Rivera, and María Varela, 1991, *Rural Environmental Planning for Sustainable Communities*, Washington, D.C.: Island Press, 7.

Selected Bibliography

American Academy of Arts and Sciences. 1973. The No-Growth Society. *Daedalus—Journal of the American Academy of Arts and Sciences* 102,4: 1-245.

Audirac, Ivonne, Anne H. Shermyen, and Marc T. Smith. 1990. Ideal Urban Form and Visions of the Good Life: Florida's Growth Management Dilemma. *Journal of the American Planning Association* 56,4: 470-82.

Beatley, Timothy. 1994. Ethical Duties to the Environment. In *Ethical Land Use: Principles of Policy and Planning* by Timothy Beatley. Baltimore, Maryland: The Johns Hopkins University Press.

Blaesser, Brian W., and Alan C. Weinstein, editors. 1989. *Land Use and the Constitution: Principles for Planning Practice.* Chicago: Planners Press.

Bollens, Scott A. 1992. State Growth Management: Intergovernmental Framework and Policy Objectives. *Journal of the American Planning Association* 58,4: 454-66.

Bosselman, Fred, David Callies, and John Banta. 1971. *The Taking Issue: An Analysis of the Constitutional Limits of Land Use Control.* Washington, D.C.: U.S. Government Printing Office.

Bosselman, Fred, and David Callies. 1971. *The Quiet Revolution in Land Use Control.* Washington, D.C.: Council on Environmental Quality.

Brower, David J., David R. Godschalk, and Douglas R. Porter, editors. 1989. *Understanding Growth Management: Critical Issues and a Research Agenda.* Washington, D.C.: The Urban Land Institute.

Brown, Becky J., Mark E. Hanson, Diana M. Liverman, and Robert W. Merideth, Jr. 1987. Global Sustainability: Toward Definition. *Environmental Management* 11,6: 713-9.

Brown, Lester R. 1981. *Building a Sustainable Society.* New York: WW Norton.

Brown, Lester R., and Jodi L. Jacobson. 1987. *The Future of Urbanization: Facing the Ecological and Economic Constraints*, Worldwatch Paper 77. Washington, D.C.: Worldwatch Institute.

Brown, Lester R., and Hal Kane. 1994. *Full House: Reassessing the Earth's Population Carrying Capacity.* New York: WW Norton.

Buchsbaum, Peter A., and Larry J. Smith, editors. 1993. *State & Regional Comprehensive Planning: Implementing New Methods for Growth Management.* Chicago: American Bar Association.

Burrows, Lawrence B. 1978. *Growth Management: Issues, Techniques, and Policy Implications.* New Brunswick, New Jersey: The Center for Urban Policy Research, Rutgers University.

Calavita, Nico, and Roger Caves. 1994. Planners' Attitudes Toward Growth. *Journal of the American Planning Association* 60,4: 483-500.

Chinitz, Benjamin. 1990. Growth Management: Good for the Town, Bad for the Nation? *Journal of the American Planning Association* 56,1: 3-8.

Clapp, James A. 1975. Growth Management: Practices and Issues. San Diego, California: San Diego State University.

Commission on Population Growth and the American Future. 1972. *Population and the American Future.* New York: Signet.

Council of State Governments. 1976. *State Growth Management.* Washington, D.C.: U.S. Department of Housing and Urban Development.

Council on Environmental Quality and the Department of State. 1982. *The Global 2000 Report to the President: Entering the Twenty-First Century.* Middlesex, England: Penguin Books.

Cranston, Mary, Bryant Garth, Robert Plattner, and Jay Varon. 1973. *A Handbook for Controlling Local Growth.* Stanford, California: Stanford Environmental Law Society.

Daly, Herman E. 1973. The Steady-State Economy: Toward a Political Economy of Biophysical Equilibrium and Moral Growth. In *Toward a Steady-State Economy*, edited by Herman E. Daly. San Francisco: W. H. Freeman and Company.

Daly, Herman E. 1991. Sustainable Development: From Concept and Theory Toward Operational Principles. In *Steady-State Economics: Second Edition with New Essays* by Herman E. Daly. Washington, D.C.: Island Press.

DeGrove, John M., and Patricia M. Metzger, editors. 1991. *Balanced Growth: A Planning Guide for Local Government.* Washington D.C.: International City Management Association.

DeGrove, John M., and Deborah A. Miness. 1992. *The New Frontier for Land Policy: Planning and Growth Management in the States.* Cambridge, Massachusetts: Lincoln Institute of Land Policy.

DeGrove, John M. 1993. The Emergence of State Planning and Growth Management Systems: An Overview. In *State and Regional Comprehensive Planning: Implementing New Methods for Growth Management*, edited by Peter A. Buchsbaum and Larry J. Smith. Chicago: American Bar Association.

Easley, V. Gail. 1992. *Staying Inside the Lines: Urban Growth Boundaries.* Planning Advisory Service, Report No. 442. Chicago: American Planning Association.

Ehrlich, Paul R., and Anne H. Ehrlich. 1981. *Extinction.* New York: Random House.

Ehrlich, Paul R., and Anne H. Ehrlich. 1990. *The Population Explosion.* New York: Simon and Schuster.

Ehrlich, Paul R., and Anne H. Ehrlich. 1991. *Healing the Planet: Strategies for Resolving the Environmental Crisis.* New York: Addison-Wesley.

Fagin, Henry. 1955. Regulating the Timing of Urban Development. *Law and Contemporary Problems* 20,2: 298-304.

Finkler, Earl. 1972. *Nongrowth as a Planning Alternative: A Preliminary Examination of an Emerging Issue*, Planning Advisory Service, Report No. 283. Chicago: American Society of Planning Officials.

Finkler, Earl. 1973. *Nongrowth: A Review of the Literature*, Planning Advisory Service, Report No. 289. Chicago: American Society of Planning Officials.

Finkler, Earl, and David L. Peterson. 1974. *Nongrowth Planning Strategies: The Developing Power of Towns, Cities, and Regions.* New York: Praeger Publishers.

Finkler, Earl, William J. Toner, and Frank J. Popper. 1976. *Urban Nongrowth: City Planning for People.* New York: Praeger Publishers.

Fischel, William A. 1990. *Do Growth Controls Matter? A Review of Empirical Evidence on the Effectiveness and Efficiency of Local Government Land Use Regulation.* Cambridge, Massachusetts: Lincoln Institute for Land Policy.

Gale, Dennis E. 1992. Eight State-Sponsored Growth Management Programs: A Comparative Analysis. *Journal of the American Planning Association* 58,4: 425-39.

Gale, Dennis E., and Suzanne Hart. 1992. Public Support for Local Comprehensive Planning Under Statewide Growth Management: Insights From Maine. *Journal of Planning Education and Research* 11,3: 192-205.

Gleeson, Michael E., Ian Traquair Ball, Stephen P. Chinn, Robert C. Einsweiler, Robert H. Freilich, and Patrick Meagher. 1975. *Urban Growth Management Systems*, Planning Advisory Service, Report Numbers 309 and 310. Chicago: American Society of Planning Officials.

Glickfeld, M., and N. Levine. 1991. *Growth Controls: Regional Probems—Local Responses.* Cambridge, Massachusetts: Lincoln Institute of Land Policy.

Godschalk, David R. 1992. Defense of Growth Management. *Journal of the American Planning Association* 58,4: 422-4.

Godschalk, David R., David J. Brower, Larry D. McBennett, and Barbara A. Vestal. 1977. *Constitutional Issues of Growth Management.* Chicago: The American Society of Planning Officials.

Goldsmith, Edward, Robert Allen, Michael Allaby, John Davoll, and Sam Lawrence. 1974. *Blueprint for Survival.* New York: Signet.

Hill, G. Richard. 1993. Forward to the Revised Printing: *Lucas* and Regulatory Taking Doctrine in the 1990s. In *Regulatory Taking: The Limits of Land Use Controls*, edited by G. Richard Hill. Chicago: American Bar Association.

Hughes, James W., editor. 1974. *New Dimensions of Urban Planning: Growth Controls.* New Brunswick, New Jersey: Center for Urban Policy Research, Rutgers University.

Johnson, Warren A., and John Hardesty, editors. 1971. *Economic Growth vs. the Environment.* Belmont, California: Wadsworth.

Kelly, Eric D. 1993. *Managing Community Growth: Policies, Techniques, and Impacts.* Westport, Connecticut: Praeger Publishers.

Kravitz, Alan S. 1970. Mandarinism: Planning as the Handmaiden to Conservative Politics. In *Planning and Politics*, edited by Thad Beyel and George Lathrop. New York: Odyssey Press.

Landis, John D. 1992. Do Growth Controls Work? A New Assessment. *Journal of the American Planning Association* 58,4: 489-508.

Lawrence, Nathaniel S. 1988. Regulatory Takings: Beyond the Balancing Test. *Urban Lawyer* 20,2: 389-443.

Lélé, S. M. 1991. Sustainable Development: A Critical Review. *World Development* 19: 606-21.

Leonard, H. Jeffrey. 1983. *Managing Oregon's Growth: The Politics of Development Planning.* Washington, D.C.: The Conservation Foundation.

Lubchenco, Jane, Annette M. Olson, Linda B. Brubaker, Stephen R. Carpenter, Marjorie M. Holland, Stephen P. Hubbell, Simon A. Levin, James A. MacMahon, Pamela A. Matson, Jerry M. Melillo, Herold A. Mooney, Charles H. Peterson, H. Ronald Pulliam, Leslie A. Real, Philip J. Regal, and Paul G. Risser. 1991. The Sustainable Biosphere Initiative: An Ecological Research Agenda. *Ecology* 72,2: 371-412.

McHarg, Ian. 1969. *Design With Nature.* New York: Doubleday/Natural History Press.

Meadows, Donella H., Dennis L. Meadows, Jorgen Randers, and William W. Behrens. 1972. *The Limits to Growth.* New York: Signet.

Meadows, Donella H., Dennis L. Meadows, and Jorgen Randers. 1992. *Beyond the Limits.* Post Mills, Vermont: Chelsea Green Publishing Company.

Meyer, Judy L., and Gene S. Helfman. 1993. The Ecological Basis of Sustainability. *Ecological Applications* 3,4: 569-71.

Moss, Elaine, editor. 1977. *Land Use Controls in the United States: A Handbook on the Legal Rights of Citizens,* National Resources Defense Council. New York: The Dial Press/James Wade.

Nelson, Arthur C., James B. Duncan, Clancy J. Mullen, and Kirk R. Bishop. 1995. *Growth Management Principles and Practices.* Washington, D.C.: Planners Press.

Niebanck, Paul L. 1984. Dilemmas in Growth Management. *Journal of the American Planning Association* 50,4: 403-4.

Porter, Douglas R. 1986. *Growth Management: Keeping on Target?* Washington, D.C.: The Urban Land Institute.

Schiffman, Irving. 1989. *Alternative Techniques for Managing Growth.* Berkeley, California: Institute of Governmental Studies.

Schnidman, Frank, Jane A. Silverman, and Rufus C. Young Jr., editors. 1978. *Management & Control of Growth: Techniques in Application,* Vol. IV. Washington, D.C.: The Urban Land Institute.

Schnidman, Frank, and Jane A. Silverman, editors. 1980. *Management & Control of Growth: Updating the Law,* Vol. V. Washington, D.C.: The Urban Land Institute.

Schumacher, E. F. 1973. *Small is Beautiful: Economics as if People Mattered.* New York: Harper & Row.

Scott, Mel. 1969. *American City Planning Since 1890.* Berkeley: University of California Press.

Scott, Randall W., David J. Brower, and Dallas D. Miner, editors. 1975. *Management and Control of Growth: Issues, Techniques, Problems, and Trends,* Vol. I-III. Washington, D.C.: The Urban Land Institute.

Seneker, Carl J. 1974. *Land Use Regulations for Urban Growth Control: Selected Legal Principles,* Environmental Quality Series No. 20. University of California. Davis California: Institute of Governmental Affairs.

Shearman, Richard. 1990. The Meaning and Ethics of Sustainability. *Environmental Management* 14,1: 1-8.

Steiner, Frederick. 1991. *The Living Landscape: An Ecological Approach to Landscape Planning.* New York: McGraw-Hill.

Stone, Katherine E., and Robert H. Freilich. 1991. Writing a Defensible Growth Ordinance. In *Balanced Growth: A Planning Guide for Local Government,* edited by John M. DeGrove and Patricia M. Metzger. Washington, D.C.: International City Management Association.

Van der Ryn, Sim, and Peter Calthorpe. 1986. *A New Design Synthesis for Cities, Suburbs, and Towns: Sustainable Communities.* San Francisco: Sierra Club Books.

Williamson, III, C. Thomas. 1980. Constitutional and Judicial Limitations on the Community's Power to Downzone. *Urban Lawyer* 12,1: 157-182.

Index